TEACHING BOYS

AMANDA KEDDIE & MARTIN MILLS

TEACHING BOYS

Developing classroom practices that work

ALLEN&UNWIN

First published in 2007

Allen & Unwin
83 Alexander Street
Crows Nest NSW 2065
Australia
Phone: (61 2) 8425 0100
Fax: (61 2) 9906 2218
Email: info@allenandunwin.com
Web: www.allenandunwin.com

National Library of Australia
Cataloguing-in-Publication entry:

Mills, Martin.
Teaching boys : developing classroom practices that work

Bibliography.
Includes index.
ISBN 978 1 74175 242 7 (pbk.).

1. Boys – Education – Case studies. 2. Motivation in
education – Case studies. 3. Academic achievement – Case
studies. 4. Sex differences in education – Case studies.
I. Keddie, Amanda. II Title.

371.823

Index by Russell Brooks
Set in 11.5/14 pt Bembo by Midland Typesetters, Australia
Printed in Australia by Southwood Press, (02) 9560 5100

10 9 8 7 6 5 4 3 2 1

CONTENTS

SERIES EDITOR'S FOREWORD

Amanda Keddie and Martin Mills's *Teaching Boys* deals with a significant contemporary educational issue, namely boys and schooling, and does so in a theoretically informed and research-based way. *Teaching Boys*, however, rejects what Eva Cox, the Australian social commentator, calls a 'competing victim syndrome' in relation to boys and girls and schooling. It is located in a perspective that recognises the need to focus our educational concerns on *both* boys and girls and to reject a zero sum account here. It also rejects backlash and essentialising accounts of boys which treat them all the same, as if they are all disadvantaged through schooling. Instead, *Teaching Boys* works with an understanding of the interweaving between social class, ethnicity, sexuality, masculinities and gender justice and recognises masculinities as socially constructed in a relational way with femininities.

What is impressive about *Teaching Boys* is the way in which Keddie and Mills pull together the best research on boys and schooling with the best research on pedagogies. Martin Mills was a co-author of another book in this series, *Teachers and Schooling Making a Difference*, which dealt with a research-derived model of productive pedagogies. This model of pedagogy was characterised by intellectual demand, supportiveness, yet demandingness, connectedness and working with and valuing difference. The research upon which productive pedagogies was based found that such pedagogies made a difference to both academic and social outcomes for all students, including those usually classified as disadvantaged. However, and this is the rub here, that research also found that in approximately 1000 classroom observations of pedagogies, while they were inevitably supportive, there was not enough of the other dimensions. One could hypothesise why this was the case and such hypotheses would include the amount of curriculum coverage required, the pacing of curriculum and pedagogy, policy pressure for high attainment on a narrow range of outcomes and restrictive political context in respect of matters to do with difference. Indeed in terms of working with difference, in the so-called 'age of terror' the Australian government appears to have worked with and upon 'fears of difference', rather than with a critical multiculturalism complemented by cosmopolitan aspirations.

Teaching Boys takes the productive pedagogies research and the (pro)feminist work done by both authors—Amanda Keddie and Martin Mills—on the issue of boys' education—and considers what pedagogies will work for different groups of boys. As would be expected by the authors' significant contributions to the boys' debates in contemporary education policy and practice, the case presented works with a 'which boys?' approach, that is, they reject an essentialist, and biologically reductionist account of boys as being inevitably the same and requiring pedagogies which are boy-friendly. Instead, what we have is a sophisticated dealing with the research on what pedagogies work with an account of masculinities as socially constructed and multiple and a ready recognition that hegemonic masculinity is a significant part of the problem for boys and girls in contemporary schooling, particularly in relation to many boys' attitudes to things academic and to harassment of girls and boys practising non-hegemonic masculinities. Indeed,

Teaching Boys deals with the complex and perplexing matter of how one connects pedagogies to boys without reinforcing dominant constructions of masculinity. Keddie and Mills seek for pedagogies that will enhance academic and social learning for all boys, but also produce citizens who will challenge injustice. All of these matters are dealt with in respect of a number of classroom teachers in different schools and schooling systems, who worked with boys in ways akin to that suggested by the productive pedagogies research.

Teaching Boys then is located in what we might call sociology *for* education, rather than sociology *of* education, with this distinction turning on practice/theory and normative/analytical distinctions. The former is committed to interpreting/translating research or making research available for teachers, the latter understanding the way schools function in relation to larger social system matters. *Teaching Boys* is very much grounded in research, but also committed to utilising research to inform teacher pedagogies. Its stance is one which lays out a research-based model of effective pedagogies for boys (and implicitly for girls for that matter), yet recognises that this needs to be rearticulated by teachers for their own classrooms and schools. There is always a danger of the narrowing and reductive effects of mandating a systemic pedagogies policy. Acutely aware of this truism, *Teaching Boys* establishes a dialogue with teachers rather than an algorithmic 'how to' manual.

The sociology *for* education approach is also evident in what we might call the method of the book, that is, its reliance on positive stories of good classroom practices from actual classrooms. The approach is also that of sociology *for* education in its optic of schools as sites for social justice, as against a view of schools as simply sites of injustice, as sites of the reproduction and legitimation of inequality. Here *Teaching Boys* works with the other side of reproduction theory, but in a realistic fashion. Schools can make *a* difference in terms of opportunity and in terms of the outcomes achieved by all students, irrespective of sex or ethnicity or Indigeneity or social class background. Pedagogies can help construct citizens disavowed of injustices, locally, nationally and globally. *Teaching Boys* recognises this and sees the quality of pedagogies as an important social justice matter. At the same time, it sees that schools alone, particularly in a time of retrenchment of redistributive and social justice policies at national and system levels, and the instantiation of a Gradgrind approach, almost fetish, for accountability and standardised testing, cannot achieve socially just outcomes. Nonetheless, education systems are beginning to see that structural reform which doesn't affect classroom practices is unlikely to achieve better outcomes. Systems are also beginning to recognise that teachers and their practices are the most significant factors in the quality of schooling experienced by young people and that educational leadership needs to be focused on aligning the three message systems of schooling, curriculum, pedagogies and assessment. Here there is an emergent space for the pedagogies considered by Keddie and Mills, as a research-based challenge to the defensive pedagogies, which are the usual effect of test driven systems of schooling.

Schools can make *a* difference and pedagogies are central to that purpose. *Teaching Boys* works with a politics of hope, despite a macro politics, which might lead progressive educators towards despair. This disposition of hope is deeply embedded in this text. However, this is a realistic rather than romantic or possibilitarian construction of hope. Raymond Williams, the British cultural theorist, observed that progressive politics should always be about making hope practical rather than despair convincing. This is an evident disposition in *Teaching Boys* with its positive stories and accounts of persistent practices of hope. In this way, *Teaching Boys* will be of great interest to teachers and teacher educators who have to deal in more pressing and immediate ways, than researchers, with what to do on Monday morning.

At a time when education research is being challenged to justify its legitimacy and relevance or connectedness to matters of professional practice, *Teaching Boys* demonstrates the practicality of good educational research on pedagogies and masculinities, and the significance of ongoing teacher learning to enhancing the outcomes from schooling. It also epitomises the practicality of good theory. *Teaching Boys* demonstrates that productive pedagogies, nuanced by an understanding of multiple practices of masculinity, can make a difference and contribute towards better outcomes for boys (and girls) and towards a more just gender order, necessary goals for an effective knowledge economy.

Bob Lingard
Series Editor

PREFACE

Jason is an excessively fidgety twelve-year-old boy with a mischievous grin who insists on writing on his arms and gently stabbing himself with his pen. While his teacher is talking, he is consistently off-task, smirking and nudging Jeremy, the amused boy next to him. His teacher reprimands him a number of times, eventually separating him from Jeremy later during whole-class reading time so that he and his mate are sitting on the mat at least 3 metres apart. While momentarily sullen, Jason is not to be deterred—furtively glancing between the desired spot next to his friend and his teacher, he surreptitiously inches his way back to sit beside Jeremy.

Adam, also twelve, says he hates coming to school and would like to 'get rid of all the teachers'. One game he plays to 'outsmart' his 'high and mighty' teachers involves skipping class. Instead of going to music class, Adam and his friend Tim sometimes hide in the school grounds for the duration of their music lesson, returning to their regular class group at the appropriate time. On one occasion, Adam smuggled sixteen cans of Coke into school in his backpack (Coke is banned at his school). He and his friend Tim drank the whole sixteen cans during lunchtime and laughed at their teacher's surprise when they needed to visit the toilet all afternoon to 'wash their hands'.

In a Year 9 classroom, Ben is trying to get a laugh from his classmates. He extracts a rubber band from his backpack and attaches a thick felt pen to it, stretching the band back in a launch position. He skilfully aims the projectile at the roof but misses and hits the fan instead—the felt pen ricochets and hits another student. He muffles a swear word but laughs at the positive response from his classmates—his audience is delighted by his antics. Attempting to prevent further disruptions, his teacher moves him to sit beside a quiet girl named Prue—she is not impressed.

Three serial pranksters in the same Year 9 classroom, who regularly partake in a strange habit of 'humping the air' in unison and simulating sex behind girls' backs to get a laugh, are colluding in a dare. One of the pranksters, Chris, dares his mate Josh: 'I'll give you a buck to pinch Kelly's arse.' Josh—who, according to one girl, 'hits on any female who is warm and vertical'—after accomplishing his task on this stunned girl, walks away casually, only the smirk on his face and his mates' raucous laughter giving him away.

In a primary classroom, three small Year 1–2 boys are plotting an attack on their enemy Brian, an eight-year-old from another class who, according to the boys, is a 'fish-face dork' who 'screams like a girl'. After the three of them 'lay into' Brian at recess, the chief instigator, Adam, brags to his peers about the incident, describing in detail how he 'bashed the crap' out of his enemy and drew blood when he bit through Brian's shirt.

Whether they are low-level disruptions or more serious altercations, such stories involving boys are familiar and, whilst not representative of all boys, are certainly typical of particular boys' behaviours. Here we see the boy who refuses to engage with schoolwork and continually disrupts those around him for a 'laugh'; the boy who rejects teacher authority as a test of masculinity; the boy who teachers attempt to 'civilise' by seating him beside a girl; the boy who thinks that sexual harassment of girls is a joke; the boy who is led on by the peer group; the boy who is a perpetrator of violence against a student who is 'different'; the boy who is a victim of other boys' violence; and the boy who does not participate in either violence or sexual harassment, but colludes and encourages other boys to do so. These behaviours are sometimes excused through the all-too-familiar—and dangerous—notion that it is just 'boys being boys'. However, these behaviours are often harmful to others. Certainly Kelly, on the receiving end of a sexual dare, and Brian, the victim of group violence, are cases in point. Indeed, far too often such behaviours have dire consequences. While writing this preface, we are alarmed by the main story in a local newspaper (Fynes-Clinton, 2006). The story tells of an attack on thirteen-year-old Daniel Browne. Daniel, an anaphylactic who is allergic to peanuts, is the victim of a bullying incident. As payback for an earlier altercation he has had with another boy, who is aware of Daniel's sensitivity to peanuts, he is pelted and taunted with the remnants of a peanut butter sandwich. Moments later, Daniel suffers acute anaphylactic symptoms, is rushed to hospital and spends the next five hours in emergency before he is finally stabilised.

One does not need to go into many classrooms to observe the importance of addressing issues of masculinity in the education of boys. Common to all these stories is a version of dominant and subversive masculinity that is detrimental to the learning success of *all* students. The problematising of such ways of being a boy, we contend, is imperative to pursuing the goals of gender justice in schooling, and should be central to the teaching of boys. It is such teaching that we foreground in this book. In *Teaching Boys: Developing classroom practices that work*, we highlight those educational issues that involve boys—both as a social group and as individuals. Through the in-depth stories of Jennifer, Ross, Rachel and Monica,[1] we provide insight into

---

1 Pseudonyms are used for the names of all the teachers, schools and students mentioned throughout the book.

how such issues might be addressed in gender-equitable ways. Drawing on these stories, we offer teachers and others research-based and constructive suggestions as to how the 'problem' of boys can be addressed through classroom practices that encourage boys to appreciate a diversity of masculinities, whilst challenging the more 'toxic' forms that limit their and others' educational experiences. We also stress the need not to lose sight of the many educational issues still facing girls in schools. Thus, central to *Teaching Boys* is an acknowledgement of and concern about how social privilege continues to be inequitably distributed within the broader gender order.

With these considerations in mind, the book offers teachers a framework for developing contextually driven and sustainable approaches to addressing issues of boys' education. While we do not offer prescriptions for working with boys, *Teaching Boys* provides practical suggestions and associated professional development material that reflect our focus on pedagogies, critical reflection and gender justice. We realise that in addressing issues related to boys' education there are no quick fixes, and that teachers and others working with boys in schools will need to be persistent in their attitude to the challenges they face while maintaining hope that change is possible. To these ends, the teacher stories provide stimulus for a series of professional development activities and discussion points which we hope will assist in the development of strategies that will address significant aspects of boys' education in local contexts. While it is not intended to 'solve' all the issues involved in teaching boys, we hope this book promotes discussions about pedagogy and gender justice, and that it is useful in developing a practice of persistence and hope along the path towards gender equity.

Amanda Keddie and
Martin Mills

ACKNOWLEDGEMENTS

There are many people we would like to thank for their support during the writing of this book.

We especially want to thank those teachers and students who allowed us to visit their classrooms. We are particularly grateful to those teachers who so generously gave up their time to be interviewed by us. We are very well aware of how precious time is for teachers.

Our friends and colleagues have provided wonderful support. Whilst acknowledging friends and colleagues there is always a danger of inadvertently leaving someone out. However we do want to thank Carmen Mills, Maria Delaney, Wayne Martino and Bob Lingard who all read earlier versions of this book and made constructive criticisms. Their friendship and support have meant a lot to us. Discussions with others over many years have also helped to shape some of the ideas that are developed in this book. These include, Jenny Nayler, Maree Hedemann, Emma Charlton, Deb Hayes, Pam Christie, Kirran Follers and Maria Pallotta-Chiarolli.

We would like to also thank the various people at Allen & Unwin who have been fantastic from the time we first took the idea of this book to them through to its final production.

Amanda would like to thank her wonderful family

Alexandra, Maree, Adam, Sally and Jane and her partner Rick for their love, support and encouragement.

Martin would like to thank Ali and Tara (who are both always so patient and understanding), Ros and Glenda for their love and what they have all individually taught him over many years.

We would also like to thank each other for making this a collaboration that has been supportive, fun and intellectually and politically stimulating.

1 GENDER JUSTICE AND TEACHING BOYS

There was a time, in the not too distant past, when teachers, students and academics working in the area of education could walk into any good bookshop, go to the women's studies section and find numerous books on key equity and social justice issues relating to the education of girls. In the early 1990s, in most bookshops, 'women's studies' sections morphed into 'gender studies', and books on men and boys have—almost Triffid like—come to dominate many of the shelves in these sections. Educationalists now, instead of finding books on girls, are confronted with books on how to raise boys, how to teach boys, how to mentor boys, and so on. These books include appeals to 'protect', 'save', 'shape' and 'rescue' boys. Many of these texts are grounded in a politics, found in books on other shelves in the same sections of the shop, suggesting that there has been a 'war on boys', that 'male power is a myth' and that men have been 'stiffed'. We have found most of these books highly troublesome in relation to the ways in which they have negated the unequal distribution of power between men and women, have been silent on gender differences in post-school options, have ignored issues of sexual harassment in schools, have reinforced dominant constructions of masculinity that are harmful to boys themselves (and also to others), and have treated boys and girls as unitary groups unaffected by issues of class, race, ethnicity, sexuality and physical abilities. We have also been concerned by the way in which some of these books have had low expectations of boys, by arguing that innate qualities in boys prevent them from performing well in similar tasks to girls.

Of course, these are not the only books on boys; there are some that do not construct boys as victims, and there are many excellent books dealing with both girls' and boys' educational issues. These books have, amongst other things, addressed the ways in which masculinities are formed in school, acknowledged differences *amongst* girls and boys as well as *between* girls and boys, considered the effects of various structural arrangements designed to address gender inequities, foregrounded girls' current educational needs, analysed statistical data on achievement in nuanced ways, and provided policy studies of various government responses to the current 'boys' debate. Some of these books have drawn heavily on theory, while others have theorised data collected from teachers, students and other sources. Importantly, these various texts have all served to provide a much-needed counter to the prevailing concerns represented in what has come to be known as the 'what about the boys?' debate. We draw on many of these works throughout this book.

In writing *Teaching Boys*, we were mindful of the need to reject what Eva Cox (1995) refers to as a 'competing victim syndrome' in presenting our case for why the education of boys needs to be taken seriously. In so doing, we also adopt a similar stance to these latter texts. In our work with teachers, we have found that it is those teachers with complex understandings of gender who have been able to broaden the options for both girls and boys in their classrooms. These understandings have mostly been informed by teachers' engagement with feminist ways of thinking. We have added to this literature in *Teaching Boys* by providing a detailed account of the work of teachers who are having success with boys in their classrooms. Here, through a selection of teacher stories, we define 'success' not only as academic achievement, but also as opening up possibilities for boys to construct non-dominant masculinities for themselves, for developing an understanding of how some of their behaviours oppress others, and for encouraging them to challenge injustice. While our focus in this book is explicitly on gender, we acknowledge that gender does not operate in isolation from other identity relations such as ethnicity and social class.

In presenting these teachers' stories, it becomes evident that a 'tips for teachers' approach—so apparent in many of the current assortment of 'boys' books—will not work. Instead, what we have found is that teachers who make a difference for boys do so within a framework that involves long-term persistence and that does not sink into despair over a failure on the part of some boys to change. They remain hopeful that change is possible. Their practices of persistence and hope mean that they seek to broaden the limited options currently open to boys, are concerned with the ways in which boys' behaviours affect each other and girls, reject deficit models of boys through having high expectations of them, both academically and socially, and acknowledge the ways in which gender is affected by matters of class, race and ethnicity.

We recognise that writing about masculinities in schools is problematic and there is a danger inherent in writing a book about teaching boys. We are concerned that our book, in being—as its title indicates—about boys, will represent yet another colonisation by boys' issues of the space available to feminists to talk about girls' issues. We do think that the upsurge in masculinity studies has had the effect of taking the focus off men (and boys') privileges and placing it on their disadvantage. We do acknowledge that such a focus, to the extent that it recognises and addresses genuine disadvantage in relation to, for example, Indigenous men, working-class men or non-Anglo men, is warranted.

Notwithstanding this concern, in this book we recognise that privilege is not a zero-sum game, and that constructing typologies of disadvantage whereby a person's sex, sexuality, race, ethnicity and geographic location are all taken into account in order to determine who is the most disadvantaged is a foolish exercise. But we do want to stress the need to take into account difference and social justice in working with boys' education. This means we do not want to shy away from feminist principles that help to provide an understanding of how society is organised in ways that privilege men as a group over women as a group. One only has to look at issues of gender in relation to distributions of income, positions of influence and authority in powerful economic and political organisations, users of domestic violence centres, and so on to see that this is the case. At the same time, issues such as racism, homophobia and poverty have to be considered in the teaching of boys. Hence we want to stress that the teaching of boys has to be concerned with a social justice agenda that recognises such inequalities.

There is a further danger in writing a book called *Teaching Boys*. The implication of many books with similar titles is that there are innate differences between boys and girls, thus requiring different pedagogical approaches. We reject such biological assertions, and the concomitant pedagogical implications, and remain unconvinced by arguments about boys' innate differences from girls. We have seen enough boys performing well and girls performing badly at a variety of tasks often deemed to be feminine—for example, expressive writing—and vice versa to feel that neither sex has a monopoly on particular behaviours. However, this is not to say that gender is unimportant. Gender is read within particular contexts and when boys behave in ways deemed feminine in some contexts, they can be punished. For example, in some school environments it is not 'masculine' to like English (see, for example, Martino, 2000), and consequently boys who demonstrate a passion for English may well be constructed as 'gay' or a 'girl'. In other situations, while the social ramifications might be less cruel and repudiating given the broader privileging of the masculine, girls who demonstrate a passion for activities stereotypically associated with boys—for example, skateboarding—may well have their skills trivialised, experience sexual harassment and/or be constructed as a 'tomboy' (i.e. not a real girl) (see, for example, Thorne, 1993; Reay, 2001).

These concerns aside, we do think it is important to consider how educators teach boys. The ways in which gender is constructed and policed in various schools, and broader contexts, makes considering a pedagogy for boys important. Hence we argue throughout this book that there are issues which need to be considered in relation to the teaching of boys. Becky Francis (2000, p. 129) asks the question, 'Do boys need to change?' We think, as do many of the teachers we have interviewed, that some boys *do* need to change. Some boys' behaviours and engagement with schooling have dire consequences for their learning and the learning of others; some boys' and girls' school experiences and safety are affected—in some cases at an extreme level—by certain boys' behaviours; some academically successful boys achieve with no concept of social justice and understanding of the various privileges that they have inherited by being a particular kind of boy; and some boys' life experiences and options are highly restricted by their, and others', conceptions of what constitutes an acceptable masculinity.

In claiming that some boys do need to change, we do not want to lay all the responsibility on boys themselves. They are, after all, boys—not adults—and as such cannot be held solely accountable for adopting various forms of masculinity that are the product of a broader set of social relations. Hence we also see the need for schools to change in ways that do not valorise those masculine characteristics that perpetuate an unjust gender order. This will entail those in schools working to identify structures and behaviours, such as approaches to discipline and curriculum organisation, which work towards normalising certain gendered behaviours. It will also involve developing structures within a school that help to create a supportive environment where students who do not fit 'normalised' constructions of gender feel safe. The gendered behaviours of teachers in schools also need to be taken into account. As many of the teachers in our research indicate, changing boys will involve treating them with respect, and whilst recognising that some boys' behaviours do need to change, adults within a school community have to work towards creating a safe environment within which this can occur. Thus this book is also based on the presumption that adults in schools have to take some responsibility for the ways in which boys have come to accept certain behaviours as 'boys being boys'.

In this chapter, we provide a brief account of the context in which the work of teaching boys occurs. The current moment in boys' education—sometimes characterised by what Susan Faludi (1992) has referred to as 'backlash'—has to be considered as it is clearly affecting the take-up of boys' education in many countries (see Weaver-Hightower, 2003, for an analysis of the 'boy-turn' in current gender equity debates). Whilst concerned that there has been a simplification of the issues involved in boys' education in the media, policy and many popular books on boys, we do consider that there is a warrant for considering boys' education which we provide in this chapter. We also outline in this chapter the research methodology employed in this book and the ways in which we think this book might be used in a variety of different contexts.

Current context

Whilst the concern about boys and their educational experiences during much of the 1990s was largely to be found in newspaper articles and on current affairs programs, alongside an explosion in the above mentioned pop psychology-style books about boys (see, for example, Biddulph, 1995, 1997; Pollack, 1999; Kindlon & Thompson, 1999; Gurian, 1999), there has since the turn of the century been an increase in policy concerns about boys and related issues. For instance, in Australia there have been national policies such as the *Boys' Lighthouse Schools Project* (Department of Education, Science and Training, 2003); *Success for Boys* (Department of Education, Science and Training, 2005a); and the parliamentary inquiry, *Boys' Education: Getting it Right* (House of Representatives Standing Committee on Education and Training, 2002; for critiques of this last inquiry see Mills et al., 2007); and some state-led initiatives such as Queensland's *Male Teachers Strategy* (Education Queensland, 2002; for a critique of this policy see Mills et al., 2004). In the United Kingdom various government departments have released documents to instruct on the ways in which boys' educational needs can be advanced. These include, as Francis and Skelton (2005) indicate, *Using the National Healthy School Standard to Raise Boys' Achievement* (DfES, 2003); *Yes He Can—Schools Where Boys Write Well* (Ofsted, 2003a); and *Boys' Achievement in Secondary Schools* (Ofsted, 2003b). It is unfortunate that much of this recent policy agenda, which has real material effects in terms of drawing resources away from initiatives relating to girls and other equity areas, has been cloaked in a victim politics. Largely generated by reductionist and selective accounts of gender and crude indicators of success and failure, such a politics has generated a panic around boys' schooling performance, promoting a 'failing boys' discourse and a sense that all girls are now outperforming all boys. This context has generated a 'crisis' discourse around issues of masculinity, and has worked to homogenise boys as an equity group requiring affirmative action and special treatment.

In this book, we locate issues of masculinity and teacher practice within a context of social justice that highlights the inequities involved in presenting boys as a disadvantaged group (see also Martino & Meyenn, 2001; Epstein et al., 1998; Lingard & Douglas, 1999; Lingard, 2003; Lesko, 2000; Skelton, 2001; Francis, 2000; Francis & Skelton, 2005; Gilbert & Gilbert, 1998). Our interpretation is that the popular justification for such a focus is unconvincing. In particular, we understand the amplified concern about boys' educational performance in media and policy discourse, as fuelled by a backlash politics against feminist gains in education and as coinciding with the marketisation of schooling and culture of performativity (dominant in most Western environments from the mid-1990s). Such cultures have generated an obsession with academic outcomes and the measurement of specific and easily quantifiable aspects of education (Mahony, 1998). We contend that this competitive environment, where market forces of efficiency and economy are increasingly driving school priorities and narrowly defining success and achievement, is fertile ground for legitimising a focus on boys and distorting issues of gender equity through the selective presentation of particular outcomes—generally those associated with literacy and retention rates (Lingard, 2003; Taylor & Henry, 2000).

Such an amplified and selective concern based on standards rather than social justice, as Francis and Skelton (2005) point out, not only ignores the long history of the 'under-achieving boy'—falsely presenting it as a 'new' phenomenon—but also disguises and deflects attention away from issues of genuine inequity, especially in relation to girls. We are particularly concerned with how the current 'boy turn' in education (Weaver-Hightower, 2003) continues to ignore the enduring structural disadvantages and power differentials experienced by females as a category within broader society in terms of males' greater access to positions of power and socio-economic security (Lingard, 2003; Collins et al., 2000; Francis & Skelton, 2005). We contend that the tendency for the 'turn' to ignore the complexity of how gender intersects with other identity relations—such as social class, ethnicity, rurality and sexuality—

and to exacerbate issues of educational disadvantage for particular groups of male and female students within but also beyond the contexts of schooling, is highly problematic (Mills et al., 2007; Mills, 2003; Gill, 2005; Lingard, 2003). In this respect, while we do acknowledge the general educational under-performance of boys in some countries, and in particular the phenomenon of boys' under-performance in literacy, we also acknowledge many boys' continued high educational performance and their relative successes post-school. To these ends, we reject a competing victims approach to issues of gender equity and instead draw attention to the evidence that, in most Anglophone contexts, issues such as social class and ethnicity—not gender—are the most accurate predictors of educational disadvantage (Collins et al., 2000; Connolly, 2004; Francis & Skelton, 2005).

In this book, we seek to disrupt the victim politics contained within current gender debates. In so doing, we highlight the social injustice of narrowly defining school effectiveness to particular academic outcomes and of reducing gender equity issues to academic performance (Collins et al., 2000). From an understanding of the current climate of efficiency, economy and performativity in education as sidelining social issues in schools and thus as not conducive to enhancing the goals of social equity, we support calls for a re-focus on the social and emotional dimensions of schooling (Lingard, 2003; McLeod, 2004). However, within the context of the ever-increasing broader social complexities and uncertainties that characterise the contemporary lifeworlds of teachers and students, finding spaces for such a re-focus is far from unproblematic. We, like others (hooks, 2003; McLaren & Farahmandpur, 2005; Giroux, 2006), are concerned with how current social diversities are being addressed through recourse to what we view as a regressive rather than progressive focus in terms of the purposes of schooling. Over at least the last decade or so, and amplified by the new narratives of security within education and culture of fear more broadly engendered through the so-called 'war on terror', this regressive climate has resulted in increasing attacks on progressive education and the stifling of the socially critical pedagogies of hope so crucial to pursuing the goals of social equity in education (Rizvi, 2004; hooks, 2003). While, within this neo-conservative environment, the critical teaching foregrounded in this book might be challenged as overly progressive, complex or too multicultural, we strongly position the pedagogies of persistence and hope foregrounded here as all the more crucial in assisting students to effectively navigate futures of social justice and peace in these volatile contemporary times.

We have both worked in the area of boys' education for some time, and have drawn heavily upon our experiences in that work to construct the arguments in this book (see, for example, Keddie, 2003, 2005, 2006b; Mills, 2000, 2001). However, what we have done here—rather than draw on multiple interviews and observations from over that period (although in Chapter 2 we do draw on a range of interview data collected from a broad surveying of teachers)—is to present four in-depth teacher narratives to demonstrate what teachers who make a difference for boys (and girls) in their care are actually doing in the classroom. We think that this is important. It is very easy to make decontextualised suggestions as to what teachers *should* be doing. It is also easy to critique efforts to address gender issues in school and to indicate what teachers are doing wrong. We do not think either of these approaches is especially helpful to teachers. What the teacher narratives provide is a series of teacher experiences that may be helpful in other contexts, and that may provide teachers with some suggestions as to how to approach a variety of educational issues in their own classrooms, as well as demonstrating practical applications of complex gender theory. In particular, these narratives also foreground those educational issues that do involve boys—both as a social group (Young, 1990) and as individuals—to consider what may be effective ways of addressing such issues through the classroom without ignoring how advantage is distributed within the current gender order. With this in mind, we focus on pedagogy and issues of gender diversity, social power, privilege and marginalisation.

We understand issues of gender and achievement in ways that do not dislocate the learner from broader gendered power relations, and draw on our teacher stories to illustrate the importance of exploring how the social construction of gender, and in particular masculinity, impacts on schooling performance (Francis & Skelton, 2005; Connolly, 2004; Lingard, 2003). Like key research in this area (Thorne, 1993; MacNaughton, 2000; Skelton, 2001; Francis, 2000; Francis & Skelton, 2005; Connolly, 2004; Martino & Pallotta-Chiarolli, 2003), we understand the 'gender gap' in achievement, in terms of boys' general under-performance, as associated with their take-up of dominant constructions of masculinity. Aligning with important work in this sphere (Connolly, 2004; Davies, 2000), and as demonstrated explicitly in our own research (Keddie, 2006a, 2007; Mills, 2001), we see these constructions as tending not to align with the formal demands of schooling. We thus call for a deconstruction of 'masculinity' so that certain aspects of learning are not seen as gendered and boys especially are 'not invested in performing particular ways of learning, and maintaining different interests and practices to delineate their gender identities' (Francis & Skelton, 2005, p. 134). Francis and Skelton (drawing on Warrington & Younger's 2002 work) point out that 'decreasing gender difference and expectations around differentiated gendered behaviours is a vital pre-requisite and first step before any other strategy may be fruitful' (2005, p. 102). Indeed, as these authors point out, boys perform at their best within schools that 'challenge gender cultures, and encourage boys and girls not to see aspects of learning as gendered' (2005, p. 134).

Against this backdrop, while we are mindful of the current tendency of some anti-'laddish' discourses to demonise particular groups of boys (see Francis, 2006), we align ourselves with research and writing in the area of gender justice that seeks to broaden boys' understandings of masculinity to be more inclusive of difference and diversity (Alloway et al., 2002; Jackson, 2006; Lingard et al., 2002; Martino & Pallotta-Chiarolli, 2003; Francis & Skelton, 2005). More specifically, and consistent with Lingard and Douglas (1999), this book draws on feminist principles in calling for boys to:

> broaden their modes of expression to encompass what has been traditionally seen as feminine, instead of progressively limiting their options as they attempt to continue to define themselves in contrast to girls, women and their identification with the feminine (1999, p. 152).

Here, like others (Lingard & Douglas, 1999; Francis & Skelton, 2005), we associate an improvement in boys' academic outcomes with a greater encompassing of qualities traditionally associated with femininity. We see, for instance, that qualities such as attentiveness, diligence, conscientiousness, pride in one's work and the ability and desire to work collaboratively (qualities generally constructed as feminine and stereotypically associated with girls) are what many under-achieving boys need to raise their achievement levels (Francis & Skelton, 2005).

Our agenda is framed within broader conceptualisations of justice that acknowledge how gender intersects with social processes in ways that produce cultural domination, non-recognition and disrespect within an enduring patriarchal world that continues to associate successful masculinity with power, domination and non-emotion, and to devalue and demean activities connoted as feminine (Connell, 2000; Kenway & Fitzclarence, 1997; Fraser, 1997; Keddie, 2005). Along these lines, we—like many others—are concerned by arguments demonstrating an anxiety about boys being 'feminised'; by the ways in which schools and other institutions reinforce and normalise inequitable understandings of gender;

by the silence surrounding the sex- and gender-based dimensions of bullying and violence in schools; and by the sidelining of the many issues of disadvantage and injustice that continue to characterise the school experience of many girls (Martino & Pallotta-Chiarolli, 2005; Francis & Skelton, 2005).

As others do, we acknowledge here the resistance that such agendas generate in terms of broader misogynistic and homophobic cultures and discourses within and beyond schools (Kenway et al., 1998; Mills, 2001; Francis & Skelton, 2005, Martino & Pallotta-Chiarolli, 2005). As many attempting to pursue the goals of gender justice have noted, there remains a clear aversion to 'feminising' boys. Francis and Skelton (2005), for instance, argue that—despite the tendency for girls to educationally outperform boys—policy-makers, schools and teachers 'are far from advocating that femininity is the socially accepted model and boys should emulate feminine behaviour' (2005, p. 131). Certainly, broader social structures and practices that continue to legitimise and assign power to hegemonic masculinity and heterosexuality while invalidating and trivialising femininity support this resistance to encouraging boys to behave more like girls. Indeed, such structures and practices, as Francis and Skelton (2005) point out, have tended to support frameworks and strategies that essentialise boys and reinscribe inequitable understandings of gender.

In working against this reinscription, a central premise of this book is that 'privilege' as it relates to gender has to be a key concern of the pedagogical decisions made in relation to the teaching of boys. However, at the same time, the ways in which some boys experience discrimination based upon factors such as race/ethnicity and sexuality, alongside some boys' failure to live up to idealised forms of masculinity, and many boys' experiences of powerlessness by being discriminated against because of their youth (McLean, 1997; Denborough, 1996; Mills, 2000), have also to be considered. Our approach, then, is one that suggests both schools and classrooms—where they are not doing so—have to change to meet the needs of all students, including boys of various ethnicities, sexualities and physical abilities. Here we acknowledge that there are ways in which *some* boys are not served well by many aspects of the schooling process (see, for example, Sewell, 1997, 1998; Connolly, 1998; Wright et al., 1998; Simpson et al., 2001). That it is only some boys who experience school as such makes it difficult to make claims about boys without also asking 'which boys are we talking about?' (Teese et al., 1995; Lingard et al., 2002; Connolly, 2004; Francis, 2000). For instance, Connolly (2004) demonstrates the differences in the sorts of pressures that are faced by middle-class and working-class young boys in two different Belfast schools. These include their exposure to sectarian violence, poverty and health issues. Then there are the differences that are placed upon boys of various ethnicities and religions (see, for example, Sewell, 1997, 1998; Archer, 2003). In a recent paper, Becky Francis (2006) notes that much of the current research shows it is difficult to speak of 'boys' and 'girls' without taking into account differences *amongst* boys and girls as well as differences *between* girls and boys.

It is the differences amongst boys that make it very difficult to identify a pedagogy which is appropriate for *all* boys. Therefore, we recognise that it is dangerous territory to suggest that there may be a pedagogy specific to the teaching of boys. For such a claim has the potential to be read in similar ways to those essentialising pedagogies shaped through the 'boys as victims' discourse (see, for instance, Gurian & Ballew, 2003). In avoiding such pedagogies, we have turned to the productive pedagogies model (see Table 1.1). This pedagogical framework has been demonstrated to provide a high-quality education for *all* students (Lingard et al., 2001, 2003; Hayes et al., 2006). However, the principles of this framework can be applied to the specifics of boys' education (see, for instance, Lingard et al., 2002; Martino & Berrill, 2003; Keddie, 2006b).

Table 1.1: The productive pedagogies framework

Intellectual quality	
Higher order thinking	Students are engaged in higher order thinking and critical analysis.
Depth of knowledge	Central concepts and their complex relations are covered in depth and detail.
Depth of students' understanding	Students' work and responses provide evidence of understanding of concepts or ideas.
Substantive conversation	Classroom talk breaks out of the initiation/response evaluation pattern and leads to sustained dialogue between students, and between teachers and students.
Knowledge as problematic	Students critique and second-guess texts, ideas and knowledge.
Metalanguage	Aspects of language, grammar, and technical vocabulary are foregrounded.
Connectedness	
Knowledge integration	Teaching and learning range across diverse fields, disciplines and paradigms.
Link to background knowledge	Teaching and learning are connected with students' background knowledge.
Connection to the world beyond the classroom	Teaching and learning resemble or connect to real-life contexts.
Problem-based curriculum	Teaching and learning focus on identifying and solving intellectual and/or real-world problems.
Supportive classroom environment	
Students' direction of activities	Students have a say in the pace, direction or outcomes of the lesson.
Social support for student achievement	Classroom is a socially supportive, positive environment.
Academic engagement	Students are engaged and on-task.

Table 1.1: The productive pedagogies framework *cont.*

Explicit quality performance criteria	Criteria for student performance are made explicit.
Student self-regulation	The direction of student behaviour is implicit and self-regulatory.

Working with and valuing difference	
Valuing non-dominant cultural knowledges	Diverse cultural knowledges are brought into play.
Public representation of inclusive participation	Deliberate attempts are made to increase the participation of all students from different backgrounds.
Narrative	Teaching draws on narrative rather than expository styles.
Group identities in learning community	Teaching builds a sense of community and identity.
Active citizenship	Active citizenship is fostered.

Source: Adapted from Hayes et al. (2006)

We do not make this suggestion about the productive peda-gogies model based upon supposed essentialised or biological differences between boys and girls, but rather on the basis of the different pressures relating to normalised constructions of being a boy or a girl (see Martino & Pallotta-Chiarolli, 2005) and the different social and political positioning of boys and girls within gendered relations of power operating within schools and the broader society. In considering a pedagogy for boys that promotes a language for talking about multiple differences at one time (Yeatman, 1995), we see this framework as particularly appropriate given that its social justice focus takes into account issues of difference and power relations within and beyond the classroom. In this book, we draw on our work with teachers to consider the ways in which the productive pedagogies frame-work can be utilised in the teaching of boys while at the same time raising some concerns about the ways in which such a pedagogy might be used to reinforce problematic constructions of masculinity.

With these considerations in mind, the book aims to provide a framework for developing practical, contextually driven and sustainable approaches to improving boys' educational outcomes. To these ends, the four in-depth teacher stories and a variety of teacher voices from broader contexts presented in this book are intended to provide the stimulus for a series of professional development activities and discussion points at the end of each chapter that tells a teacher story. This framework is structured in a way that we hope supports teachers to examine how the 'personal theories' underlying their actions in classrooms might be implicated in either enabling or constraining boys' (and also girls') academic and social outcomes (Martino & Berrill, 2003). A key purpose of this book, then, is to assist teachers in moving beyond a narrow focus on boys' educational strategies to a broader focus on pedagogies and critical reflective practice (Lingard et al., 2002). Of significance is the research-driven but practice-oriented framework of this text, which takes up calls to bridge the gap between heavily theorised approaches to addressing issues of masculinity and schooling on the one hand, and 'commonsense' 'tips for teachers' approaches on the other (Lingard et al., 2002; Martino & Berrill, 2003; Apple, 2001).

This gap, as Apple (2001) points out, has generated the space for under-researched approaches to colonise teacher practice in this sphere. The problem here is that under-researched or 'quick-fix' approaches invariably do not align well with addressing issues of masculinity in schools in sustained and socially just ways. 'Boy-friendly' strategies—for example, along the lines of increasing 'masculine' curriculum content, resources and teaching styles; increasing the number of male role models in boys' lives; and the implementation of single-sex classes—are often deployed within understandings of gender as difference and opposition (Alloway, 1995; Epstein et al., 1998; Francis, 2000; Gilbert & Gilbert, 1998; Lingard & Douglas, 1999;

Martino et al., 2004; Keddie, 2006b). Such understandings treat all boys as being the same and as being different from girls. As such, these strategies—while potentially effective in addressing some issues of masculinity in schools—can be counter-productive in terms of gender justice because they tend to normalise, reinforce and leave unquestioned a narrow and often problematic version of masculinity (Connell, 1995, 2000; Davies, 1993; Keddie, 2003; Mac an Ghaill, 1994; Martino & Pallotta-Chiarolli, 2003; Martino et al., 2004). Furthermore, in their prescriptive approach, these strategies fail to account for contextual factors and broader issues of gender and power, and in this sense the often inequitable social processes and discourses that interplay to construct and maintain particular versions of masculinity are ignored (Martino et al., 2004).

We are aware that many teachers, and others in the field of education, are struggling to come to grips with the 'what about the boys?' issue. In an era where teachers are often expected to do 'more with less', teachers are often looking for 'quick fix' solutions to the 'problem of boys'. In terms of enhancing boys' educational outcomes, while we certainly acknowledge that there is no such thing as a quick fix, we also acknowledge the clear need for more effective translations of critical theory for teachers working on the ground (Apple, 2001; Francis, 2000; Lingard et al., 2002; Martino & Berrill, 2003; Skelton, 2001). In bridging this gap between heavily theorised approaches and quick fix solutions, this book is explicit in its focus on pedagogical reform.

Our focus on quality pedagogy seeks to illustrate how environments conducive to enhancing effective learning and engagement can be created (Lingard et al., 2002). Through gender justice lenses, we feature pedagogies that seek to challenge and broaden those constructions of masculinity that damage the educational outcomes of students—girls and boys—and the boys performing such masculinities. We provide teachers and others with research-based and constructive suggestions as to how the 'problem' of boys can be addressed through classroom practices that encourage boys to appreciate a diversity of masculinities, whilst challenging the more 'toxic' forms that limit their and others' educational experiences. In so doing, we address ways in which the academic and social achievements of boys marginalised within schools by, amongst other things, race/ethnicity, sexuality and class can be improved. We also stress the need not to lose sight of the many educational issues still facing girls in schools. Thus, in challenging dominant constructions of masculinity, we promote a gender relations approach that does not ignore girls' educational needs (Francis & Skelton, 2005).

This book positions teachers as central to positive outcomes for all students (Lingard et al., 2000, 2002; Hayes et al., 2006). However, we are also cognisant of broader social relations that have a major impact upon students' outcomes. We do not want to over-state the difference that teachers can make. As with Hayes et al. (2006), we contend that teachers make *a*, not *the*, difference in assisting students to achieve high-quality social and academic outcomes. However, what teachers do in their classrooms with their students *does* matter! The teachers we have foregrounded in this book are teachers who have demonstrated a commitment to making such a difference in their students' lives.

The teacher narratives

The four teacher narratives presented in Chapters 3 to 6 are fashioned from interviews and observations that sought to explore and represent philosophies and practices in relation to teaching boys. The selection of these four teachers was generated from a broader surveying of teachers from a range of secondary and primary schools in Australia situated in a variety of locations. Subsequent to a contact person at several of the participating schools supplying us with the names of teachers whose practice they believed aligned with the principles of gender justice and quality teaching, we contacted over 70 teachers to inform them about our study and to invite them to participate in an interview. This initial contact informed the potential participants about the aim of the research—to 'bring to life' a diversity of teacher perspectives about issues relating to boys and education—and identified the areas that would be focused on during the interview. These areas related to exploring teacher philosophies or beliefs about what is important in the teaching of boys; issues associated with masculinity within and beyond the classroom and their implications for practice; and broader structures within schools that help or hinder work with boys. Drawing on these areas as a loose scaffold where teachers were encouraged to explore and provide examples about how particular issues of masculinity impacted on their practice, the 35 teachers who agreed to participate were each interviewed for up to 75 minutes. From this group of teachers, a further sub-group was selected for observation and an extended interview. These observations took us to schools in depressed former mining towns, to schools surrounded by sugar cane fields, to schools in impoverished urban areas, to urban middle-class government schools and to highly privileged boys' private schools.

While a diversity of teacher voices generated from these interviews is dispersed throughout the book, we foreground the stories of four teachers (Jennifer, Ross, Rachel and Monica). We write this book with teachers in mind, and hope these stories will connect with key aspects and themes in their experiences of teaching boys. The four teachers were selected from the latter cohort of teachers because their understandings and practice tended to align with gender justice and the pedagogical framework we have adopted for this book, and because each of them presented something different to add to understandings of the issue of boys' education. In terms of their teaching content areas, Jennifer, Ross, Rachel and Monica share a distinctly humanities focus, and certainly the capacity for this focus to be amenable to pursuing gender justice imperatives shaped our selection of these teachers. However, beyond the subject-specific, we believe that all teachers interested in gender justice can learn from the stories that feature in this book—particularly, for instance, in terms of the insight they offer in relation to the construction of socially supportive and connected learning environments and mutually respectful teacher–student relations.

After our initial interview with each of these teachers, we conducted several follow-up interviews and observations in each of the teachers' school contexts. The follow-up interviews sought to further explore some of the issues each teacher raised in relation to the focus areas. These interviews also explored issues we raised in relation to our observations of each teacher's practice, and tended to be rather informal and dynamic. The main purpose of our observations—which tended to include several classes for each teacher—was to corroborate and enrich our interpretation of the interview data.

Throughout the data-collection period, particularly in terms of how we fashioned the stories that feature in this book, we were concerned with highlighting enactments of quality pedagogy and gender justice. Here we drew on the dimensions of the productive pedagogies model (connectedness, supportive classroom environment, intellectual quality, and valuing and working with difference) as a framework of analysis that guided our foregrounding of teacher practice that we interpreted, as connected to students' experiences—their biographies and the world beyond the classroom; socially supportive in terms engendering mutually respectful teacher–student relations; intellectually demanding with regard to facilitating students' problematising of knowledge and their deep rather than superficial understanding of particular topics and issues; and valuing and working with difference in terms of valuing non-dominant cultural knowledges and generating a tenor of inclusion and respect for diversity (Lingard et al., 2001). In Chapter 2, we explore these dimensions in more depth in relation to how they support pedagogies of gender justice.

In constructing these stories, and consistent with the social justice agenda outlined earlier, we were also concerned with foregrounding understandings of gender and gender justice that might be implicated in disrupting and broadening restrictive and essentialist versions of masculinity (and femininity). Here our analytic frame draws on Giroux's (2003) positioning of the teacher as public and oppositional intellectual who takes seriously 'the supposition that in order for social arrangements to be otherwise, teachers must be able to think and act against the grain' (2003, p. 6). In this regard, in relation to issues of gender justice, we seek to illuminate the:

> . . . political nature of teaching, the importance of linking pedagogy to social change, connecting critical learning to the experiences and histories that students bring to the classroom, and engaging the space of schooling as a site of contestation, resistance and possibility (Giroux, 2003, p. 6).

The social arrangements that we foreground in this book as those that must be contested and resisted—that should be 'otherwise'—are largely associated with the gendered dimensions of classroom/school interactions that reinforce a privileging of males and 'the masculine'. We are concerned that such gendered dimensions have changed little over the past three decades in relation to issues of power and control—a discourse of entitlement prevails in terms of many boys' continued domination of classroom and playground space and resources, as well as of teacher time and attention, and the perpetration of sexual, misogynistic and homophobic harassment (Salisbury & Jackson, 1996; Mills, 2001; Mahony, 1985, 1998; Skelton, 2001; Francis & Skelton, 2005; Martino & Pallotta-Chiarolli, 2003, 2005).

Issues and key themes: Problematic constructions of masculinity

Problematic constructions of masculinity and their implications for pedagogy are explored in considerable depth in subsequent chapters in relation to the four main teacher stories. Notwithstanding this, we present some of these issues here as they were key themes in our broader interview data and provide compelling insight into the gendered power dynamics that we seek to trouble and disrupt in this book. Indeed, several teachers were explicit in their concern about boys' ways of being as associated with issues of power and control. These ways of being work to ensure that it is boys, as noted by early feminist educators, who tend to colonise the space in the classroom. The following comments from a teacher at an all-boys' Catholic school and one at a rural primary school are illustrative:

> I think boys tend to articulate things without thinking and I think a lot of it is based in terms of power—who's got the vocal power, who's got the verbal power, in the classroom. 'Who can we put down and get away with it?' (Maree)

> A lot of boys that I've taught and seen in schools—the only way they seem to be able to assert their personality, the strength of their personality, is this sort of power play which often leads to physical demonstrations of strength but it's also that occupying of physical space, occupying of teachers' time and so on. 'Look at me—you've got to look at me' and 'I'll do anything so that you do look at me'—and they do. Yeah—it's a way of demonstrating . . . it's a way that they think that that's how you be a boy. It's very rare that girls will behave that way. I'm not saying that some of them don't, but as a group boys tend to. (Phoebe)

More specifically, and consistent with important research in this area, a dominant theme in these broader interviews related to boys' investments in and exertions of power as associated with their group identity (Connell, 2000; Mac an Ghaill, 1994; Martino, 1999; Martino & Pallotta-Chiarolli, 2005). A number of teachers commented on the potency of boys' peer cultures in shaping their restrictive behaviours. Sally, a teacher from an all-boys' school, made the following remark:

> Someone told me that there is no such thing as 'mob mentality'—somebody said that to me the other day, but you do see that in the yard, particularly from the jocks, that still exists and there has been quite a few problems in the yard with those boys. (Sally)

Interestingly, another teacher from the same school commented upon how this 'group culture' was particularly worrying in an all-male context:

> Yeah, all-male environment—the boys' behaviour, say just from in the yard, having taught in co-ed, they just would not behave that way in a co-ed school . . . I don't know why. I think the girls are a calming influence. You see fights and everything, and that will happen everywhere but it just seems a bit more, it's the 'boyo' extremism—the pack mentality. If there's going to be something wrong at lunchtime, there's going to be a fight, well, there's 400 of them running towards the fight. In a co-ed school the fight probably wouldn't have happened, and if it did, not all of them would run to it. The physical presence in the yard, there are no quiet calm spots. (Alexandra)

It seemed that many of the teachers we interviewed understood these expressions of masculinity as associated with the need for many boys to prove themselves in pursuit of self-legitimation, status and prestige within the peer group's 'pecking order' or hierarchy (Connell, 2000; Mac an Ghaill, 1994; Martino & Pallotta-Chiarolli, 2005). As one teacher from a regional government high school stated:

> . . . definitely one of the issues is that, particularly with the Year 8s, they have to prove they're guys. They've got to prove their masculinity. (Jane)

Within this peer context, but also more generally, boys' tendency to dominate other boys physically was raised as a key issue in most of the schooling contexts:

> There's still the mentality I guess that boys will be boys—that there's certain things that they can get away with, so to speak . . . they like to punch each other and wrestle and all that sort of stuff . . . they're constantly having digs at each other too. You know they call it mucking around—but they always seem to be paying out on each other. (Penny)

> . . . once again it's about proving masculinity . . . the boys are very physical with each other. Very, very physical. Not even just fighting but you know lots of really rough, rougher play and it's not all negative. It's not all fighting, it's just what—apparently what boys do—to just sort themselves out. (Jane)

> . . . especially when it comes to oval play . . . I do notice the boys rove the ball. They'd get the ball and then whoever had ownership of the ball could make the rules . . . that presented problems not only for the girls who wanted to kick the ball around but also for other boys who had to do what somebody else said—'Oh it's my ball, it's my game, I got to the ball first' and when he gets the ball first he's in charge and I have to do what he says so he can do what he wants . . . Getting control of that ball is really important . . . it's the same with the cricket bats . . . so you find a lot of them will prefer not to eat or not

to complete eating and finishing their drink at lunch time because they want to get to the game . . . the actual being there at the beginning of the game when everything's organised— they have to be there at the beginning otherwise it's sort of like they go down—down the ladder. (Debbie)

Such concerns illustrate the competitive and hierarchical dynamics—especially evident in all male peer environments— that shape boys' investments in what can be a particularly harmful version of competitive and belligerent masculinity that seems to be synonymous with power, control and domination.

Consistent with research that explores how dominant constructions of masculinity can limit boys' repertoires in terms of expressing emotions in positive ways (Connell, 2000; Kenway & Fitzclarence, 1997; Fitzclarence, 2000), a number of teachers associated issues of power and boys' physical expressions of masculinity with aggression and anger. The following comments from teachers in both rural and urban schooling contexts are illustrative:

. . . a lot of the boys tend to—they like to push and shove each other a lot. And if they get angry about something, they are really quick to rise to the anger. (Michelle)

. . . like boys will punch each other for no reason. Like they'll just turn around and boom . . . often that's an aggressive anger, a pent-up anger getting out. Sometimes it's playful but some- times it's just an anger thing. (Alexandra)

Along these lines, a few female teachers relayed to us specific instances of aggression and violence perpetrated by male students. One female teacher with 30 years' experience in primary schools expressed concern about the regularity of such violence where particular boys have attempted to exert their power to display their physical strength. Indeed, this teacher described such physical assault as 'more common than you think. It happens a lot.'

Against this backdrop of masculinity and issues of power and legitimation, a dominant issue several teachers in both urban and rural environments raised related to some boys' tendencies to denigrate females and femininity. This was apparent in many teachers' concerns about boys' perpetration of sexual harassment and misogynous behaviours:

> . . . one thing that really does concern me is their disrespectful attitude to women and sex and—they're not emotionally ready . . . yet that's what they're exposed to and so that's what they think is cool, or the norm—you know for their behaviour, for their standards, for their attitudes to girls. (Belinda)

> I don't pretend to think for a second that, you know, they're not fairly macho, a lot of them, in their attitudes towards women and that sort of thing . . . or girls of their own age, you know, like, I see them at the dances that I organise and that sort of thing. I know what their behaviour is, is like . . . I do hear them talk about sex and girls sometimes, in a way that's not respectful. And I don't like that. I don't like that at all . . . expressions like, you know, 'Oh she'd be a good root', or something like that. (Adam)

> You hear horrendous stories about the boys when going to watch the Rugby. Fighting and drinking and . . . yeah, you hear that sort of thing all the time . . . and I wonder how you eventually get through to them that acting like a mob like . . . yelling out, 'Bunch of skanks'. I mean, it's because they don't have any kind of, a lot of them don't have the social skills to deal with girls. So it's either pash tongue down the throat or . . . Do you know what I mean? That, because they don't know how to talk to them—it's let's pay out on them and call them every name under the sun . . . they just don't seem to deal with girls very well. (Sally)

. . . you just have to have a fundamental principle in place like respecting others' beliefs and behaving respectfully—to women and girls. That sort of stuff applies to all of them but you have to really keep an eye on them because boys can do things that are really inappropriate like making comments of a sexual nature, sexual harassment . . . especially as they get a bit older. (Maree)

. . . the way that they relate to the opposite sex . . . some would still think that it's OK to be, to act in a really disrespectful and cruel manner toward girls—an over-reliance on appearance and things like that, like a girl who mightn't measure up to a certain look, you know, is less worthy. Even though, as I point out to the boys, it doesn't seem to be an issue for you, but it seems to be an issue, you know, the girls have to look a certain way. (Rick)

In these comments we can see how some boys draw on oppositional or binary understandings of gender as difference to legitimise their 'masculinity' at the expense of 'femininity'. We can also see from these comments how such understandings are supported by a framework of compulsory heterosexuality (Alloway, 1995; Davies, 2000; Martino & Pallotta-Chiarolli, 2003, 2005). Several teachers also associated boys' oppositional understandings of gender with their rejection of school. Such misogynous attitudes and behaviours can have negative consequences for some boys' academic success and engagement with schooling. As one teacher stated:

. . . there are kids here who are self-selecting themselves out of an academic future and they're making those decisions at eight and nine because school's uncool and it's a feminine pursuit and that's what we've got to really address. (Carmen)

For many female teachers, teaching boys foregrounds their inequitable positioning within broader discourses of gender and power (Robinson, 2000; Kenway et al., 1998; Reid, 1999; Epstein & Johnson, 1994). As Robinson suggests, the representation of gender in schools (through, for example, gendered work specialisations, staff hierarchies, curricula and extra-curricula activities, pedagogy and classroom management practices), in generally reflecting broader power relations that authorise 'maleness', often work in ways that de-legitimise female authority. In particular, accessing these discourses makes it possible for boys to subvert the traditional adult–child /teacher–student power binary to undermine their female teachers (Clark, 1993; Epstein & Johnson, 1994; Kenway et al., 1998; Robinson, 2000). The following teachers were particularly concerned about this issue:

> I think sometimes the boys are a bit dismissive of you because you're female, and you know, if I was one of the Rugby coaches I can guarantee that I would have very very few run-ins with very few boys . . . because they don't want to get on the bad side of the Rugby coaches . . . But, yeah, I mean you get, sometimes you get boys who are a bit dismissive and a bit, I don't know, just a bit anti-you. (Sally)

> Sometimes we come across boys who . . . who just tend to for some reason not really like women, or women who are seen to have some sort of power—a position of power—and they're the ones that often challenge you the most in the classroom—behaviour-management wise. (Penny)

> We have a lot of female teachers here, who in my twenty years of experience are often complaining about the ways the boys in particular speak to them. Definitely a lack of respect for some of the female teachers and it's coming from the male students. (Carmen)

A number of female teachers commented on how particular boys used their larger size to undermine the teacher's authority. As many commentators note, where power and legitimate authority are associated with the hegemonic masculine body and dominant masculine characteristics, and conversely powerlessness with the female body and femininity, the professionalism of female teachers—particularly in the areas of discipline and behaviour management—is frequently undermined (Davies, 1988; Clark, 1993; Kamler et al., 1994; Robinson, 2000). In this respect, it is commonplace for teachers—especially young, female teachers—to experience power battles, rebellion and uncooperativeness with particular male students (Robinson, 2000), as these comments indicate:

> They try to intimidate you. But like I just stand my ground and make sure I maintain eye contact and things like that and often boys are taller. Like the senior boys—the fifteen, sixteen, seventeen-year-olds are often taller than we are—so they try to use that as well . . . (Penny)

> He was a really tall lad and he came and confronted me about something, I can't even remember what it was, but he stood over me, and yelled and pointed, you know . . . at the time I wasn't scared but then afterwards when I looked back I thought, 'that was a little bit...' I probably should have moved somewhere where someone could see me, because that was a little bit scary, you know, in the fact that he was standing over me and he was yelling at me . . .
> This [other] boy in particular has got a chip on his shoulder, he's kind of renowned for being rude . . . he's got this kind of attitude . . . he's very dismissive . . . his head of house spoke to me and said he has a real issue with females, he won't be told what to do by a female. He has a terrible relationship with his mother and he seems to take that out on

her, the head of house. You know, he says all the time, 'Oh, you've got it in for me', and that kind of thing . . . (Sally)

It was not only older boys who sometimes sought to intimidate female teachers. One teacher in a rural primary school also outlined to us a frightening experience she had with a boy at her school:

He was actually assaulting one of the girls in the playground. I was on duty so I went up to intervene. I mean this is a boy who has had a lot of very long suspensions, a very troubled kid—I had quite a good relationship with him actually but once he got agitated he just lost all control of his behaviour basically and first he moved away from me and then I think he decided he'd take me on because he was as big as me. Like I'm only five foot one and he was that big. And he tried to grab me around—I suppose he was going for my throat—but he actually got me around the shoulders. I pushed him away. Of course we're not supposed to touch students but you know when you are being threatened you are allowed to use reasonable force to preserve your dignity. And he just—he was 2 centimetres from my face. I could see his tonsils, you know, telling me to 'fuck off' and other such charming things. Calling me all sorts of names and the principal had to come out to intervene and he struggled with him as well. I mean the principal is a great deal bigger than me and a lot stronger and was able to hold him. (Phoebe)

Along similar lines in terms of boys drawing on broader discourses of gender and power to subvert the traditional teacher–student binary, a few of the female teachers—particularly within the all-boys' school—spoke of how such attitudes worked as a surveillance mechanism in terms of their physical presentation:

I'm very conscious of what I wear in front of them. It's nothing tight, nothing low V-neck, I try to look professional . . . I try to look smart, neat and respectable every day, nothing short, do you know what I mean? Nothing tizzy, but try and look professional and try and act professional in front of them because we have had people in different schools who don't do that, and the boys, the boys don't miss a beat. They talk about, 'See what miss has got on?' and like, you know, I'm really conscious when I go and buy a pair of trousers or a skirt for work, about the underwear not showing through, the old VPL (visible panty line). But you know, the boys will pick up, you know, 'She's wearing a G-banger (G-string) today miss'. They notice. Especially the young females, they notice. They don't miss a beat. (Alexandra)

I'm very aware of the fact that I'm female here . . . coming here as a female is a bit of a tough task because immediately that you walk into the room they're sizing you up—they do look at what you wear and they do make comments about your hair or, you know, that kind of thing . . . (Sally)

A powerful way in which particular (even very young) boys continue to subvert the teacher–student binary and reinforce the discourse of gendered authority is through sexual harassment. As Robinson (2000) states:

Boys from a very early age are aware that accessing hegemonic masculinity privileges them to certain resources and institutionalised power that neither girls nor women will equally share in particular contexts. In schools, boys have learnt that practising sexual harassment does work to gain power . . .(2000, p. 88).

In further relation to how dominant constructions of masculinity can work to police female teachers' behaviours, a few of the teachers relayed disturbing personal experiences of sexual harassment. In the first instance, a teacher details her experience in an elite private boys' school:

. . . last year I had some really horrible emails sent to me . . . really sexually explicit stuff that was sent to me, probably about four emails altogether. The first one started off very low-level, and as each one got worse, the last one was just disgusting . . . it was all about sex and where this boy wanted to have sex with me and what he wanted to do to me . . . to cut a long story short without going into all of the politics of it all, I decided that I would see the police about it and see if they could do anything. And that was . . . it was a pretty big step I think from the school's perspective for me to go to the police, and anyway, the police had put the traces out and everything. And then just last week they caught the person who did it, and it was a boy who this year would have been Year 10, but he did it when he was in Year 9, and he now, he doesn't even go to the school anymore . . . I had him in my volleyball team two years ago. And so they caught him and he'll be cautioned and he has to write a letter of apology and all that kind of thing. But that was very scary in terms of being female here . . . It was horrible but, you know, as well it just makes you think about, 'Oh, what am I wearing, you know, should I be more careful with what I wear?' And when I came here I was told, you know, 'Because it's a boys' school be careful with what you wear—don't wear anything too revealing, don't wear anything too tight, don't wear anything too short', all those kinds of things. So, I mean, when I first came here I wouldn't even have worn, I bought shirts that were, you know, a size bigger than what I'd normally wear because I was so paranoid about it 'cause I, you know, I didn't know what to expect. (Sally)

In the second, a high school teacher from the government sector tells us that:

. . . when I was . . . a younger teacher, this particular boy used to do intimidating things to me—walking very close to me, touching my hair, that sort of stuff—trying to I guess, well

some of it was a little bit—I guess sexual is the word to use—
he was sixteen and I would have been 23 and just that sort of
stuff, like trying to intimidate me—when I was making him
work or he was doing the wrong thing or that sort of stuff.
(Penny)

It is unfortunate that such experiences by women teachers have
been used by sections of the boys' lobby to call for more male
teachers. The arguments have consisted of claims that men
would have more authority with boys than women, that boys
would respect men more, that men are more able to tolerate
so-called boyish behaviours and that men are more likely to have
a calming influence over boys (see, for example, Kindlon &
Thompson, 1999). However, we suggest that such claims treat
boys as deficit. First, they ignore the evidence that not *all* boys
behave in such ways. Second, they implicitly suggest that boys
do not have the ability to learn how to change their behaviours
in order to act more appropriately. And third, they are suggesting that boys are unable to work for women—not exactly
helpful in terms of preparing them for the workplace. Such
claims also deny the political nature of such behaviours on the
part of some boys to maintain a particular gender order that
favours the interests of men and boys in a society based on
inequitable gender arrangements.

Mac an Ghaill (1994, p. 92) refers to such practices of sexual
harassment as 'crucial elements in setting the parameters' of
schoolboy masculinities. In so doing, such practices work to
construct normalised versions of femininity and masculinity,
whereby femininity becomes associated with vulnerability,
sexual objectification and passivity; and masculinity becomes
associated with predatory behaviours, power over girls and
women, and sexual desire. Sexual harassment, as these interview
data indicate, also serves to police women's behaviours in that
they are constantly having to consider issues such as what to
wear, how to remain safe and how to avoid confrontational

situations with boys. It thus works to constantly remind women of their femininity and the power that men *and* boys have over women—even women who are positioned in authority over them.

Mac an Ghaill and many others (see Martino, 1999; Mills, 2001; Connell, 2000; Martino & Pallotta-Chiarolli, 2003, 2005) also illustrate how homophobia works in similar ways to regulate and police boys' behaviours and, in particular, their investments in dominant constructions of masculinity. From the range of different schools, several teachers expressed their concern about the prevalence of homophobia in their school:

> . . . it comes through in machismo, it comes through in homophobia. I'm often hearing comments—those derogatory terms, you know, 'faggot', 'gay', that sort of thing. (Carmen)

> . . . they use the expression, 'fag', you know, or, 'that's gay', 'that's gay'. 'That's gay' has become . . . and I have no idea where that came from, but it happened within the last four years . . . And so now you're constantly fighting a battle about, 'Oh don't be gay', they say to one another. And I think, 'What did you just do?', like 'What happened?' (Adam)

> . . . they use the word 'gay' a lot . . . everything's gay or—gay's very derogatory—it's a put-down. (Penny)

> A big thing—an epidemic in Year 8s we have is the use of the gay insults—'he's gay', 'he's a fag'. He's . . . you know various renditions thereof . . . we have a lot of fights and tussles . . . I don't mean full-on fights, I mean boys giving each other a little bit of a nudge or a shove or something when they're lining up or they're walking between classes or something—stems from the idea of who's gay and who's not—the kind of shoes you wear, the kind of, y'know all that sort of thing and to proving well if you're—for example one, one boy had quite long hair.

You know not long, long but just I suppose longer than most [boys'] hair and he copped for a month the teasing that he was gay—that's why he had long hair! Of course the next—you know three and a half weeks later it's cut short. He tried to cope with that.

. . . We do Ancient Greece and that sort of thing where these issues will arise and they, you know, complete shutdown, 'nup—it's unnatural, it's wrong, they're wrong, they're unnatural'. And yes—we'll do things like Ancient Egypt where there's incest—you know—pharaohs marrying their half sisters. And they're open to exploring the concept and why the pharaohs did that—you know, the political reasons behind it—yet they won't be open to the other thing . . . there's this—I can't say for all . . . but it wasn't female homosexuality that shut them down. It was male homosexuality. That's what they were saying was unnatural. That's what they were saying and that . . . seems to be a theme in that men are very—or boys at least are quite threatened by that. They find that very threatening . . . something that seems other than what is male in their minds becomes, becomes a super duper threat, becomes a big scary . . . you know 'men are this!' and anything that isn't—you know—it, it really disturbs them and very much makes them uncomfortable because it's not—it's a direct threat. (Jane)

We have presented an extensive amount of data here to demonstrate the importance of addressing issues of masculinity with boys. However, this is only a sample of the data we have collected. What these data show, combined with the fact that we could have filled page after page with similar observations of classrooms and comments from the interview material given to us, is that there is a warrant for undertaking work with boys in schools. While these comments came from very diverse schools—in isolated areas, rural towns, wealthy suburbs, industrialised areas and inner-city areas—and they relate to boys from a variety of social and economic backgrounds, there appear to be some very strong commonalities about the ways in which many boys in these diverse locations perform their masculinities. It is these teachers' concerns about issues of power, aggression, violence, sexism and homophobia that shape how we understand and problematise masculinity throughout this book.

We would like to note also that, while such behaviours cause obvious problems for many teachers and other students, both boys and girls, some of these behaviours also have negative repercussions for some boys. For instance, those working-class boys who construct schoolwork as 'feminine' and seek to demonstrate their masculinity by refusing to cooperate with, or indeed actively resisting, the academic curriculum are unlikely to benefit from the schooling process (see Epstein, 1998; Jackson, 2006). We thus acknowledge that there are some boys who are being failed by the school system and that schools do need to address such boys' lack of academic success. We further contend that the model of pedagogy that we advocate in this book, whilst challenging those toxic forms of masculinity that cause boys to be a problem for others, by also encouraging all students—boys and girls, high and low achievers—to be stretched intellectually will have positive effects for all students. However, while acknowledging some boys' lack of academic success, we do not accept that there is a crisis in masculinity that has advantaged girls at the expense of *all* boys.

Our general sense from the data we have collected leads us to see, as Martino and Pallotta-Chiarolli (2005) do, that the 'real crisis of masculinity' is associated with:

> the misogynist reaction to any perception of so-called 'female' thinking and behaviour, the accepted hegemonic culture of male violence and power and the fear . . . of sexual diversity and non-hegemonic masculinities (2005, p. 7).

With a transformative framework that seeks to disrupt such ways of thinking in mind, we present the stories of Jennifer, Ross,

Rachel and Monica in the following chapters. Importantly, in each story we highlight the key research-based understandings about gender, masculinity and schooling imperative in teachers critically reflecting on the nature of their strategies and their potential effects within a social (gender) justice framework (Lingard et al., 2002; Martino et al., 2004). We recognise that such an approach requires that teachers have a deep knowledge and critical understanding of how gender identities and inequities are constructed, both within and beyond the contexts of schooling. Through the teacher stories we illustrate these knowledges and understandings—particularly as they relate to challenging, rather than reinscribing, the structures and practices that normalise and perpetuate gender inequity (Francis & Skelton, 2005; Martino & Pallotta-Chiarolli, 2003; Martino et al., 2004).

Structure of the book

In the next chapter, we outline the pedagogical framework—productive pedagogies—that we draw on to highlight those practices that improve the academic and social outcomes of schooling. It is a framework that is associated with high-quality academic and social student outcomes (Lingard et al., 2001; Hayes et al., 2006; Allan, 2003; Munns, 2007; Marsh, 2007). It has been a key pedagogical framework recommended to improve the educational experiences of boys within a social justice framework (Lingard et al., 2002; Keddie, 2006b; Mills & Keddie, 2007). However, we do have some concerns about how this framework might be interpreted and implemented in the absence of the gender knowledges demonstrated by the teachers we have foregrounded in the following chapters. We cover some of these concerns in this chapter.

In Chapters 3 to 6, we present the stories of four teachers who have given thought to the education of boys. These are all teachers who do not have deficit models of boys—they believe that they can all learn. They seek to stretch their students intellectually by making them think through complex and difficult issues, and they are not prepared to give up on students whose behaviours make them a problem to others and to themselves. In many ways, they are also teachers who are firmly located within the current 'education wars' where progressive education has been under attack for an apparent lack of rigour, failure to engage with the canon and for substituting process for content. What these teachers indicate—and we would suggest that they are indeed 'progressive' educators—is that academic or intellectual rigour is very much part of their practice, and that they are not necessarily opposed to introducing aspects of the canon into their classrooms (albeit in connected and meaningful ways); for them, content is just as important as process. We would thus assert that these teachers are far more likely to motivate their students into achieving higher level (academic *and* social) outcomes than would be the case with teachers who emphasise the learning of canonical content in traditional expository ways that are then tested through standardised testing processes.

In Chapter 3 we present Jennifer's story: 'A "fresh look" at taken-for-granted ways of being', where we explore how her respectful approach and intellectually challenging classroom environment position her students with agency and legitimacy and provide a highly generative context for pursuing gender justice. Jennifer teaches Years 11 and 12 in a large inner-city P–12 coeducational government school. We look at how she tries to broaden students' understandings of masculinity and femininity and to problematise dominant and dominating ways of being male through her resistance of the power inequities inherent in traditional teacher–student relationships and her scaffolding of critical literacy. Her story foregrounds how particular ways of thinking about gender, power and inequity, as social constructions that are amenable to change, enable spaces for social action and transformation.

In Chapter 4, 'Ross: Afflicting the comfortable and comforting the afflicted', we highlight how a commitment to the principles of social justice frames a teaching approach that seeks to challenge students' narrow views, particularly in relation to issues of class and culture. Ross teaches in a large, well-established and prestigious boys' Catholic school. We explore Ross's understandings of masculinity as a hierarchical construction, particularly as this relates to his challenging of students intellectually on a range of social issues. Here Ross tries to transform the sense of elitism, materialism and ethnocentrism that he sees as characterising the lifeworlds of many of his students. We draw attention in this chapter to issues of hierarchical masculinities and a pedagogy that promotes 'thinking from another angle' to foreground the 'missing voice'. In Ross's story, we also explore issues relating to boys and gender role models, and more specifically to the ways in which particular types of role models can work to reinscribe but also disrupt traditional notions of gender.

In Chapter 5 we present Rachel's story: 'Challenging "power-driven" notions of being male'. Rachel teaches in an edge city government coeducational high school. Her story brings to life a passion for gender justice that drives a commitment to fighting against the gender stereotypes that she sees as constraining boys' lifeworlds. We explore how Rachel's desire for her students to 'break out of the box' of restrictive gender stereotypes frames behaviour-management strategies and classroom pedagogies that challenge and seek to broaden boys' 'power-driven' notions of being male. To these ends, we examine Rachel's one-on-one interactions with boys and her respectful pedagogy in the classroom. Here we identify how she tries to offer alternative ways of thinking and acting through a conciliatory approach that scaffolds boys' examinations of being male and a transformative practice that explores issues such as homophobia and sexism.

In Chapter 6, 'Monica: Schooling children for life beyond school', we identify how accounting for specific social and cultural issues and factors of inequity relevant to a particular context is imperative in terms of working for gender justice. Monica is a teaching principal in a remote government primary school situated in an economically depressed area. We draw attention to how Monica does this in her present teaching situation, where the predominance of boys in her class and the broader gendered assumptions and understandings of the rural community mean that she must focus on ensuring that girls in her class 'can be heard'. Monica's story also draws our attention to how broader social factors constrain her efforts to teach in socially just ways. In working 'against the grain' of these factors, we explore how Monica attempts to broaden her students' 'horizons' and challenge limited notions of masculinity and femininity through teaching for and about active citizenship within a context of enhanced community–school relationships.

At the end of each of these teacher narratives, we outline a series of activities, which draw on the teachers' stories, to assist in the development of strategies to address various aspects of boys' education in local contexts. These activities are not designed to 'solve' issues in teaching boys, but to promote discussions about the appropriateness of various ways of addressing issues of boys' education. We hope that these activities will be useful for teachers, both in terms of developing socially just classroom practices and in relation to the development of school structures that promote gender equity.

In selecting the contexts and the scope of teachers within the broader interview cohort as well as these particular teachers, we were mindful of representing a range of issues, experiences, curriculum areas and year levels. In terms of the four main teachers, and given that our book does not draw on data from students, we were especially mindful of ensuring that our teacher stories resonated with the concerns raised by students in other research in this area. Here we drew in particular on recent extensive empirical work conducted by Martino and Pallotta-Chiarolli (2005) that surveyed over 700 adolescent students about 'what it means to be a boy and a girl at school, what it means to be "cool" and "normal" and the effect of these social constructions on learning and relationships' (2005, p. xi). We saw it as critical that our key teacher stories demonstrated an awareness of the issues that are important for students in terms of gender diversity and schooling.

As such, and consistent with an abundance of other gender and pedagogy research (Davies, 1993; Gilbert & Gilbert, 1998; Lingard et al., 2002; Martino & Pallotta-Chiarolli, 2003; Keddie, 2006b), we were concerned that the teacher stories demonstrated awareness, in particular, of how gender regimes can work in oppressive ways to police and normalise particular behaviours and constrain achievement, and how inequitable relations of authority, power and control negatively impact on students. Acknowledging students' concerns in these areas, and consistent with the data presented in this chapter, we highlight in particular teacher knowledges and practices in terms of issues of sex- and gender-based harassment, especially in terms of transforming the harmful impacts of homophobia, (hetero)sexism and misogyny, and issues of authority and control—particularly in terms of disrupting the traditional teacher and school practices that endorse gender inequities and, more specifically, dominant constructions of masculinity.

We conclude the book with a hope that the current moment of boys being constructed as victims is coming to a close. We are eager to see an approach to the education of all students that encourages them to engage with the world in ways that will make it a better place for all to live in. While at times we are not overly optimistic about this eventuality, we do draw hope from the work that many teachers do with the students in their care. We have seen teachers in this, and other, research who make a difference to students' lives. They are teachers who strive to ensure that their students' opportunities are not limited by restrictive notions of gender, and that their students understand and challenge their own privilege, as well as having an understanding of their own rights. They are teachers who reject deficit models of students; they believe that all of their students can achieve, and they refuse to lower standards and expectations based on spurious notions of gender difference. These teachers also are concerned to ensure that the work undertaken in class has meaning for their students, being well aware that many students—boys and girls alike—who are under-achieving are doing so because they see no relevance to schooling. These teachers make schooling meaningful. And most of all, and importantly for students in their classrooms, they *care* about their students. They create a classroom environment that scaffolds students' learning, that encourages students to take risks, and where being different is not perceived as a problem. We thus present the teacher narratives in this book based on the presumption that what teachers do in the classroom matters and that their work can contribute to a more just and equitable world.

2 BOYS AND PRODUCTIVE PEDAGOGIES

Introduction

In this chapter, we draw on the productive pedagogies model to consider some of the key issues and strategies for improving the academic and social outcomes of boys. As detailed in Chapter 1, our focus here is on assisting teachers to move beyond a narrow focus on boys' educational strategies to a broader focus on pedagogies and critical reflective practice (Lingard et al., 2002). To these ends, we draw on transformative gender justice lenses, and the teacher voices from our research, to illustrate sustainable pedagogies that will work to broaden boys' narrow understandings of identity. Organised around the four dimensions of the productive pedagogies framework, the following examines issues of gender equity and masculinity in relation to connectedness, intellectual engagement, social support, and valuing and working with difference. Articulating how our gender justice principles support gender-just pedagogies, this chapter provides a context for how we present and analyse the teacher stories and professional development activities in the remaining chapters.

The 'productive pedagogies' framework

'Productive pedagogies' is a framework of teaching and learning developed as part of a large Australian research study, a three-year examination of the links between classroom practice and improved learning (Lingard et al., 2001, 2003; Hayes et al., 2006). This study, drawing on the work of Newmann and Associates (1996) in the United States, and complemented by other research (for example, Boaler, 2002; Darling-Hammond, 1997), demonstrated that students' academic and social outcomes are enhanced through classroom pedagogies and assessment tasks that connect with students' lives, promote intellectual engagement, are undertaken in socially supportive environments, and value and work with difference. The four dimensions of the model reflect these imperatives of quality teaching and learning.

Elements within the 'connectedness' dimension are intended to enhance learning through linking particular understandings and knowledges to students' interests and experiences—their biographies and the world beyond the classroom. The dimension of 'intellectual quality' involves facilitating students' deep knowledge and understanding of particular topics and issues through a view of knowledge as problematic in its social, political and cultural construction. The 'supportive classroom environment' dimension is characterised by social support and mutually respectful relations while the legitimation of non-dominant cultural knowledges underpins the 'valuing and working with difference' dimension. Evidence from the major research project from which this model was developed suggests that, when the various elements from all four dimensions of the model are present in classroom practices, the academic and social outcomes of all students—especially those from traditionally under-achieving groups—improve. This model of pedagogy, with its focus on social outcomes as well as academic outcomes, and its demonstrated effectiveness in improving both, is an ideal platform from which to consider issues of gender justice and the teaching of boys (see, for example, Lingard et al., 2002; Keddie, 2006b).

We draw heavily on this model because of its social justice possibilities—of particular importance in relation to encouraging boys to consider their own privilege and to engage in activities that work to challenge gender injustices. However, we do have some reservations about how some aspects of the model can be taken up with boys if not supported by an understanding of gender justice. In this chapter, we outline this model and comment on some of the dangers of using its principles in working with boys without taking into account the relational nature of gender constructions. In so doing, we examine each of the four dimensions in turn to focus on key issues and strategies associated with boys, gender justice and schooling.

Connectedness

Much has been made of the supposed way in which current school curricula fail to connect with the lives of boys. The 'feminisation' of schools and teaching is typically blamed for this apparent disconnection, and indeed has been a pervasive explanation for boys' 'disadvantage' (see Francis & Skelton, 2005; and Skelton, 2002, for critiques of this argument). Here the supposed gender gap in achievement is explained as arising from schooling environments favouring girls', rather than boys', ways of learning and relating. A secondary teacher in our work seemed to sum up this particular view:

> I really do believe that the school system very much favours girls . . . you know the whole idea of being in control, disciplined, well behaved, doing the right thing . . . I think that girls have been pushed to an advantage even further . . . I believe that boys lose out. (Brenda)

Consistent with our gender justice framework and our rejection of a competing victims approach to such issues, we do not endorse this view. Notwithstanding our contention that schools in many ways—given their increased focus on management regimes—are becoming increasingly masculinised (Mahony & Hextall, 2000), we take issue with the way such a view casts 'feminisation' in a negative light. As we pointed out in Chapter 1, we associate an improvement in boys' academic outcomes with a greater encompassing of qualities traditionally associated with femininity, and thus qualities such as being 'disciplined', 'well behaved' and 'doing the right thing' are not necessarily a bad thing for boys—although we recognise that discourses that valorise these behaviours can be used in punitive and problematic ways (Mills, 1996, 1997). We also take issue with how such a view essentialises gender. One of the key assumptions underpinning the association of boys' poor academic performance with a feminisation of schools and teaching relates to how an over-representation of female teachers, particularly in primary classrooms, equates to an excessively 'feminine' environment—such a suggestion rests on the premise that only males can 'do masculinity' and only females 'femininity' (Francis & Skelton, 2005). We believe this premise to be untenable, not least because our research—consistent with the work of others (Robinson, 2000; Reid, 1999)—notes many female teachers' compunction to 'masculinise' their management practices in order to be seen as authoritative and to be taken seriously, particularly by male students. As one of the secondary teachers in our research pointed out:

> . . . I have used my voice, and when I speak very loudly I can make my voice go very low and very loud to defuse any situation that's not appropriate. I remember doing it one day and I thought 'Who was that who just yelled then?' and it was me . . . it was so deep and so loud and I thought, 'Oh my god, I've lost any sense of femininity'. Sometimes I think the boys have

allowed the feminine side of me to go. I feel that I'm a bit blokey bloke with them. [I mean] . . . you're not going to go [*said in high soft voice*], 'Excuse me boys, separate'. Ain't gonna do a thing. (Alexandra)

In exploring issues of masculinity and connectedness in learning, we take further issue with how assumptions about the feminisation of education imply that schools and teaching *are* connected with girls' lives. While our research tends to suggest that girls are much happier than boys to 'play the game', we contend that this willingness to 'play the game' does not mean that schools and teachers are effectively connecting with girls, nor does it mean that girls are not resisting. In terms of a general sense of resistance and disengagement with school and classroom life, girls and boys express *similarly* negative views, but girls' resistance tends to be enacted in more tacit ways and not necessarily through the overt disruption that tends to characterise boys' resistance (Martino & Pallotta-Chiarolli, 2005).

Mindful of the imperative of connecting learning to the lifeworlds of *all* students and the importance of broadening particularly boys' understandings of gender, our focus in this section is on how connectedness issues have been taken up within the current boy-turn in schools. In particular, we problematise the common response to the assumption that schools and teachers are excessively feminine and thus disadvantage boys—the uncritical take-up of 'boy-friendly' strategies. While we acknowledge how such strategies might be effective in engaging *some* boys, we want to highlight how they ignore boys' and girls' gender diversity and invariably normalise and leave unquestioned a narrow and often problematic version of masculinity (Connell, 1995, 2000; Davies, 1993; Keddie, 2003; Martino et al., 2004; Francis & Skelton, 2005).

Within a context that seeks to make learning more relevant and connected to boys, calls for more 'masculine' curriculum content and resources are familiar. The major emphasis here in terms of enhancing boys' engagement and motivation to learn relates to teachers connecting with their real-world interests and preferences beyond the classroom (Lingard et al., 2002; Alloway et al., 2002). Certainly, in our experience, teachers are mindful of this. Many express the view that boys' educational outcomes can be improved through greater efforts to construct environments that are interesting and relevant to them. Particular teachers we have interviewed talk, for instance, about how they negotiate curriculum content around boys' interests in sport, popular culture and issues that concern them.

There have, however, been numerous instances where, in attempts to connect with and engage boys in the learning process, there has been a reinforcement of traditional forms of masculinity (see, for example, Connolly, 1998; Francis, 2000; Skelton, 2001; McGregor & Mills, 2006; Roulston & Mills, 2000). For instance, it was brought to our attention by a senior policy officer in an Australian department of education that one advocate for boys had been showcasing an online magazine that would help boys to enjoy reading. This magazine has pictures of scantily clad young women draped over cars, alongside other material about 'chicks', sport and cars. This form of reading material serves to reinforce narrow definitions of what it means to be a boy (including holding misogynous attitudes towards women and girls). This also, rather ironically, serves to reinforce those attributes amongst some boys that have caused them to already disengage with the learning process—and it serves to limit their life experiences and breadth of knowledge about the world. Do we want, for instance, to encourage boys who spend most of their free time playing football to then read only about football? There is often the presumption that at least boys are reading. This is true. We are prepared to accept, as many of the teachers we have interviewed do, that it is useful for boys to develop the technical skills of reading by reading material in which they are already interested; however, not misogynous and homophobic materials! This argument that it doesn't matter what boys are reading as long as they are reading has been made to us on numerous occasions.

But, as most teachers know, reading is also an intellectual practice where readers make assumptions, hypothesise as to meaning, and are emotionally affected, engaged, intrigued, and so on. Teaching reading has to involve students being exposed to a wide range of ideas and thoughts to expand their knowledges. Making classroom practices connected then need not only relate to that which students are already interested in. There is, of course, value in building on students' background knowledge. There is a significant body of research that makes this point (Newmann & Associates, 1995; Darling-Hammond, 1997). However, 'connectedness', as indicated by the productive pedagogies research, also involves connecting to 'real-world' issues and problems (see, for example, Ashman & Conway, 1993, 1997; Apple & Beane, 1999a, 1999b) and launching classroom units with the intent to engage with such problems. One secondary teacher we interviewed, in teaching about issues of violence and war in various historical periods, drew on current real-world events and issues to connect with his students to raise issues of gender justice:

> We talked about violence in the war and the comfort women, and we talked about that ad that runs on Australian television and what that says about our society—the one that the government's put on about women being battered—violence against women. And so you try and bring it into the now a little bit, and that's what I've been trying to do . . . and they tend to remember that as well as the content. They still remember the content, but they can relate it to things. (David)

Earlier, we indicated some of our concerns about attempts to achieve connectedness by reinforcing dominant constructions of gender. We are likewise concerned that an emphasis on connectedness might lead to creating a curriculum that fails to challenge students intellectually. For instance, we would be concerned about the introduction of vocational education programs as a means of engaging low-achieving boys when such programs fail to engage at an intellectual level. However, this is not to say that vocational education programs cannot be built around intellectually challenging tasks. Along these lines, one of the secondary coeducational teachers in our research connected his classroom work with work in his school's broader farming community to stimulate particular boys' interests and to encourage greater intellectual engagement:

> . . . I really try and tap into their interests like—a project that I do comes from a client-service project. I act out a role play where I act like a customer . . . I say, 'OK you're a small welding company. I've got $2000. I want you to build me a pig rack for the back of the ute [utility truck].' And so they have to ring the local steel dealer, they measure it and they come up with all the quotes, all the materials, that sort of stuff. And on the day they will drive their utes into the school ground, dress up in all their work gear, as if they're actually at a welding company and they say—you know, 'Well this is one we've prepared earlier' and 'This is pretty much what yours would look like' and—like I just walk up to them and say, 'G'day, I'm such and such. How did you go with my pig rack?' You know 'What have you come up with?' And then I just keep on asking them questions and they'll end up talking for 15–20 minutes like an oral . . . and they talk comfortably and confidently and so you can end up giving them a good mark especially if you can just ask a few leading questions. (Brad)

While we would express caution about the ways in which the content for this activity may reinforce limited versions of masculinity, it is clear that its written and oral communication and personal relationship elements have clear potential for connecting with these boys without compromising intellectual engagement.

The provision of such a context is consistent with the work of Rosenstock and Steinberg (1999), who argue that vocational education curriculum should broaden, rather than limit, creative intellectual work and should not be reduced to job skills training that only erects more barriers to high-quality education for students from traditionally low-achieving backgrounds.

This provision of intellectually challenging work is critical to the improvement of educational outcomes for students. We do want to stress the importance of providing students with material that engages their interest. This is particularly important for those students, including boys, who have clearly disengaged from the learning process. But as Darling-Hammond (1997, p. 109) has argued: 'Just creating interesting tasks for students is not enough.' There has to be a focus on developing 'deep understanding' in worthwhile and meaningful contexts that takes students 'beyond recall and reproduction of information to evaluation, analysis, synthesis, and production of arguments, ideas and performances' (1997, p. 107). These concerns of Darling-Hammond are taken up in the following section.

Intellectual engagement

Providing intellectually challenging work that promotes deep knowledge and understanding of important disciplinary concepts is imperative for all students to perform well academically (Lingard et al., 2001, 2003; Hayes et al., 2006; Apple & Beane, 1999a, 1999b; Darling-Hammond, 1997; Newmann & Associates, 1996; Boaler, 2002). However, in relation to issues of equity and raising the performance of boys (and of course girls) from traditionally under-achieving backgrounds—that is, Indigenous students in Australia, Afro-Caribbean students in the United Kingdom, and students from low socio-economic backgrounds generally—we want to stress that intellectually challenging work is of particular importance. Like most educationalists, we are aware that high expectations are required of students if they are to achieve well—and the converse is true: low expectations of students are likely to lead to low achievement (see Lingard et al., 2003). As mentioned earlier, we are concerned by the move towards 'boy-friendly' curricula which have the potential to treat various groups of boys as deficit by watering down the curriculum for these boys.

Within many of the current claims about teaching boys, there is an argument that boys struggle with the complexities and difficulties of a postmodern curriculum where there are multiple answers to problems (see, for example, submissions to House of Representatives Standing Committee on Education and Training, 2002). Criticism of supposedly postmodern curricula has been a recurring theme in various conservative commentaries on contemporary education (see, for instance, Donnelly, 2004). However, this is a very limited, and limiting, view of education and its purposes, and of knowledge itself. As Hargreaves (2003) has argued, we now live in a *knowledge society*, and schools need to be equipping students for life in such a society. A feature of this society is the amount of knowledge available to all, often at the click of a mouse, on a multiplicity of topics.

Referring to this aspect of the knowledge society, a history teacher we interviewed talked about how his students are 'drowning' in content, because there is 'so much information'. This teacher also talked about how this knowledge-rich and complex environment demands far beyond the 'low-level' intellectual skills of rote and recall (which, for instance, a watered-down curriculum might generate). Indeed, we contend that the information explosion within our increasingly complex, dynamic and globalised world demands the high intellectual critical engagement and deep knowledge that postmodern curricula support. Significantly, several of the secondary English teachers in our work argued that such curricula were integral in terms of enhancing the academic performance of traditionally lower achieving students. As one remarked:

> ... if we settle for mediocrity, we're gonna get mediocre students ... when we do this work with them, it extends even those boys who are traditionally C students and we're not just talking about jumping through hoops to get marks but they're able to talk about things in such a more sophisticated, supported, valid and discerning way than ever before. (Adam)

It is clear that a knowledge society demands sophisticated, supported and discerning learners, as this teacher suggests—which should, we would add, reflect students' understandings of knowledge as not fixed, but socially produced. Such kinds of learning are especially important for pursuing the goals of gender justice because they allow the processes that produce dominant and restrictive gender knowledges to be challenged and transformed.

In terms of negotiating ways forward for improving boys' educational outcomes in particular, significant gender justice work calls for a problematising of gendered knowledge and cultures. From the 'embryonic' deconstruction in MacNaughton's (2000) work designed to scaffold children's gender awareness in the early years to Martino and Mellor's (1995) work for older students, improved academic and social outcomes are possible through boys' exploration and critical analysis of what it means to be 'masculine' (Alloway et al., 2002; Davies, 1993; Lingard et al., 2002). With the aim of broadening understandings of masculinity and femininity, Martino and Mellor (1995), for instance, provide a framework for assisting students to understand how gender difference and diversity can be produced and maintained, but also challenged and transformed through examining the social production of knowledge. Their work focuses on facilitating students' awareness of how language operates to produce particular versions of reality, and more specifically, how texts and contexts work to construct and regulate taken-for-granted assumptions about gender that position people in inequitable ways. In challenging and transforming these gender(ed) assumptions, their work illustrates the importance of students recognising how texts and contexts can be read or interpreted in multiple rather than singular ways—ways, as Davies (1997) suggests, that highlight the gaps and silences around particular issues and identity relations.

Along these lines, a secondary history teacher from our research talked about how he facilitated awareness of the ways in which particular representations of war promote a particular reality of dominant masculinity, and in so doing create gaps and silences surrounding alternative realities:

> . . . the course that I do which runs through from World War I to World War II has a series of documentaries which show these very old men talking about war. Not about, you know, the old glorify thing, [but] talking, breaking down, crying, you know, some of those things in the Holocaust and the death in the camps where people talk about their experience and how it shook them to the core, and how it's all right to be upset and scared by that, it's all right to be emotional, because if you aren't, OK, forget about being male or female, you're not human . . . I spend a fair bit of time on that . . . the last of those survivors—they don't speak about anything else but what an absolute waste and how scared they were and the tears rolling down the cheeks and the kids sit there in absolute awe of people speaking like this because what they see from, you know, documentaries . . . is the sort of blood and guts and we did this and we took this and we stormed this. (David)

Another secondary teacher we interviewed talked about textual choices in English and how he deliberately chooses texts that 'deal with' the realities and interpretations of 'others'. Within the all-boys' environment of his schooling context, this teacher saw it as important that he select written and visual forms of the same text such as *The Hours* for study with the boys, as these texts could in some way fill the 'silence' surrounding issues of femininity in these boys' lives.

So I do choose texts which will look at female interpretations and female writers. I really like Gwen Harwood's and Sylvia Plath's poetry . . . and when I do *In The Winter Dark* by Tim Winton . . . in that text I ask the boys to become the female, to become either Ronnie or Ida and to take on their role and to use their voice to fill a gap or a silence or some point of marginalisation within the text. (Adam)

Such scaffolding illustrates how the dynamic interaction with texts can make transparent the inequitable power relations surrounding particular issues of gender and provide a context for understanding the social constructedness of knowledge. In particular, students taking on a particular role and using their voice to fill a point of marginalisation within a text can foreground the multiple ways possible for thinking about, responding to and transforming these issues.

This sort of questioning is central to promoting a critical awareness of how we construct knowledge and how our particular 'social baggage' can shape the way we represent and interpret things (Lemon, 1995; Davies, 1998). Delving deeper into how multiple perspectives about particular issues can be explored, another secondary English teacher we interviewed talked about the importance of identifying with students how an individual's prior experience impacts on how they read and interpret texts, and the extent to which they are likely to 'take up' the invited readings within particular texts:

. . . we talk about how things are represented in texts but also the extent to which different readers are likely to take up the invited readings of texts and the reasons for that. So, for example, if you've had a bad experience with some form of bureaucracy, you will be even more suspicious of Big Brother–type intrusions into your existence than other people might be. If you're had a carefree life and are very trustful of those things, you might not even think about it. [Such analysis] is important because it encourages kids to think about the reasons for different interpretations and different readings of texts. (Merrilyn)

These processes of critical analysis and deconstruction can make transparent the constitutive force of the social and help to fracture some of the taken-for-granted truths that we have about gender (Davies, 1997). Through these lenses, gendered assumptions can lose their apparent inevitability because they become visible as fiction. This opens up possibilities for new ways of thinking, speaking and acting (Davies, 1997). In terms of drawing on this framework in ways that encourage a critical reflection of the self, several of the teachers we interviewed talked about the importance of students understanding them-selves as socially and politically constructed—as living texts. One particular teacher associated such critical understandings with making a difference in people's lives. She talked about the significance of students being aware of how particular social processes or discourses subject them in ways that they can either accept or reject, as she explained:

> . . . once you understand where you are then you can either accept where you are or it can become a potential site of resistance. It's a powerful concept isn't it? . . . it's all about making a difference in people's lives, not as a teacher but just giving them the framework so that they can act on it them-selves—they can use it, they can understand where they fit in to society. They can choose to go on with that or they can understand that they have the capacity to change things—that notion of agency. (Merrilyn)

Davies (1998) talks about how such critical self-reflection highlights the relationship between the construction of the self and the construction of knowledge and 'truth'. She presents understanding this relationship as central to enabling 'the capacity to read against the grain of dominant discourses, and against the grain of the privileged positions constructed within them' (1998, pp. 12–13). For gender justice, this allows us to see how particular 'truths' about gender speak us and others into being, and how conventional and constraining ways of being male or female might be resisted and transformed by alternative language practices. One of the teachers in our work, whose story is foregrounded in Chapter 5, helped boys to explore this relationship between themselves and constructions of knowledge and 'truth' about masculinity in a unit she designed for her Year 8 students called 'Boys' Stuff'. In particular, she asked the boys to identify their thoughts about issues of dominant masculinity by positioning themselves on a human continuum (from 'strongly agree' to 'strongly disagree') in relation to assumptions such as:

• Boys are naturally more aggressive than girls.
• Crying is for wimps.
• It's better for a girl to be a 'tomboy' than for a boy to be a 'sissy' or a 'wimp'.
• Achieving well is not cool for boys.

This activity highlighted the boys' understandings of dominant truths about masculinity—an activity that can also highlight how such truths, rather than being fixed and universal, are multiple and shifting depending on particular interpretations and on what it means to be male in various contexts and historical periods. Against this backdrop, this teacher supported the boys' examination of how truths about masculinity are reproduced and policed through, for example, the words and actions of friends, family and female peers, as well as the media and leisure activities such as sport. In making transparent some of the ways in which the dominant truths about masculinity are spoken into existence, such scaffolding high-lights the relationship between the construction of the self and the construction of knowledge, and opens up possibilities in terms of thinking and acting against the grain of dominant discourses (Davies, 1998).

Such explorations help to develop awareness of how speaking-as-usual constructs our sense of self (Davies, 1998). However, breaking the 'enchantment of the compulsory struggle towards dominant and hegemonic forms of masculinity' requires acknowledging the 'desirability and joyful sense of power that boys gain from being positioned within dominant forms of discourse which hand them ascendancy over others' (Davies, 1997, p. 15). Consider the following work sample—a dialogue snippet from a Year 11 drama activity that supported boys' exploration of male identity. In small groups, and following visual and textual scaffolding around issues of masculinity, the boys were required to write a script around the focus question 'What is masculinity?' The snippet is set in a shed and involves three men.

WORK SAMPLE: THE SHED

John: (about to walk off stage) Honey, I'm just heading down to the office, I have to . . . (hesitant) file some papers. Be back later. Bye. (walks off stage)

Tom: (about to walk off stage) Babe, I'm just heading down to the corner store. I will be back in an hour. Bye. (walks off stage)

Later, Tom and John are outside a shed.

Jerry: Password please?

John and Tom say the password and enter the shed.

John and Tom: Hey, mate!

Tom: (relaxing) Back in the shed! I've missed this place.

John: Yep, this good old place. I've been dying to come here. I just want to get away from everything, especially the wife.

Jerry:	Yeah, I know what you mean. It's hard sometimes just to try and get away from them. They're always on your back every minute of the day.
Tom:	Tell me about it (*rolling his eyes*). My wife calls me every day at work.
Jerry:	You think that's bad? Well mine comes and visits me every day just to make sure I'm at work. She's paranoid. If only they could understand what it means to be a man.
John:	They will never understand—they're women.
Later . . .	
Tom:	So how's everything with the wives?
John:	You mean with the sex?
Tom:	Yeah.
John:	It's as rare as a steak tartare.
Jerry:	Me too, the wife is always too tired or not in the mood.
Tom:	Well you've only been married for three years. Sally and me have been married for ten years. Ten long years and I can tell you the sex is even more rare than a steak tartare, it's as dry as a baby's bottom.

While only a brief snippet, this work sample can be read in multiple ways—for instance, as a playful parody of dominant constructions of masculinity that works to ridicule such constructions or as a normalising text that reinforces traditional gender constructions. Notwithstanding, the script brings to life the enchantment of masculinity and the joyful power of dominant forms of masculinity (Davies, 1997). Here these boys tap into well-established and taken-for-granted discourses about women, wives and sex to collude in the legitimation of their maleness at the expense of femaleness, even whilst making fun of such discourses.

Such texts can provide stimulus to consider with students the ways in which normalised versions of masculinity can limit their relationships with others as well as oppressing others. However, within the context of exploring a broad range of possible ways of being male, the imperative is for teachers to recognise affirmative or socially just spaces and work with these spaces in connected and meaningful ways. This means teachers being able to identify how students' actions and silences either support or challenge inequitable gender definitions (MacNaughton, 2000). In relation to broadening boys' understandings of masculinity, teachers can make visible these challenges and position them as legitimate alternatives to dominant constructions (Martino & Pallotta-Chiarolli, 2003). This is an ongoing challenge that involves facilitating boys' awareness and appreciation that alternative ways of being can be rewarding and positive, and continually encouraging boys to resist the dominant and perhaps more convincing and familiar social processes and discourses of masculinity that speak them into existence (Davies, 1993, 1997).

We have argued in this section that intellectual work which engages students in critical literacy-type activities that problematise traditionally gendered ways of seeing and knowing the world is important for improving social justice outcomes. As with the connectedness dimension of productive pedagogies, the intellectual quality dimension is not sufficient to improve boys' academic and social outcomes. Boys are only likely to take up alternative versions of masculinity in socially supportive environments where they are provided with the explicit skills to do so.

Social support

The importance of positive and supportive teacher–student relationships is a major focus for boys. Whilst not wanting to construct boys as victims, there are many boys—especially from low socio-economic backgrounds—who have disengaged from schooling as a result of poor relationships with teachers and other authority figures within their schools. Whilst the same is true of many girls from such backgrounds, for many of these boys their disengagement is grounded in a masculinity politics that positions them in an antagonistic relationship with the formal processes of schooling (see Epstein, 1998; Mills, 2001; Martino & Pallotta-Chiarolli, 2005; Francis, 1999; Jackson, 2002, 2006). In this section, we are mindful of these politics in our consideration of the ways in which teachers construct relations of support with their male students. Principally, we explore issues of support associated with teachers positioning their students with greater autonomy over their everyday school lives. However, we also explore how the engendering of high levels of support requires an examination of the hostile relationship many disengaged boys have with 'official' schooling. In terms of creating socially supportive and respectful learning environments, we take a critical view of the 'ways in which power relations and constructs around domination and authority are being played out and systematically legitimated within school structures and classroom practice' (Martino & Pallotta-Chiarolli, 2003, p. 208). In particular, we look at how such structures interact with masculinity politics in ways that can limit work for gender justice.

Many of the disengaged boys who we have come across feel angry at 'the system' and the formal structures of the school. They often feel that they have no voice—that they are often punished unfairly and that no one in the school cares about them (see, for example, Mills, 2001). To some extent, these concerns can be justified. We—like many others—have witnessed the authoritarian structures within some schools that seek to stifle any dissent (Mills, 1996, 1997; Keddie, 2006a, 2007). And, as Darling-Hammond (1997, p. 138) has noted: 'Authoritarian systems that rely on heavy-handed sanctions ultimately increase the level of student alienation and misbehaviour and reduce possibilities for addressing problems constructively.'

In developing positive and mutually supportive relationships, the importance of breaking down the traditional power imbalances between teachers and students is central, particularly given many boys' resistance to being overpowered and controlled. Boys' social and behavioural outcomes are enhanced through democratic disciplinary approaches that position students with greater legitimacy and agency in their everyday school lives. A key emphasis here relates to teachers adopting a more connected and conciliatory approach with students—an approach that many teachers we have interviewed regard as being supported by engaging and collaborative pedagogies such as, for example, those embedded in new multi-modal ICT technologies where the students are 'teaching the teachers'. In providing a context for these ways of teaching, a number of teachers we have interviewed talk about the importance of a co-learner approach, as the following illustrates:

> I really go to great pains to point out to them that we're co-learners, and I'm learning from them as much as they're learning from me and that none of us should ever be afraid to say we don't know anything. I say to them: 'Look boys . . . I'm no more intelligent than you. I'm still learning.' (Maree)

Considering how authoritarian teacher relations are likely to affirm—and indeed exacerbate—boys' take-up of dominant constructions of masculinity, we can see the importance of democratising the classroom in these ways. We are aware, however, of the research (see Keddie, 2003; Davies & Laws, 2000) suggesting that some teachers almost expect boys to misbehave and, in trying to gain respect and authority, respond to these students in excessively controlling ways. As one of the primary teachers in our research remarked:

> . . . some teachers expect that they are going to have a battle of wills with boys and the teacher must win. Whereas with girls I think that sometimes the way they talk to them automatically indicates that they are expecting this girl to cooperate. Whereas sometimes when they are talking to the boys they're just, 'You're not going to cooperate with me so you're just going to have to do what I want'. (Debbie)

As some of the data we presented in Chapter 1 illustrated, we are also aware that these expectations regarding boys' potential to misbehave are, in particular cases, warranted—especially in terms of many boys' 'anti-female' attitudes and their disrespect for and resistance to female teacher authority. Along these lines, one of the teachers in our work felt that, to develop some 'street cred' with the boys in her class in her early career, she had to be excessively strict:

> I think I've gone from being a really strict nasty disciplinarian, you know, Miss Witch in the classroom, from the beginning stages, 'cause I felt I had to do that, to get my street cred with them. I really felt as a female that was the hard yards. I would be very strict and very firm, and, you know, 'don't smile till Easter'. (Alexandra)

Notwithstanding the importance of problematising some boys' resistance to female teachers' authority, we acknowledge—as this teacher does—how excessively controlling teacher–student relations 'make for a really nasty classroom environment', particularly when considering the masculinity politics of power and domination that frame many boys' misbehaviours. With this in mind, we can see how disrupting and reworking teacher–student power relations to make them more equitable might facilitate a broadening of boys' understandings and enactments of masculinity through legitimising alternatives to dominance (Alloway et al., 2002). Along the lines of a co-learning and anti-authoritarian approach that provides such alternatives, many of the teachers in our research have talked about the importance of presenting themselves as fallible, as the following illustrates:

> . . . if I've done something that I afterwards think, 'Oh, that was a bit out of line, I shouldn't have', I always apologise and it's really important to me that they realise that I am sorry, and that

just 'cause I am a teacher doesn't mean I can walk all over you and your feelings. (Sally)

An important concern in creating a democratic learning environment relates to teachers being transparent about why students are asked to engage in particular tasks. Key issues raised by our research relate to the importance of allowing greater student input in what, how and when they engage in particular tasks. With the aim of providing students with multiple opportunities to experience success in their learning, the teachers in our research consistently highlight the significance of providing a range of choices for students in terms of content and presentation formats. One of the secondary teachers we interviewed, for example—while acknowledging some of the difficulties of such an approach—talked about how such learning was important:

> . . . building in choices is absolutely fundamental in the way that kids feel about learning. You have to build in, as far as is practical and appropriate, choices . . . and sometimes it's not an easy thing to do—to give kids choices with books for example, because it means that teachers may have two major novels on the go in Year 11 and 12. So you've got to think of different ways of teaching because you can't have the same degree of input into things you normally would. We say to them you have this choice but this is what it will mean—that you will have to work a bit more independently . . . but I think that choice is very important—so important that a few things can be traded off for it. And it also ties in with people taking responsibility for their own learning, which is something that you really want to encourage. (Merrilyn)

Against this backdrop of student choice and input, an overwhelming number of the teachers in our work have highlighted the significance of demonstrating their personal interest in students beyond formal schooling contexts. Such interest can enhance the teacher–student relationship and, consequently, the learning engagement of students. A few of the teachers in our study mentioned specific strategies that they understood to be invaluable in terms of demonstrating such interest. The following is an example:

> . . . it's really important, particularly for the boys, that the teacher knows them outside of school or is interested in them beyond the subject area. So I thought, well, the first two lessons I will put aside to getting to know these kids . . . and what I did was on the first day I said, 'OK I don't know you, you don't know me . . . the quickest way I think I can find out about you and what your lives are like is for you to fill in this little questionnaire' . . . it was about what they liked about English, what they didn't like, what they loathed doing . . . five things about them that I should know. And when I got the sheets back I looked through them and made up a quiz about the class. For the next lesson—it was a competition and with lolly prizes: 'Who knows their classmates the best?' And so I asked questions like, 'OK, in this room there are five people who ride horses on a weekend—who can pick those five people?' That sort of thing. Well by the end of the lesson I actually had boys carrying my books from class and come over to meet me because I knew their dog's name. It was just phenomenal. I could get on really well with the class and I've never actually had a discipline problem with that class. It's just—I think I started off on the right foot. I just put the books away for a couple of lessons to get to know the kids and that made such a difference . . . like they told me topics they were interested in and I could go up to them during the year when they were scratching their head about what to write about in their short story and say 'Well you know you like mythical creatures—why don't you incorporate that?' And you could just see their eyes light up that I would actually know that. (Carmen)

While recognising that student interests have to be incorporated in to school, that their voices have to be heard in respectful ways, we are also tentative in our suggestions about the importance of this for boys. A focus on engaging boys through demonstrating an interest in their lives, showing a concern about their views and trying to build relationships with them, especially in the form of 'male bonding', may have negative consequences for girls. We are, for instance, aware that such engagement can work to perpetuate and reinscribe inequitable understandings of gender, and can involve male teachers colluding with boys against the interests of girls and women. A young male teacher in our study, for example, talked about how a celebration point system was a 'major success' in encouraging his predominantly male English Communication students to read:

> . . . we do a celebration chart and basically for every kid that reads they get a point and when they rack up enough points they get to use those points to spend them, so to speak on a reward . . . they could choose to spend on whatever. Like if they racked up a million points I had to buy them a carton of rum; if they racked up you know a hundred thousand points I think I had to bring in a stripper or something like that—you know they were never going to get . . . when they suggest well what can we spend our points on? You just put anything up but then you say—but that will cost you a million points . . . but it's a good bit of fun. (Brad)

Here we can see how connecting with boys might collude with and valorise a particular version of masculinity that, in this instance, positions drinking alcohol and the objectification of females as rewards. Indeed, some of the teachers in our work talked about the dangers of such collusion in terms of producing relationships where boys 'overstepped the mark' in terms of their attempts to manage behaviour. We are certainly not suggesting that dominant masculinities associated with the harassment of girls or female teachers and sexist and homophobic jokes and comments should be tolerated. Rather, we are suggesting that a democratic classroom (and school) environment be created where all who are participants in the everyday life of the school are treated with respect. Such respect requires that boys be taught how to be members of a democratic environment within which power differentials based upon class, gender, sexuality, race/ethnicity and physical (dis)abilities are challenged (see Mills, 2001). Learning how to become a member of a democratic classroom does not, as with most academic and social dispositions, come naturally—such skills have to be explicitly taught.

Much has been made about the need for explicit criteria in the classroom and the ways in which those familiar and at ease with the mores and nuances of what makes a 'good' student are at an advantage over students who are not at ease with the schooling process (Bourdieu & Passeron, 1977; Cope & Kalantzis, 1995). For these latter students, the need for explicitness has been stressed. This means making it obvious to students what is expected of them. These expectations have to be both related to their schoolwork *and* to their behaviour—and here we broaden the notion of a 'good student' to include one who is concerned not just about academic achievement but also with being a positive member of a democratic community. In our work with teachers, the routines, boundaries and clear expectations of particular behaviour-management programs and strategies, and broader pastoral care systems support their efforts in this regard. More specifically, a number of teachers to whom we have talked see processes like William Glasser's (1992, 1998) 'choice theory' and the 'responsible thinking process' as useful in managing the behaviour of boys, particularly in terms of minimising disrespectful behaviours such as 'pay-outs' and 'put-downs'.

While we are cognisant of how these sorts of processes are helpful, we are also cautious of how they can be taken up in overly prescriptive and clinical ways. Such rationalist practice is inclined, for instance, to dislocate behaviour from its broader social context and, in this sense, tends not to be sensitive to the dynamic nature of human social relationships—defining students' identities within conservative, narrow and incomplete paradigms. Indeed, it is argued that prescriptive, systematic and controlling strategies can work to perpetuate violent cultures because the world of emotions and feelings is devalued (Fitzclarence, 2000; Kenway & Fitzclarence, 1997). Highlighting the limitations of such measures, in terms of their potential to be used as 'mechanical devices' that lack human connection, one of the secondary teachers we interviewed made the following significant remark:

> . . . we do obviously have behaviour-management policies and things like that—the problem with them is that if they are just treated like a mechanical device and the outcome is just pre-ordained the kids will just jack up against it and that's it—without any sort of relationship there the procedures just won't work. (Paul)

In their tendency to ignore the broader social context, such prescriptive systems often disregard the sex- and gender-based (as well as the class- and race-based) dimensions of bullying and violence in schools. In this respect—and particularly, of course, given the overwhelmingly high proportion of boys who are recipients of such systems—we would see it as critical that these approaches be accompanied by a recognition of how boys' behaviours are situated and invested within broader inequitable power relations and discourses that work to construct and maintain their ways of being. A gender-just framework of choice and responsible thinking about behaviours, then, would not only reflect a non-authoritarian approach that respects student agency and autonomy, but also a self-critical problematising of the power relations of gendered knowledge along the lines featured in the previous section on intellectual engagement.

We have so far outlined and commented upon three of the dimensions of productive pedagogies: intellectual engagement, connectedness and socially supportive classrooms. The fourth dimension, valuing and working with difference, is critical for promoting social justice within and beyond the classroom. This is especially the case when teachers are attempting to broaden gender options for students and challenge those policing mechanisms that reinscribe dominant constructions of masculinity and femininity.

Valuing and working with difference and diversity

Davina Cooper (2004), in her discussions on diversity and equality, explores some of the problems with expressions such as 'valuing diversity'. For example, questions relating to whose diversities are worthy of support, and whose are not, have to be confronted. Such questions are clearly central to how issues of masculinity might be understood and addressed in schools. As we have highlighted in this book, key agendas within the sphere of boys' education will understand and present issues associated with the valuing of diversity in quite different ways. For gender justice, the implications for different understandings about areas of diversity worthy for support are significant. In this book, we promote a valuing of difference that enables students' critical awareness of the inequitable power relations in our social world. Here valuing difference is not simply about encouraging boys to uncritically value diverse ways of being male, but to draw on social justice imperatives to trouble the inequitable power relations that unfairly discriminate.

Such considerations are central to raising boys' awareness

about the ways in which patriarchal sets of relations shape the construction of privilege, but also constructions of marginalisation that are generated by such social ills as racism, religious intolerance and poverty. To a great extent, we believe that engendering such awareness is key to teaching for democracy—that is, to providing students with the skills and knowledges necessary for them to act as responsible members of a democratic community. Darling-Hammond (1997, p. 141) argues that this awareness centres on schools providing students with 'access to knowledge that enables creative thought and access to a social dialogue that enables democratic communication and participation'. In our experience, there are many significant ways in which teachers are attempting to engender in their students such commitments to democratic community. In terms of concerns associated with boys and masculinity, a focus on issues of group identity and on building boys' commitments to inclusivity and active citizenship is characteristic of these attempts. It is against a backdrop that seeks to value non-dominant gender-just cultures that we explore understandings of difference and diversity in relation to issues of peer group identity, consciousness-raising and extra-curricula activities, and the issue of male role modelling.

Boys' collective or group identities are an important focus of secondary and primary masculinities and schooling research (Connell, 2000; Martino, 1999; Mac an Ghaill, 1994; Connolly, 2004; Keddie, 2003). This research illustrates the significance of 'groupness' or peer culture in shaping boys' behaviours. One of the teachers in our research, who works in an all-boys' environment, describes the potency of such 'groupness' in her account of the school's playground area:

> You know that big area in the centre of the school? Up until about two years ago all the boys had morning tea and lunchtime there and it was like a bubbling cauldron. Just, you know, 1200 boys in there, just brewing over at lunchtime. It was nasty. (Alexandra)

This teacher further describes how such groupness can work to amplify hierarchical masculine conventions. Her observations illustrate how boys' group identities can enforce narrow understandings and practices that work in exclusive ways to subsume and disparage difference and diversity (Hickey & Keddie, 2004; Keddie, 2003):

> At my last school there was this area that they used to call the 'jock wall' and that's where the footy jocks sat for that year and they were pretty nasty kids . . . sitting there, and passing comment. [Here] we have the 'veranda group', and they're the same—a cluster of mainly Grade 12s . . . they're the 'boyos' . . . and then you've got the 'undercross' group and they're the dead-heads—they sit near the tuckshop . . . there's a dozen or so kids . . . there's some extremes in behaviours . . . they're excluded but they're not nerds, they're not your study kids—they're your kids who are probably on the edge. They would be the kids who would push the boundaries in the classroom, and probably push the boundaries with drinking and stuff on the weekend . . . they just seem to push the whole time and their behaviour is socially just bizarre some days. Like they think it's really cool to make noises when anyone walks past them. And that can be noises from mooing like a cow to stamping their feet. (Alexandra)

It is because peer group behaviours—especially those of boys—can be disruptive in these sorts of ways that teachers tend to break peer groups up in classrooms—often to the extent that they are sometimes not even recognisable. However, as this teacher points out, such groups are invariably visible in the playground where they can be very oppressive to other students. Hickey and Fitzclarence (2004) argue, in this respect, that in schools taking their role in the development of responsible decision-making seriously, they must rethink approaches that deny or dilute groupness. Indeed, these authors contend that 'while pedagogies of separation continue to dominate mainstream education, peer groups will continue to exist as the natural enemy of teachers' (2004, p. 61).

It is clear that issues of 'groupness' cannot be ignored. We are aware that there are times when teachers do need to break up particular arrangements of students who are disrupting the learning of others, and provide students with broader connections with other members of their classroom group. However, at the same time students need to 'learn' how to function in their peer groups in ways that are not oppressive to others. While the peer group's disciplining force can be seen as shaping behaviour in negative ways, it can also be seen as enabling of social collectivities, moral bonds and political agency (Seidman, 1993). In understanding group identity or peer culture in this regard, we can view this context as a productive space for identifying and exploring positive alternatives to narrow constructions of gender (Hickey & Keddie, 2004). In terms of generating an active and inclusive citizenship, for example, we might tap into this space to foster boys' sense of community, connection and responsibility for the welfare of others (Hayes et al., 2006).

Within a gender justice framework, key masculinities literature suggests ways in which schools can generate such positive group identities and active citizenship. Informed by anti-sexist, anti-racist, anti-classist and anti-homophobic principles and organised around group structures (within the context of mentoring, pastoral care, leadership or student representative programs, for instance), many of these suggestions revolve around consciousness-raising activities that promote diversity and difference, and challenge discrimination and marginalisation (Pallotta-Chiarolli, 1995). Many of the teachers in our work talk of the importance of such activities. The boys in one school, for example, were regularly exposed to strong visual imagery of individuals less fortunate than themselves and asked to contribute financially to various causes such as St Vincent de Paul and Amnesty International. While noting the positive impacts of such initiatives, however, one particular teacher was

clearly sceptical about the ways in which they were orches-
trated and understood at this school. To these ends, she
questioned the extent to which these activities made a difference in terms of the boys' capacities for empathy and their
commitments to social justice and active citizenship:

> There's been a big push this year in the service side . . . trying
> to get some service points up but it kind of annoys me a little
> bit, the way that it's been done is you get a bronze medallion
> or you get a silver, it's like they have to get something, you
> know, you don't do anything for anybody unless you get some-
> thing. I don't believe in sort of, you know, hitting them with a
> stick to get them to give money . . . I will never ever say,
> 'Come on, where's your money?', I just don't believe in that.
> But it does happen . . . it's a bit of a competition, like whose
> homeroom's got the most money and everything. But I'll often
> say to my homeroom, and they're a nice bunch of kids, 'There
> are so many people less fortunate than you—you really don't
> realise and appreciate how well you've got it here', you know,
> all those kinds of things. And yet still the money doesn't come
> . . . I don't think you can get kids to empathise unless they've
> seen it, unless they've really been to those places where the kids
> are struggling for money, or if they've seen the homeless. And
> I think that's something that we really need to work on. (Sally)

This teacher's concerns highlight the difficulties in moving
beyond a superficial engagement with consciousness-raising
activities, particularly if they reflect a disjointed or prescriptive
element of school culture. Indeed, the danger in these strategies—and others that might raise awareness about gender
issues around events like International Women's Day or Lesbian
and Gay Pride Week, for instance, or the public and positive
recognition of prominent people who identify as 'marginalised'
(see Pallotta-Chiarolli, 1995)—is that they may actually perpetuate narrow constructions of identity through reinscribing

simplistic notions of difference as 'other'—as unfamiliar and disconnected from the boys' lifeworlds. As this teacher begins to suggest, a genuine commitment to inclusivity and active citizenship will require connecting with boys' realities to heighten their capacities to appreciate injustices and mobilise their sense of responsibility for the welfare of others (Gilbert & Gilbert, 1998). In attempting to facilitate such capacities, a number of teachers in our work have noted the success of facilitating such awareness in activities beyond the school context. Two of the teachers whose stories appear later in this book talk about how consciousness-raising activities conducted in the broader community, where students interact with many different types of issues, people and attitudes, help to challenge and broaden narrow views and stereotypes (see Chapters 4 and 6). One of these teachers, Ross, describes how he attempts to mobilise his students' collective political agency through fieldwork that engages with 'different ethnic groups and people of different faiths'. As part of the project that he runs, the boys at his school—who tend to come from very middle-class backgrounds—are encouraged to work and mix with people from marginalised communities. Whilst such activities are potentially paternalistic, they can provide a useful scaffold for, as mentioned in reference to intellectual engagement, recognising, connecting with and legitimising positive ways of thinking and being that are relevant to boys' personal and group experiences of difference and marginalisation.

Schools showcasing and celebrating a diverse range of academic, sporting and socio-cultural achievements are also presented by many teachers as an imperative in generating inclusive group identities that legitimise difference and diversity and foster active citizenship along these lines. Significantly, many of the teachers in our research recognise the importance of promoting alternatives to the dominant and sometimes harmful masculinities of combative sports, such as Rugby and other codes of football—especially within broader school and social environments that tend to support, and indeed celebrate, such cultures. As the following teachers remarked:

> Every assembly, lots of it's taken up with sporting presentations and information and, 'here's the Rugby video, or here's the soccer video', and, you know, I think sometimes they value sport a little too highly . . . I don't always know if that's healthy for the boys, you know, it's just reinforcing that masculine thing of, 'you're a man if you're in the first fifteen', you know, 'you are cool'. (Sally)

> . . . the promotion of things like culture and music and service are really important and I don't think we bow to the great Rugby god as much as we used to . . . (Adam)

One of the most critical factors in the lives of boys is their engagement with sport—either positively or negatively (Mills, 2001). The link between sport and masculinity has been well made (see, for example, McKay et al., 2000; Burstyn, 1999). A key task for teachers is thus to disrupt this link, not to denigrate the role of sport in young people's lives, but to problematise essentialist connections between sport and masculinity and to trouble the role of sport in creating masculine hierarchies. One teacher spoke of how her school was seeking to do this:

> They're getting better, as the years have gone on there seems to be a lot more focus on cultural activities like music and drama and sometimes we have this house competition, theatre sports and that's excellent—the kids love it. I think that's really doing wonders for the arts because those kids are sort of becoming the popular kids because they're outgoing and funny and they say stupid things and everyone laughs and, in fact, I think one of the boys who is one of the college leaders this year is a drama student, and I think he's also a debater so that's really good. And the music program here is excellent . . . but when

they play at assembly often there's this kind of like low moan when they say, 'And here we have the music, you know, the choir are going to sing'. So I think there's a long way to go in terms of raising their profile, but I think it certainly, it's getting better. (Sally)

Along these lines, many of the teachers in our research highlight the importance of their school's recognition and celebration of non-dominant gender cultures associated with, for instance, poetry, drama, creative arts, music and dance, and activities like debating and 'tournament of minds'. The following teacher articulates her views in this regard:

> . . . one of the members of staff in Expressive Arts Week directed a talent show. So he got all these Islander kids from PNG and the Torres Strait and I think he got some of the Samoan boys to do a combination of traditional dances . . . so he had 20 boys up on stage in grass skirts dancing. And oh my god, it was awesome, and it brought the house down. The kids responded so well. They just clapped and clapped and clapped, it was awesome and the respect they got out of that . . . (Alexandra)

There is, of course, a danger here of exoticising the 'other' with such performances without addressing real issues of racism that impact upon 'Islander' children in many communities. There are some simplistic take-ups of 'valuing difference'—a 'spring rolls in the tuckshop' response to multiculturalism—in schools. However, at the same time such presentations also work to demonstrate the diversity of male performances across a variety of cultures, thereby working to disrupt essentialised notions of gender. Thus, within a transformative agenda, these examples can be seen as offering boys diverse possibilities for expressing themselves and alternatives (to narrow versions of gender) which are known not to be harmful or belligerently competitive and which are not sexually exclusive. Most importantly in this respect, dominant masculine constructions can be disrupted and reimagined in relation to a sense of being to which boys can aspire (Gilbert & Gilbert, 1998).

In further reference to this sense of being to which boys can aspire, and constructed by some as an issue of inclusivity for boys within supposedly female-dominated schooling environments, much of the current literature on boys has focused on the issue of male role models. This has been most evident in the call for more male teachers—a widespread 'remedy' aimed at improving boys' educational outcomes (see Mills et al., 2004, 2007, for a critique). Amid current discourses that position boys as victims, such remedies are also presented as a panacea for broader social 'ills' like the increasing prevalence of single-parent, female-headed households. In our experience, many teachers seem to share this sentiment, as the following comment articulates:

> . . . we've got a proportion of boys who have no significant male in their lives. I was actually asking some of the boys in my class the other day—the ones who have been here from Kindy to Year 9—and there was a good handful of them who said they had never had a male teacher until they hit Year 8. And that concerns me—especially if they come from a single-parent family where there's mum—a lot of them don't have men in their lives and you know, there's a lot to be said for having a man in your life where you can go out and do those old traditional masculine things like going camping and boating and all that kind of stuff—some of these kids are missing out. (Kim)

While it is possible that exposure to a variety of masculinities performed by a diverse range of men could broaden boys' understandings of masculinity to be more inclusive of difference and diversity, we—like many other commentators—have serious misgivings about the anti-feminist/anti-female tenor that invariably frames this issue. Certainly such sentiments and strategies tend to position females in boys' lives as inadequate and tend not to discriminate as to the kind of males who would be positive role models for boys. As this teacher's comments bring to light, simplistic assumptions about gender as difference and opposition tend to inform how this issue is approached— for this teacher, boys need men in their lives who can go out and do those old traditional masculine things like camping and boating. Such simplistic assumptions tend to be problematic because they are generally based on recuperating or reinstating an idealised form of conventional white, middle-class and heterosexual masculinity (Connell, 1995).

To these ends, we would not endorse a simplistic or uncritical approach to increasing the number of males in boys' lives, as such an approach could normalise, rather than disrupt, boys' investments in limited understandings of masculinity. Notwithstanding the well-established argument that in the sphere of schooling, it is the quality of the pedagogy, rather than the gender of the teacher, that makes a difference in boys' lives (Lingard et al., 2002), we would endorse an increase in the number of male teachers only if it helped to broaden boys' understandings of masculinity in gender-just ways and was brought about through a disruption of those misogynous and homophobic discourses that devalue teaching because it is 'women's work' and that construct men who want to work with children as 'deviant'. This would mean acknowledging how such initiatives are situated within broader inequitable power structures that continue to privilege dominant forms of masculinity (Skelton, 2001).

Conclusion

This chapter has raised pedagogical issues in the teaching of boys. It has drawn on the productive pedagogies framework to stress the importance of connectedness, intellectual engagement, supportive classroom practices, and valuing and working with difference in teaching boys. It recognises that the pedagogical practices contained within the concept of productive pedagogies are critical for improving the academic and social outcomes of *all* students. However, there are particular considerations peculiar to working with boys. These peculiarities are not linked to essential characteristics of masculinity, but arise from the need to consider issues of gender justice and the relational nature of masculinity and femininity.

We have stressed that, while it is important to connect with boys' interests in order to engage them in classroom activities, a gender-just approach to boys' education requires that such a connectedness should not work towards reinscribing traditional constructions of masculinity and femininity. Hence we shy away from those claims which argue that schools need to be made more 'boy friendly'. Such claims fail to take into account issues of privilege, social justice, the relational aspects of gender, post-school options and boys' often misogynous and homophobic attitudes and behaviours. We have also expressed a concern that connectedness should not displace an intellectually challenging environment. For us, the importance of connectedness lies in making classroom experiences relevant to students' worlds and to real-life issues in ways that lay the groundwork for challenging inequitable social relationships.

It is through intellectually challenging students' understandings of the world through problematising existing knowledges that moves towards gender justice can be made. We have focused on critical literacy in this regard. There are significant case studies that demonstrate how such work can be used to engage students intellectually in problematising various gendered knowledges. As many of the teachers we have interviewed have indicated, such practices are not limited to the English classroom. They can be present in a range of learning areas. We have argued that challenging boys' preconceived notions of gendered behaviours, including essentialised understandings of such behaviours, should be integral to approaches to boys' education if such an education is to open up possibilities for boys to resist and reject those forms of masculinities that are oppressive to others, and often harmful to themselves. We have also stressed that, in ensuring that students who are under-achieving receive intellectually challenging work to improve, that deficit models of boys whereby they are perceived to require less challenging work than girls (for example, claims that they are better at short responses rather than extended pieces of writing) have to be rejected.

The productive pedagogies emphasis on supportive classroom practices is important for boys, as it is for all students. We have written of the need to undertake challenging boys' understandings of gendered behaviours in respectful ways. We recognise that many boys construct their masculinities in an oppositional relationship to the authority structures of schools and classrooms. We are concerned that attempts to 'control' boys will exacerbate those forms of masculinity, which thrive on conflict. Hence we have stressed the need for students to be given a voice in the classroom. However, we again put a rider on this in that giving boys a voice should not open up, or fail to close down, space for misogynous and homophobic discourses which oppress others. The teachers we have interviewed who have managed to work with boys in respectful ways have also sought to build their relationships with students by coming to know the students in their care. This form of 'knowing' enables teachers to build on student interests to 'model' respectful relationships. Such respect underpins democratic classrooms where students are taught explicitly about how to relate to each other and how to be a member of a democratic community.

This notion of a democratic community is picked up on in the difference dimension of productive pedagogies. Here we have stressed the importance of students developing a critical awareness of the ways in which social relations work in favour of and against the interests of particular groups of people because of their ethnicity, gender, race, sexuality, age, socio-economic status, religion, and so on. Such critical awareness, we contend, is crucial in a democratic community. Within the productive pedagogies framework, a valuing of and engaging with difference has a concern with developing students' sense of social justice and developing the requisite skills and knowledges for addressing such inequities. However, a valuing of difference does not mean treating all students as individuals: 'groupness' is also important for students and does need to be valued. We have argued that this dimension of the productive pedagogies framework is critical for encouraging boys to consider the variety of ways in which gender can be performed, and the consequences of some performances of masculinity for others and for themselves.

In this chapter, we have drawn on numerous teacher voices to expand upon, illustrate and support our arguments regarding the importance of pedagogical practices framed by gender-just principles. In the chapters that follow, we focus on just four teacher stories. We could have told other teachers' stories—we have come across many teachers who can articulate and/or demonstrate the characteristics of productive pedagogies alongside a commitment to the principles of gender justice in their work with students. We have chosen only four teachers because we wanted to provide in-depth and detailed accounts of their work, which can become lost when many teacher voices appear in the one space. These four teachers demonstrate particular practices, often performed by other teachers, from which we as researchers and others as practitioners can learn much. We do not always agree with everything they say or do—and that is as it should be. However, we have been impressed by their commitment and their knowledges, and by the changes they effect in their classrooms. What these teachers demonstrate, alongside many others we have interviewed and observed over the years, is that teaching is both a caring exercise requiring significant amounts of emotional labour and an intellectual enterprise. We hope that these teacher narratives are useful in stimulating discussion in a variety of contexts about issues of gender justice and the teaching of boys.

3 JENNIFER: A FRESH LOOK AT TAKEN-FOR-GRANTED WAYS OF BEING

Introduction

Jennifer's purple-themed English and Philosophy classroom is captivating. The physical surrounds bring to life an eclectic and vibrant mix of student voices. Neatly and colourfully organised graffiti, cartoons, postcards and drawings cram the length and breadth of all four walls. A beautifully hand-painted and stencilled olive-green vine with deep pink flowers curls its way across the wall on top of the blackboard. Near it, a Bob Marley quote reads 'Emancipate yourself from slavery, none but ourselves can free our mind'. Silver cardboard stars cascade down the wall beside the blackboard with the handwritten caption 'Reach for the moon 'cos even if you miss you'll be amongst the stars'. A poster featuring prominent women who 'dared to pester' is affixed to the back wall. Amid assorted artwork, other poignant verses and phrases fill the wall space. From the profound to the humorous, words from well-known philosophers and writers sit amongst student prose: Gandhi's 'An eye for an eye will make you blind' is written on the wall beside the blackboard at the front of the classroom; Charlotte Brontë's 'Conventionality is not morality' is printed on the blackboard frame; a verse of a Missy Higgins song is scrawled on an adjacent window; while students' own thoughts tell more stories: 'I hateth thee Shakespeare' is scribbled between two windows; 'People in glass houses should wear pants' is written on the sill; 'Does a one-legged duck swim in circles?' appears elsewhere. The fluorescent light dangling from the roof at the front of the class has a paper cut-out label on it that reads 'Spread your love like a disease'.

Jennifer's alternative, bohemian appearance seems very well placed within the unconventional and perhaps quietly dissident surrounds of her classroom. Jennifer is in her mid to late thirties, and her purple-coloured hair, trendy silver jewellery and neck piercing is more than a little at odds with the conventional 'teacher image'. Perhaps a product of her formal training and specialisation in Drama, Philosophy and her 'passion', English, her appearance and manner convey a strong sense of artistry and intellect, and seem to be embodied in the calm, caring and respectful way in which she relates to her students. Jennifer says that supporting and demonstrating ideas of respect are central to her teaching. In our observations of Jennifer's classroom, this valuing of respect seems integral to her practice, and in particular embodies her more informal relations with students. We note here a generally inclusive and student-centred tenor where students are positioned with agency, legitimacy and autonomy. It is apparent to us that Jennifer values her students—she is encouraging and thoughtfully respectful of their input and students appear willing and at ease volunteering their interpreta-tions or questioning Jennifer's and other students' points of view. The high levels of engagement and politeness in Jennifer's classroom also suggest that the students value and respect her. Perhaps unsurprisingly, we see very few behaviour-management issues, and the one or two incidents that we do observe are dealt with in ways that do not seem to compromise students' sense of agency. For example, on one occasion between classes in the staffroom two of Jennifer's male students are sent to her for skipping assembly. While she hands a detention to the two boys, she does so in a way that does not undermine her relationships with the students—there is no hint of a moral lecture that might enforce her power over them as a teacher or any remark that might be understood as colluding with their misbehaviour—one of the boys even thanks her for the detention as he leaves!

Jennifer has been teaching Years 11 and 12 at Claymore Park College for sixteen years. Her decision to teach within the state system was a 'moral' one. She says she is 'really proud' to be a teacher at a state school, particularly as it provides her with an opportunity to 'give back' to a system that 'enriched' her as a student. Claymore Park College is a Preparatory to Year 12 co-educational state school located in a large urban centre. At 1600 students, the size of the largely Anglo-Australian student population means that the school can offer a diversity of curricula and extra-curricula programs and activities. In relation to the latter, the school has a social justice committee, a jazz and orchestra group, a cheer squad, a musicals committee, a chaplaincy group, an extensive array of sporting groups, and debating, drama, dance, garden and chess clubs. One of the distinctive things about this school is its highly regarded performing arts excellence program. Affiliated with a major university, this excellence program offers extension courses for senior students in Drama, Dance and Music that can lead to university accreditation. The school also provides excellence programs for senior students in aviation, and for secondary students in golf, tennis and soccer, and boasts an outstanding Visual Arts facility. More broadly, the college's university affiliation allows Year 12 students to commence particular degree courses during their senior year at the school.

It is against this backdrop that we present Jennifer's story. We believe Jennifer's respectful, student-centred approach provides a highly generative context for pursuing gender justice. Seeking to broaden students' understandings of masculinity and femininity, we foreground how Jennifer provides spaces in her classroom for students to safely explore 'non-traditional' aspects of their gender. We highlight how Jennifer's ways of thinking about gender, power and inequity compel her to find spaces in her teaching for social change, and in particular to problematise dominant and dominating ways of being male. From her rejection of particular conventions that reinscribe teacher–student inequities to her scaffolding of critical literacy, this chapter presents Jennifer's endeavours to create an intellectually challenging environment that engages 'the space of schooling as a site of contestation, resistance and possibility' (Giroux, 2003, p. 6).

Jennifer's story

In our interviews, Jennifer talks about how a context of respect frames her understandings of gender and identity. She explains that this means developing students' self-respect and their respect for others' views. Specifically, she notes the importance of modelling respect for her students through showing boys, in particular, that she is 'comfortable' with them 'not fitting into traditional Australian masculine stereotypes'. Similarly for girls, while she sees their gender identities as perhaps 'a little more fluid', she believes her demonstrated respect for a range of femininities is important. Jennifer understands that gender stereotypes, particularly in relation to issues of masculinity, are 'damaging' for both males and females through restricting their range of experiences and choices. By way of illustration, she talks about the 'pressures' for males 'to be dominant and active rather than passive'. As she explains, with specific reference to the subject of English:

> I think quite a few of the boys who want to be seen as attractive people feel that masculine attraction involves assertion and aggression . . . issues to do with being assertive and aggressive

to—I don't know, confirm that they're, they're men . . . that they're attractive people and [also with] English because there's a lot of—ideally there's quite a lot of emotional and introspective work that goes on to do with using language. Being seen to be articulate and able to connect with storytelling . . . I think a lot of the boys in particular—not just the boys, but a lot of the boys in particular find that that's not something that they're supposed to be good at—even though they might want to be good at it. They're under pressure not to be.

Acknowledging both the oppressive and restrictive aspects of masculinity that some boys feel compelled to perform, Jennifer describes pressures to be assertive or aggressive, rather than passive and introspective, as enacted in the 'sense of entitlement over others' that the males in her class 'seem to display'. She talks here about boys tending to dominate classroom space and time, and being inclined to lack 'consideration of other people's space, property and views'. Along these lines, Jennifer notes a general 'assumption of [male] superiority over the girls' that she sees fits with a masculine, rather than feminine, 'upbringing'. Such observations recognise that, for many boys, their efforts to make themselves attractive *as boys* often involve them oppressing others in ways that mark their opposition to females and 'the feminine'.

Such understandings are evident in Jennifer's comments about English in terms of how displays of dominant masculinity can restrict boys' opportunities. Here, as the work of Wayne Martino (2000) has demonstrated, Jennifer points to the way in which some boys' engagement with this learning area suffers as a consequence of constructions of English as an 'emotional', 'introspective' and thereby 'feminine' subject which 'real' boys should not like. These constructions are certainly drawn on in femiphobic and homophobic ways and, through an association of English with an inferior femininity, work to police the boundaries of accepted masculinity and to denigrate marginalised boys (such policing is perhaps best epitomised in the following comment from a boy that features in Martino's work (2000): 'Most guys who like English are Faggots'). Importantly, Jennifer's problematising of such constructions reflects a gender justice understanding that disrupts a devaluing of those attributes and subjects traditionally seen as feminine and facilitates a consideration of the ways in which gendered boundaries are policed by associated pressures such as those grounded in homophobic discourses.

Whilst taking a critical view of dominant constructions of masculinity, Jennifer does not take an idealised view of girls' behaviours. She recognises that some girls do become complicit in the valorisation of dominant forms of masculinity, and also the oppression of marginalised boys, when she notes that some boys' 'narrow behaviours' are 'quite often' reinforced by the girls in her class:

> . . . there are some behaviours that are non-traditional that are rewarded but there are also quite a lot of low key sort of things that the girls—not all of them obviously—discourage boys from doing because that's not what boys do.

Hence, for Jennifer, there is an implicit understanding that for constructions of what it means to be male to be challenged, 'gender relations' have to be considered in terms of the complex ways in which various girls and boys, and men and women, reinscribe (but also challenge) the current inequitable 'gender order' (Connell, 1995).

Jennifer attributes the critical lens through which she understands issues of masculinity and gender relations to her experiences as a woman and her desire for change:

> . . . the cognitive framework that I'm coming from is as a woman and so—I understand . . . issues of masculinity as being—my view of them is that they are primarily socially constructed rather than biologically based and my beliefs that they're socially constructed encourages me to feel that change can be made . . .

She articulates that her experiences as a female have impacted on how she believes gender relations should change. She explains, in this respect, that she 'would like not to have the girls behaving in the same way as the boys'. In terms of gender change, she talks here about wanting girls to 'feel entitled' too, and wanting boys to show greater courtesy and respect. Again, she draws attention to the relational nature of gender—that is, we cannot talk about boys' education without also considering that of girls, and vice versa.

Disrupting taken-for-granted ways of thinking

Drawing on these understandings, Jennifer describes her ways of thinking and teaching as 'persistent and hopeful'. While she doesn't have 'huge expectations' in terms of how she might shape gender change in the short term, she works in explicit and implicit ways in her classroom to encourage her students to move beyond 'narrow behaviours'. In particular, she wants her classroom to be a 'background influence' that 'incrementally has like an undercurrent effect that will contribute to a cumulative shaping of student behaviours in positive ways'.

Jennifer draws on her own experience of travelling overseas to illustrate her views about the importance of exposing students to a 'fresh look' at taken-for-granted ways of thinking and acting:

> . . . like when I went overseas for the first time last year—I couldn't believe how Asia smelt and I wasn't aware of the background smell of Brisbane until I got home—so that sort of giving them a fresh look at something . . . like if you were moving around in a crowded room for a number of years, it would influence the way you walked—or if the ceilings were low or where your eye level was you may not be conscious of

it, at least not after a while, but being put in another space with
different physical views and barriers might cause me to lift my
head up more or stoop less or more—so that sort of influence—it's part of the background but maybe if I'm providing
a varied background, it would just give them another thing to
help shape who they are.

This 'fresh look' at the world is tied into those pedagogical
principles which treat knowledge as something problematic, and
which disrupt what Bourdieu (1993) has referred to as a 'feel for
the game'—in this case, of particular cultural mores and knowledges: 'taken-for-granted' ways of being that she can shake up
so that students come to see other possibilities. With regard to
a 'fresh look' at gender, Jennifer says that she tries to create a
supportive 'space' in her classroom for students to 'feel comfortable' with 'exploring or experimenting with non-traditional
aspects of their gender and . . . non-stereotypical aspects of
Western Anglo culture'. She argues that such a space both 'validates' these explorations and 'provokes those who wouldn't think
in that way—to consider that other people might'. With this in
mind, Jennifer expresses the importance of challenging students
intellectually in ways that involve 'being able to think critically
. . . not necessarily in a negative way . . . but having the meta-
cognitive skills to think about what they are doing and think
about thinking about it, rather than just acting all the time'.

Jennifer talks about the subject of English, and in particular
the skills of critical analysis and deconstruction, as providing an
explicit framework to enable students to do this by exploring new
ways of thinking about themselves and others. She talks in this
regard about understanding identity as shifting rather than static:

. . . we definitely do a lot of work on multiple identities and
how—I don't usually present it as 'this is the truth' but just that
it's a current theory which seems to have a lot to recommend
it that—ourselves aren't static—and we'll be looking at text

and looking at choices or impulses and, yeah how our awareness of ourselves and other people's awareness of us would shift
from situation to situation . . .

As we suggested in Chapter 2, despite some of the conservative
resistance to critical literacy, such ways of thinking open up possibilities for gender justice in terms of helping students to
recognise the multiple rather than singular gender realities that
shape their lifeworlds. Such understandings are central to
contesting and transforming the taken-for-granted gender truths
that limit our ways of being (Davies, 1997). These understandings
were evident in a number of Jennifer's lessons that we observed.

In one of the classes, a Grade 11 English class consisting of
fifteen boys and six girls, we observed how this critical framework scaffolds the students' engagement in the play *X-Stacy*—a
tragic story, written by a local playwright, of a girl who dies at
a rave culture party. The play is very graphic and deals with a
number of difficult issues facing young people. One boy tells us
that it is 'pretty full-on'. Another tells us that it didn't relate to
him, but then went on to list the other students in his class
to whom it did. In this lesson, students are expected to use the
text as a springboard to begin their assessment for this unit,
writing an intervention or missing scene that explores potential
pathways a particular character might take in response to a
specific issue in the text. As a 'starter', Jennifer has them working
in pairs or small groups to 'write what a character might write in
a letter or blog after the play ends'. The groups that self-form are
mainly same-sex, although there is one group with two boys and
one girl and another with two girls and one boy. In scaffolding
this exercise, Jennifer supports her students to see how a particular issue can be explored and interpreted in multiple ways.

In another lesson, and drawing on a similar critical frame to
engage with texts—this time in a Year 12 Philosophy and Reason
class, consisting of seven boys and thirteen girls, on moral philosophy—the problematising of knowledge is encouraged when

students explore different perspectives on issues such as abortion and euthanasia. Here we observe interesting and substantive discussions about the disparities between moral or factual statements concerning these issues and how, for instance, an Aristotelian or Christian perspective might shape how these issues are understood. In this lesson, Jennifer walks them through how to write a 'good' essay on their topic. They are provided with very explicit instructions on how to write the essay and are given examples of the kinds of issues that have to be addressed. For instance, the sheet they are provided with raises issues relating to abortion; students are then guided through each of these, determining which are factual and which 'moral'. The students then start to raise their own questions—for instance, 'Can torture ever be right?' The atmosphere in this classroom is highly positive, with teacher and students engaging in enthusiastic, meaningful and insightful discussion. In another Philosophy and Reason lesson, this time Year 11, we observe the students argue productively about the validity of particular provocative statements regarding President Bush, corporate power and the Iraq war. In this lesson, Jennifer uses snippets from an episode of the popular television program *Arrested Development* ('Girls gone wild')—one of the girls sitting near us is particularly impressed by Jennifer's chosen stimulus to explore the soundness of particular arguments about young women and sexual exploitation; she exclaims that this is 'the best' program 'ever'.

Within this framework, Jennifer talks to us about scaffolding feminist readings of texts such as *The Crow*—a text that she describes as sexualising violence and objectifying women. Such scaffolding has provided a context for her students to explore and deconstruct taken-for-granted understandings about gender:

> . . . it was on the surface . . . an enduring love story but sort of deconstructing it, I was sharing with the kids my perception and many of them came to share it as well, but not all of them, that it was really . . . something else masquerading as a love story . . .

it was sexualising violence and objectifying women and so taking a feminist reading of the film but towards the end, quite often I would explicitly say 'Well let's have a look at what that's saying' . . . in terms of restricting the male behaviour, because it's taking for granted that the male will be the fighter, the protective one, the one who endures when the weaker female can't and sort of looking at the implications of sexism, which I'm very strong on talking about from a feminist point of view, but that it's got many damaging things for the male population as well in terms of the range of experiences that are cut off from men.

Jennifer finds that students are generally positive and interested in such activities; she says that they tend to 'provoke quite a lot of debate'. In commenting about her efforts to scaffold the critical analysis and debate of particular texts, Jennifer suggests that:

. . . maybe for many students, particularly the boys, it's maybe just a little crack in the doorway, like I've opened the door and stuck a little door wedge in there but it certainly hasn't opened the door to a whole new world but perhaps now that the crack is there, you know over time they might open up a little more . . .

Such learning experiences can be seen as particularly constructive in terms of gender justice. Consistent with our focus in Chapter 2, Jennifer's teaching—while clearly connecting with the 'real-world' concerns and interests of students—does so in a way that seeks to question and challenge, rather than endorse inequitable understandings of gender. Here she provides a context for understanding the social construction of particular realities and knowledges, and support for the recognition that such ways of being and knowing are amenable to critique and transformation.

Significantly, Jennifer seems to draw on these critical lenses in self-reflective ways—ways, as we noted in Chapter 2, that can highlight the relationship between the construction of the self and the construction of knowledge and 'truth'. In this respect, while Jennifer believes that the explicit challenging of gender stereotypes is very important, she acknowledges that 'you can be doing all this and then when you're just reacting on instinct or whatever, you behave differently'. In terms of having an impact on changing student behaviour, Jennifer sees that she must not 'merely' scaffold deconstructive exercises, but also 'try and model' gender-inclusive behaviours. In relation to her scaffolding of critical analysis, this plays out in Jennifer's endeavours to be open to and to legitimise 'multiple' and 'often unexpected' readings students might have of particular texts. As she explains in reference to *Hamlet*:

> . . . students will come up often jokingly with quite unexpected readings of Hamlet or Claudius or whoever . . . and yeah sort of allowing the students to express that and giving it perhaps a more thoughtful or respectful listen than they might have expected when they say, 'Oh maybe he's gay—he really likes Horatio' or that sort of thing—which is actually a very well-grounded reading of the text.

Thus, for Jennifer, there is an explicit attempt to disrupt, and to support students' disruptive takes on, normalised constructions of gender. However, when students actually begin to embody such disruptions, they open themselves up to all those forms of policing that have been graphically outlined elsewhere in relation to homophobic, femiphobic and misogynous bullying (see, for example, Martino & Pallotta-Chiarolli, 2003, 2005). Hence any such disruptions have to be accompanied by the creation of safe environments. This may not be possible at the societal or even school level, but individual teachers can work to make their classrooms safe places for those students who are prepared to experiment with non-dominant ways of being. For Jennifer, this is an important priority.

Creating a safe and gender-inclusive environment

Jennifer tries to 'welcome the different choices students make'. For example, mindful of her own physical appearance as alternative to the typical teacher image, she doesn't compel students to adhere to the school's dress requirements. In illustrating how this might support gender inclusivity, she refers to one particular example—a boy in the school's Dance Excellence program who, in Jennifer's words, is 'very into presenting as bi' and wearing makeup. While many teachers would ask this student to remove his makeup, Jennifer supports and validates this boy's 'experimentation with non-traditional aspects of his gender', and thus his makeup is 'not an issue' for her. That Jennifer has built strong relationships with her students, and in so doing has created a safe environment in her classroom, appears to be supported by our observations of her practice. For example, despite the disproportionate number of boys in her English classroom, the atmosphere did not feel overwhelmed by the boys, and neither boys nor girls dominated the conversation—or teacher time—in the classroom. Indeed, the lesson was largely free of behaviour-management issues (as was every class of Jennifer's we observed). Similarly, Jennifer had created an environment within which there appeared to be significant support for learning. For instance, in the Grade 11 Philosophy and Reason class, students had their first assessment piece in this subject returned. Whilst some students found the concepts new and difficult, with some boys and some girls failing, there did not appear to be too much of the masculinised bravado that sometimes accompanies school failure, or even teasing of those who achieved or failed. The same quiet, calm but stimulating environment as we had seen in Jennifer's other classes continued here.

Much of Jennifer's gender-inclusive practice involves taking incidental opportunities to use or foreground counter-stereotypical issues and language to 'provide a richer variety of experiences'. Here she tries to respond to students and situations in ways that offer 'real-world' and 'alternative ways of thinking about something that maybe haven't occurred'. For example, Jennifer talks about her 'conscious effort' to recognise and affirm difference in counter-stereotypical ways:

> . . . like if someone comes to class with a new hairdo or they're wearing—sometimes the kids wear ties that aren't school ties and rather than just saying to the girls, 'Oh you look beautiful' or whatever, but using the same words for the boys saying 'You look gorgeous' or 'You look beautiful' or 'That's really attractive' and similarly for the girls using words that I might stereotypically have applied to boys like—I don't know—'That looks really strong' or those sort of things. Yeah so just trying to use my language with less gender discrimination when I'm interacting with the students as individuals and I'm more conscious or I have been for a longer time—more conscious of doing that when I'm teaching—but yeah sort of taking it into just 'ordinary', in inverted commas, behaviour.

Jennifer also talks about being conscious of drawing on a range of representations of difference in terms of gender and sexuality when using examples and selecting materials in her teaching. In particular, she expresses concern about the Philosophy and Logic curriculum that she teaches:

> . . . it's probably reinforcing things that I don't want to have happen in some ways because the—it's unremittingly Western males in its examples of philosophers and in my head I think, 'Oh I'd love to take the time to get together a unit on females' but even then it's sort of marginal—it's ghettoising the thing, 'Oh no, we're doing a unit on the women!' I feel sometimes that I'm reinforcing an unspoken view that the best thinkers are male thinkers. Although many of the students are very articulate in criticising that and being aware that the textbook

is giving—it is reinforcing the patriarchy and not indicating that women too are thinkers and society hasn't given them the tools and the opportunity to have their views recorded and taught and that's why they're not here, not because they didn't exist, or at least that's my view and it's the view that the students who offer that up unrequited express as well.

Like many teachers who are concerned about gender issues, Jennifer struggles to understand how she might be complicit in maintaining particular representations of masculinity and femininity. In her day-to-day relationships with students, she reflects on how her behaviour might be implicated in reinforcing students' negative understandings about gender and masculinity. She talks, for example, about an incident of behaviour management in the tuckshop line where a boy used the word 'faggot' to insult another boy:

> Like the other day in the tuckshop line some boy said, 'Oh you faggot' to the boy behind him and I said, 'Oh he can go first now!' and afterwards I thought—normally I'm conscious of not treating the word 'faggot' as an insult, but it was so—he was using it in such an insulting way and clearly it was meant as derogatory but I felt like afterwards—I felt like I perpetuated the idea that the idea of being gay was bad.

Jennifer picks up on a really important point here. While we certainly commend many teachers' efforts to redress the unacceptably high levels of homophobia in schools, we are concerned—as Jennifer's comments indicate—about how the ways of addressing students' use of homophobic language can work in opposition to the intended aim—in ways, as Jennifer points out, that reinforce the negativity of the term. Maria Pallotta-Chiarolli (1995, p. 67) provides a nice example of how she confronts this issue in her classrooms by beginning each year with the statement: 'This will be a non-racist, non-sexist, non-homophobic classroom', which then sets the tone for raising issues of homophobia, issues that she never lets pass. Hence she goes on to say: 'That's all it took sometimes: just a few words, a question, some facts, an honest response to a concern, a poster, a song, a personal anecdote, and students no longer accepted that homophobia was normal and justifiable' (1995, p. 72).

Notwithstanding Jennifer's critical self-reflection of the many ways that she might be complicit in endorsing students' existing gendered behaviours, she does demonstrate similar concerns about the role of homophobia in the classroom as Pallotta-Chiarolli, and in so doing also demonstrates her aware-ness of how particular truths about gender are spoken into existence. Such awareness reflects Jennifer's philosophy about the self as 'not static'—as 'shifting from situation to situation' and, consistent with our argument in Chapter 2, enables her to 'read against the grain of dominant discourses and against the grain of the privileged positions constructed within them' (Davies, 1998, pp. 12–13). In so doing, she does broaden the gendered realities of the students in her care.

Examining Jennifer's practices, philosophies and understandings about gender

Jennifer's ways of teaching can be seen as supporting gender justice in implicit and explicit ways. The tenor of her classroom, her respectful manner with students, her efforts to value and legitimise difference, and her problematising of knowledge fore-ground a strong framework of threshold knowledges in terms of quality teaching and issues of gender and masculinity. Here Jennifer's sense of gender fairness and equity provides a context for gender justice that supports her persistent and hopeful practice. The possibilities of Jennifer shaping gender change in socially just ways are supported by her understandings of masculinity and femininity as these concepts are constructed and endorsed through inequitable social relations that can be transformed through alternative ways of thinking and being, together with her recognition and problematising of 'damaging stereotypes'—and, in particular, constructions of masculinity as synonymous with power, domination and a denigration of 'the feminine'—and her understanding of her teaching as a political activity. These ways of thinking seem to frame the gently disruptive ways in which Jennifer 'acts against the grain' for gender justice.

One of the key ways in which Jennifer enables gender justice is through her disruption of the traditional teacher–student binary. As we pointed out in Chapter 2, the inequitable power relations of this binary—and more specifically the excessive relations of hyper-rationality and control that often characterise teacher practice and school structures—have long been criticised as normalising gendered relations of power. These relations of power are seen as endorsing boys' investments in hegemonic masculinity and inciting feelings of powerlessness and disengagement. Rather than contributing to this normalisation, Jennifer's practice can be seen as legitimising and giving space to the student voice. This is perhaps best epitomised in the opening description of her classroom, where the showcasing of students' voices shapes the physical surroundings. Consistent with this clear valuing of students is the level of respect Jennifer demonstrates in her relationships with them—as, for instance, the detention scenario illustrates. Importantly, in this situation, it seems that, for Jennifer, adherence to the school's broader regulations does not have to mean positioning students as powerless. In this environment, Jennifer supports student agency in terms of gender difference through her modelling of gender-inclusive and gender-disruptive behaviours through, for example, validating multiple and perhaps subversive readings students may offer regarding particular texts, 'welcoming the different choices students make' (in terms of their physical appearance, for example) and drawing on counter-stereotypical language in her interactions with students. This, as Jennifer suggests, 'provokes those who wouldn't think that way to consider that other people might', and facilitates students' respect for others' views. Additionally, Jennifer's non-adherence to the typical teacher image can be seen as disrupting the practices of normalisation that contribute to the traditional teacher–student binary. For Jennifer, then, a supportive classroom means an inclusive and student-centred environment that recognises and respects multiple ways of interpreting that may deviate from dominant readings/cultures.

Jennifer seeks to provide a classroom that challenges students intellectually. Drawing on her understandings of justice, she wants to encourage critical thinking about issues of gender and diversity so that restrictive ways of knowing and being are challenged and broadened. In order to do this, she provides a space in which respect and validation of alternative views and perspectives can occur. Jennifer's first-time experience overseas in a context unfamiliar to her is a compelling illustration of this positive view that 'change is possible'. Her notion that 'change is possible' reflects an important attribute of high-quality teaching: the rejection of deficit models of students (Lingard et al., 2003). This is in contrast to some within the boys' lobby who argue that boys cannot change (i.e. 'boys will be boys') and hence seek to adapt the curriculum and pedagogical strategies to meet what they believe are essential qualities of masculinity. Throughout the stories told in this book, we have found that those teachers who are committed to gender justice actually have high opinions and expectations of boys in that they believe it is possible for them to achieve 'against the odds' in relation to the pressures that are exerted upon them to be particular kinds of boys.

Jennifer's 'fresh look' also enables her to appreciate the significance of thinking and understanding in different and perhaps non-dominant ways. This suggests that, for boys (and girls), there are benefits to be had by experiencing the world from a different perspective. While not wanting to buy into those arguments which suggest that boys are the new disadvantaged, it is clear that there are costs faced by some boys in trying to live up to the expectations of being a 'real' boy—such as emotional closeness to other boys, dangerous and high-risk behaviours, lack of engagement with education, and so on. This is, of course, a cost some boys are willing to pay in return for the benefits that accrue to them as a result of being a 'real boy' (see Mills, 2001). However, as the kind of teaching Jennifer performs demonstrates, not all boys benefit equally from this set of arrangements.

Drawing on her understandings of masculinity and femininity as constructed within a system of interdependent and inequitable power relations, Jennifer challenges these elements of masculinity in her desire for change (she talks here about wanting boys to show greater courtesy and respect). Such understandings are evident in her concerns about the damaging impact of gender stereotypes—particularly those associated with masculinity—for both girls and boys, and her concerns about the pressure for boys to ascribe to discourses of entitlement and superiority over girls and femininity in terms of, for example, being dominant and active rather than passive and introspective. In particular, Jennifer recognises how such pressures to conform to a narrow masculine stereotype constrain boys' performance in English—a learning area traditionally associated with femininity. Importantly, she also notes that such hierarchical understandings and relations are not just taken up and endorsed by particular boys but are also reinforced by girls (Mac an Ghaill, 1994). Such understandings highlight the complex and dynamic ways in which boys and girls actively take up and police the gendered identities that reinscribe inequities.

Significant in Jennifer's thinking is an acknowledgement that, while there may be multiple ways of being male and female, there are some ways which are privileged over others (Connell, 1995, 2000; Martino & Pallotta-Chiarolli, 2003, 2005; Mills, 2001). She talks here of supporting boys who do not fit into 'traditional Australian masculine stereotypes', and supporting girls by 'respecting a range of femininities'. Implicit here is a challenging of gender constructed along binary lines, with social power and privilege assigned to the masculine side of an oppositional binary and social powerlessness and dependency to the feminine side of the binary (Davies & Hunt, 2000), and efforts to broaden—particularly boys'—narrow understandings and enactments of masculinity (Lingard et al., 2002).

Such understandings of gender, and Jennifer's belief that she can make a difference clearly permeate her pedagogy and her relationships with students. Most importantly, these understandings and Jennifer's 'persistent and hopeful' practice link her ways of teaching to social change and engage 'the space of schooling as a site of contestation, resistance and possibility' (Giroux, 2003, p. 6). While she doesn't have 'huge expectations' in terms of transforming gender(ed) behaviour, Jennifer clearly recognises the political nature of her teaching in terms of its potential 'undercurrent effect' to shape student behaviours in positive (though also negative) ways. As Jennifer explains, she sees her practice as 'maybe just a little crack in a doorway' that opens up new ways of thinking for her students. In attempting to shape student behaviour in positive ways, Jennifer teaches 'against the grain' in her explicit contestation of stereotypical constructions of gender. This is visible in Jennifer's 'multiple identities' work, which encourages students to see themselves, including their 'choices' and 'impulses', as contextual and shifting. Such a framework is particularly significant in Jennifer's scaffolding of critical readings of visual texts such as the play *X-Stacy* and *The Crow*. The deconstructive exercises with these texts encourage students' deep understanding of gender through the exploration of multiple readings. Here, students are supported to see knowledge as problematic through examining issues of representation in relation to domination, power, marginalisation and powerlessness. Importantly, in relation to *The Crow*, Jennifer highlights the 'damaging' implications for both males and females of the sexualising of violence, the objectification of women and the promotion of a particular narrow version of masculinity. Within a framework that understands identities as 'multiple', situational and shifting, however, Jennifer presents these harmful constructions as amenable to change through alternative ways of thinking and acting. Significantly, within this context of critical engagement, Jennifer draws on texts and issues that connect with her students' lifeworlds in ways that seek to broaden, rather than endorse, limited understandings of identity.

With further reference to the problematising of gendered knowledge, Jennifer also makes transparent the political nature of curriculum materials. In reflecting on how her teaching may shape student behaviours in negative ways, Jennifer 'thinks against the grain' in highlighting how the philosophy curriculum, with its 'unremittingly Western male' perspective, reinforces 'an unspoken view that the best thinkers are male thinkers'. Jennifer understands such a perspective as silencing and marginalising the non-dominant cultural knowledges of 'the feminine'. Importantly, moreover, Jennifer's critical reflection on an alternative unit on female thinkers acknowledges that sometimes celebrating or showcasing 'difference' serves to perpetuate or, as she describes it, 'ghettoise' difference (Keddie, 2006b). Jennifer also draws on her understandings of gender justice when she critically reflects on the potentially negative impacts of her response to a boy's use of the term 'faggot' (as an insult to another boy). Here she notes that punishing this boy for using this term actually works to reinforce rather than challenge its negative connotations. Significantly, Jennifer tries 'normally' to disrupt 'the idea that being gay is bad' by 'not treating the word faggot as an insult'.

We have chosen to present Jennifer's story in this book as it indicates the importance of thinking about boys and gender relations within a gender justice framework. We find her story hopeful. It acknowledges that boys do face problems in school, and that there needs to be a focus on improving the quality of education that they experience. However, for Jennifer this does not mean reinforcing dominant images of what it means to be male (Martino et al., 2005), sacrificing the education of girls

(Charlton et al., 2007), or treating boys as deficit. Whilst Jennifer is clearly not the 'average' teacher, there is much that teachers can learn from her practice. This includes rejecting a competing victim approach (Cox, 1995) which pits the interests of boys against those of girls, rejecting deficit models of boys and girls, a willingness to trial 'new' ways of teaching, challenging students' thinking within a socially supportive environment, and encouraging and valuing diversity within the classroom.

Learning from Jennifer

Jennifer's classes are a pleasure to observe. We have seen students engaged in high-quality substantive conversations about meaningful topics. In these classes, students were stretched intellectually on topics which have purchase in their lives and which compel them to consider a range of non-dominant interpretations of traditional and conventional texts. In this, she encourages students to read against the grain and to come up with meanings from texts that problematise valorised constructions of gender. Her relationships with students are grounded in an ethics of care that is not just about being warm with the students—although this is clearly evident—but also about wanting them to achieve academically by taking risks with their learning and by providing an environment where differences amongst the students are valued. To this extent, we can see a very clear integration of the principles of productive pedagogies into her classroom practices. These principles are accompanied by an in-depth understanding of gender theories.

Broadening understandings of gender

Through the gender justice framework employed by Jennifer, she recognises a diverse range of femininities and masculinities, but challenges and seeks to transform relations of discrimination and marginalisation. Jennifer's story highlights the many ways in which this can be made possible—for instance, through the personal relationships that teachers develop with students, through behaviour-management strategies, through everyday engagements with students, and through curricula and pedagogical decisions. In the following activities, we foreground ways this might be done through the curriculum and through various pedagogical moments. In these we assume that, whilst Jennifer's focus has been on such subjects as English, Drama and Philosophy, all curriculum areas can provide similar opportunities.

EXAMINING CURRICULUM KNOWLEDGE

This exercise is designed to promote reflection on the kinds of gendered knowledge that schools present to students. The transmission of knowledge does not occur simply. Students and teachers mediate their understandings of knowledge through their various lifeworlds. Curriculum and textual knowledge need to be considered in the light of the way teachers' and students' different views of the world frame their engagement—or indeed, lack of engagement. Jennifer's story, for example, highlights how some boys construct the curriculum area of English, and specifically its demand for introspection and emotion, and its focus on storytelling and being articulate, as incompatible with their sense of masculinity. Jennifer also highlights how knowledge in particular curriculum areas—namely Philosophy—is constructed (as, in her, words 'unremittingly Western male'). Along similar lines, she talks about how students can read the gender messages in texts differently—for instance, in alternative ways, as her *Hamlet* example illustrates. Moreover, Jennifer's choice and use of curriculum materials such as *The Crow* and the television program *Arrested Development* reflect her own gender knowledges and agendas. Use the following discussion starters to stimulate conversations *within departments in high schools or* groups of year level teachers in primary schools or to consider your own individual practices:

- Reflect on the hierarchical valuing of various curriculum areas in your school. What areas are most valued/privileged? What areas are least valued/ privileged? What are the gender messages/issues and their implications for student learning?
- Reflecting on Jennifer's observation of the way that knowledge is presented as problematic in her philosophy subject, consider how knowledge is presented in your curriculum area/s. In relation to issues of gender, race, class, ethnicity, sexuality and so on, whose voices are dominant and whose are marginalised?
- How might you re-present or reorganise this knowledge to take account of dominant and silent voices in more socially just ways? For example, how would you tackle Jennifer's concerns about the Western male focus of her Philosophy curriculum in non-tokenistic ways? How, like Jennifer, might you draw on texts to offer students alternative understandings of such knowledge?

ENDORSING AND DISRUPTING THE NORM

Students sometimes present teachers with a pedagogical moment when dominant knowledges are on the one hand endorsed, but on the other challenged. For instance, Jennifer notes how dominant understandings about masculinity—as associated with an aversion to English because it is emotional and 'feminine'—are endorsed by particular boys (and girls). She also notes, by contrast, how dominant constructions of gender are disrupted, as her account of a student's alternative reading of *Hamlet* demonstrates. Discuss with others instances of when students may have offered views or readings of masculinity, femininity and sexuality that on the one hand ascribe to, but on the other disrupt, dominant views. Share some of these examples and then use the following questions as discussion starters:

- How did you respond to this situation?
- Drawing on the principles of social/gender justice, how might your ways of responding to students reinforce or challenge narrow and unjust views of gender and sexuality?
- What were the pedagogical benefits/disadvantages of this moment? Are there things you would do differently if presented with this situation again? What would they be?

Creating a safe and gender-inclusive environment: Constructing relations of cooperation, support and respect

A key platform of Jennifer's teaching philosophy is the promotion of respect for different perspectives. This philosophy informs Jennifer's endeavours to demonstrate respect for gender diversity. Importantly, Jennifer's commitment to gender justice—particularly her recognition of the harmful pressures associated with boys' ascription to dominant versions of masculinity—reflects her efforts to facilitate students' challenging of 'traditional' gender stereotypes and, more specifically, the problematising of narrow versions of masculinity. Jennifer's attempts to provide an environment that does not constrain students' alternative expressions of masculinity and femininity are evident in her support for a particular boy's wearing of makeup as an expression or presentation of bisexuality, her use of counter-stereotypical language in her everyday interactions with students (for example, her comments regarding students' physical appearance) and her endeavours to draw on a range of non-discriminatory gender representations in the texts she uses in her teaching. Jennifer's commitment to recognising difference in gender-just ways is also clear in her awareness of the potentially negative implications associated with her punishing of a boy for a homophobic remark.

A significant way in which Jennifer enables gender justice is through her disruption of the traditional teacher–student binary. As we pointed out earlier, the inequitable power relations of this binary have long been criticised as normalising the gendered relations of power that endorse boys' investments in hegemonic masculinity, and incite feelings of powerlessness and disengagement. Jennifer's practice gives space to the student voice and her non-adherence to the typical teacher image disrupts the practices of normalisation that contribute to the traditional teacher–student binary. However, such disruption does not mean that she never exercises authority.

FACILITATING GENDER-JUST TEACHER–STUDENT RELATIONSHIPS

This exercise is intended to stimulate discussion about how engagements with students often have gendered effects, and how these effects can often have consequences with regard to how safe students feel in the classroom. With one or more trusted colleagues, share what you perceive to be the key characteristics of your relationships with students. After listening to your colleague(s), consider some of the following questions to promote discussion:

- In what ways does your take-up of an 'official' teacher identity shape your relationships with students? How might this take-up constrain or enable student agency and autonomy? For example, do some of these relations reflect unnecessary or excessive levels of domination and control over students? In what ways are the broader structures and cultures at your school complicit in endorsing the traditional power inequities of the teacher–student relationship?
- Do you treat boys and girls differently? Are there particular types of boys or girls you like/dislike? Why? To what extent are your thoughts here informed by gendered assumptions? To what extent might your actions reinscribe inequitable understandings of gender?
- How does your gender affect your relationships with students? For example, consider the issues of gendered authority we foregrounded in Chapter 2, whereby the masculinised voice and body tend to be associated with authority and power and the feminised voice and body with a lack of authority and power. How have such associations impacted on your relationships with students?
- In what ways could you change your interactions (and your broader school structures and cultures) to reflect greater student autonomy and agency?

DEALING WITH A BEHAVIOUR-MANAGEMENT ISSUE

The purpose of this exercise is to consider how to deal with conflict in a situation where it is perhaps easiest to ignore the event. In schools, it is often easier to let some behaviours pass in order to avoid what seem like unnecessary conflicts with students—for instance, this appears to be the case with Jennifer in relation to the boys who sometimes wear non-school ties. However, there are also some behaviours which appear harmless to onlookers but which have significant consequences for those involved. For example, one of us in another study observed a classroom where a Year 11 boy was often the subject of homophobic teasing. In interviews, other boys indicated that it was just a case of 'joking around'. However, the boy who was the subject of the teasing, and who seemed to take it as a joke in the classroom, broke down and cried when this teasing was discussed in an interview (see Mills, 2001). Jennifer tries not to let such incidents go without intervening, as they do work against her understandings of justice. The incident described by Jennifer at the tuckshop line, where she reprimands a student for calling another boy a 'faggot', is a case in point. However, as she suggests—and along similar lines to the earlier exercise, 'endorsing and disrupting the norm'—there are also gendered problems in relation to how she responded to this incident. Using that incident as a discussion starter, respond to the following:

- What are some of the gender issues involved in this situation? Do you think Jennifer dealt with this appropriately? Why/why not?
- How do you tend to respond to students' or teachers' homophobic or sexist remarks? How do your students and other teachers tend to respond to these remarks? Consider the extent to which various responses are likely to reinforce inequitable understandings of gender and sexuality—endorsing or, as Jennifer would say, 'ghettoising' difference even further. Consider how various responses might challenge and work to transform such inequities.
- Draw up a list of principles for dealing with such events.

4 ROSS: AFFLICTING THE COMFORTABLE AND COMFORTING THE AFFLICTED

Introduction

One of the first impressions that is gained when walking into Ross's school, Elwood Green College, is that of overwhelming opulence. This is a 'good' boys' school. It is also clearly a religious school. There are statues of various religious figures displayed in prominent places. These can also be found in various gardens surrounding the old buildings. The effect of this is to create an atmosphere similar to that found in European stately homes. During our various walks around the school, we catch glimpses of white-robed figures. These are the principal—or headmaster, as he is referred to at this school—and various 'brothers' who work with the boys and in the administration of the school. While sitting in the waiting area to meet Ross for the first time, we are greeted politely by students and staff alike. There is a relaxed atmosphere at this school, where students are clearly at ease with adult company.

In this chapter we have chosen to foreground Ross's story as a male teacher who has long been committed to the principles of social justice, and who has worked closely with boys to improve their social and academic outcomes. He is a committed teacher who seeks to stretch his students intellectually through challenging their preconceived notions about a range of social issues. At the same time, he has given thought to what it means to be a male teacher working with boys around issues of social justice. What he demonstrates here is that a commitment to gender justice is the responsibility of *both* male and female teachers.

Many male teachers concerned about social justice issues in schools have been troubled by the current boys' debate. As part of this debate, as noted in Chapter 2, there have been widespread calls for more male teachers in schools. These calls—often found in media stories, populist texts on boys and, increasingly, in government policies—have worked with the presumption that boys are failing, or at least under-achieving, and that one reason for this is the lack of male teachers in schools. This places those male teachers who, over the years, have supported a gender-just approach to schooling in a difficult situation.

On the one hand, these teachers recognise that there are issues for boys in schools and that dominant forms of masculinity can cause problems for others—including women and girls—and for the boys themselves. They are also very well aware that it is impossible to talk about *all* boys in the same way, and that issues of class, race/ethnicity, geographic location and so on all impact upon the take-up of particular gendered identities. For many of these male teachers, feminism has helped to shape their view of education, and they often dismiss claims made by the boys' lobby as overstatements. However, in the current climate, male teachers are often expected to stand up for boys, to suggest that feminism has damaged boys' life chances and educational experiences, and to act as authority figures towards boys. Male teachers who are not prepared to do this can be regarded as 'traitors' to their gender (Martino & Frank, 2006). The issue of male teachers is one that has come to be associated with the education of boys (see Francis & Skelton, 2001; Mills et al., 2004), and it is one we take up later in this chapter in the context of issues that Ross raises about female teachers at his school.

Like all the teachers we have foregrounded, Ross seeks to challenge students intellectually, tries to ensure that students see the world from multiple perspectives, is concerned with building student relationships and wants to make education relevant to students' worlds. Like the other teachers whose stories we have told, we do not always agree with everything that Ross tells us. However, we think that this is a strength of Ross's story. Whilst agreeing with many of Ross's comments—and, indeed, respecting his commitment to gender justice—it is our disagreements with him that open up debates and possibilities for new ideas to emerge about the teaching of boys in gender-just ways. After a brief description of the context in which Ross works, we focus on two issues surfacing from our conversations with and observations of Ross. The first relates to his philosophical commitment to a pedagogy that encourages critical thinking and the second to the notion of male role models.

Ross's story

Ross, who has been a teacher for fifteen years, currently teaches Religious Education at Elwood Green College, a large metropolitan single-sex Catholic school for boys from Grades 5 to 12. This is a very traditional school that is proud of its 'old boys', one of who became prime minister of Papua New Guinea and another who is a current Test Cricket player. It has both boarders and day pupils. The school boasts numerous grand buildings, eight major sporting fields and an Olympic-size swimming pool. It has a proud sporting tradition. It is strict about uniform, and the boys always appear to be immaculately dressed. There are 'tea ladies' to supply the staff with morning tea, and the environment would be the envy of many working in struggling government schools. In the Catholic tradition, the school articulates a strong commitment to social justice by encouraging students to take part in the school's Social Justice and Service Program that involves such things as contributing to Amnesty International (a former student was at the time of writing the Australian national president of Amnesty International), barbecues for the homeless and holiday camps for students with disabilities. Indeed, a concern with social justice is evident in the school's explanation of its motto on its webpage, where it declares that: '"Viriliter Age— Act Courageously" challenges each person to envision a more just and compassionate world'.

In this privileged boys' school, concerns about boys' academic achievements do not appear to be particularly evident. This is a school that is quite selective. Ross tells us that every year, 400 students apply to get in and only 100 are successful. This has significance for the identity of the parents, and their children, as entry is linked to status within the local community. For instance, Ross says that this was apparent 'when you find parents who didn't get in and are crying because "What are my neighbours going to think?"' He points out to us that there are very few issues of low aspirations at this school because: 'You go into a classroom and you don't have to fight that battle of getting kids motivated or switched on because of that desire to learn and I think it's tied into "success equals university entry".' Thus, in his approach to boys' education, Ross is very aware that he is working with privileged boys— not the stereotype of the 'under-achieving boy' so prevalent in populist books and media stories on boys. Hence, for Ross, what is important for these boys is that they learn to problematise their 'privilege'—which he associates with a Christian philosophy. He makes very clear to us that what he seeks to achieve with these boys is a Christian principle of 'comforting the afflicted and afflicting the comfortable'.

Troubling the 'normal': Thinking from another angle

Ross, in discussing his approach to teaching, demonstrates his alignment with the school's commitment to social justice. He states that he seeks to challenge what he feels are his students' narrow views, particularly in relation to issues of class and race. In this respect, Ross says that he tries to transform the sense of elitism, materialism and ethnocentrism that he sees as characterising the lifeworlds of many of his students, through a pedagogy which promotes 'thinking from another angle' and which foregrounds those voices that have been 'missing' from the traditional curriculum. In broadening boys' understandings of difference and diversity, Ross tells us that it is important for schools to provide multiple and varied adult role models, but recognises that particular ways of being male and female send messages to boys that are far from positive in terms of social/gender justice. Ross talks here in positive ways about how his school reflects a diversity of 'really good' male and female teachers who work in collaborative ways to create a whole-school inclusive tenor that focuses on quality teaching and positive relationships. This issue is taken up later in the chapter.

Ross argues that, as part of this social justice approach, it is important to teach boys 'tolerance'—which for him means accepting others and appreciating diversity. He sees this as particularly important within what he describes as his school's 'mono-cultural' environment where, according to him, students are 'all from white Irish Catholic backgrounds'. He is very mindful in this respect of how the particular values of the boys' family backgrounds and the elite status of the school impact on how his students view what is important in their lives:

> In these sorts of rich elite . . . schools there is a danger of kids coming out with a view that 'the world owes me a living because I went to this school', rather than 'what can I

contribute to society because, as a Christian or whatever this is what I'm on about?' And it's very hard . . . like there's a counter-cultural thing 'cause the market forces of their parents probably wanting that elite advantage sort of thing . . .

To some extent, Ross's comments suggest that the school is not living up to its stated Christian ideals. This is perhaps not unexpected when, as he argues, contemporary market forces and parental expectations perpetuate the view that what is important in life, and what will make one happy, are good matriculation results and a high-paying job. This, Ross tries to point out to the boys, is not necessarily the case. He also claims that 'kids who come from families that "value" (i.e. "pay for") education tend to have a very narrow mind, or they think they're better than everybody else sort of thing'. He says that such thinking is contrary to the teachings of the school's church. These teachings, of course, give him leverage when he wants to challenge the boys (and indeed other teachers and parents) on their views when they conflict with his social justice principles. However, while he sees that it is important to challenge students' narrow views from 'a Catholic teaching point of view', he also sees that having their horizons broadened is also necessary in terms of them 'getting on in life'.

In order for his students to become more aware of social issues, Ross argues that it is imperative for them to develop the 'ability to be critical thinkers'. He sees this as particularly important within what he describes as a 'day and age' of excessive 'propaganda' and 'media bias', where religious and political issues are distorted. However, he claims that the boys' ways of engaging with learning sometimes make this approach quite difficult. He says of the students at this school:

. . . they've learnt the codes of behaviour of how to succeed, and to succeed here is to find out what the parents and the teachers want and give it to them. So you will have very compliant students who will do exactly what you want in terms of behaviour and homework and learning and assessment, but I find it very hard to get them to express their own opinions and to critique—for example, church teaching or societal teaching or school policy—because they see that as not beneficial to their getting into university or whatever their goals are.

Ross draws on 'liberation' and 'feminist' theology in his classroom to support his attempts to have his students critically analyse 'real-world' social and religious issues, and in particular to foreground the 'missing voice' in dominant representations of the world. Here he mentions boys' positive responses to his scaffolding of explorations about why marginalised groups such as women and particular religious and ethnic groups are 'left out of the text'. As we highlighted in Chapter 2, such scaffolding, in foregrounding the inequitable social relations that construct what counts as knowledge and what we see as 'reality', has clear potential in terms of working for gender justice—within this critical framework, the inequitable power relations that construct gendered knowledge can be made transparent, challenged and transformed.

In foregrounding this missing voice, it is perhaps paradoxical that Ross does not appear afraid to challenge some of the dominant beliefs of the Catholic Church and to wade into the treacherous waters of discussing homophobia and human sexuality, and their relationships to particular constructions of masculinity. He explains in this regard that:

I think kids know a lot of students who are openly gay or have had a gay experience and—they know the people. Whereas I think my generation—the older generation—would say—well we don't know anyone who is, as they have kept it all quiet, 'cause it was 'dirty' and not acceptable and I think it has become acceptable . . .

When asked if accepting homosexuality was contrary to some of the church's teachings, he tells us:

> . . . kids believe you can ignore church and the traditional societal thinking on sexuality and morality. They ignore them because there's not—it doesn't make sense to them. . . . The reality is that the kids are postmodern kids and most of our teachers are operating in a modern . . . People just pick and choose and ignore things. I think we're trying to say—look at a relational approach to church. It's how you treat one another and all those sorts of things. It's how do we relate to one another? And I suppose that's a shift in philosophy. But we've shifted our focus on to social evil rather than personal.

This shifting to 'social evil' rather than 'personal evil' necessitates an approach that he says tries to 'really challenge the kids to think and question' what he and others say. He does this, he says, through dialogue and debate that encourage 'thinking from the unspoken person, so like the minority group person who's missing in the debate'. He sees this as being far preferable to students 'just sitting passively and copying off the board or working from handouts'.

To illustrate his critical approach to religious studies, Ross discusses the current representations of Islam in the West. He is highly critical of what he perceives to be religious intolerance, and of the way in which the media present current concerns about terrorism:

> . . . the whole Muslim–Christian fight between the conservative government that we have and different groups, cultural groups that appear to be different because of their colour or their religious background—what's going on? Is it a religious issue or is it politics trying to manipulate the masses sort of thing?

He tells us about a deconstructive activity that he has scaffolded with his students, which explores media representations of

Muslims on the commercial and populist television program *Today Tonight* and the non-commercial television program *Media Watch*:

> Just yesterday we were deconstructing the Channel Seven, *Today Tonight* thing on the Muslim young fellas, and then looking at *Media Watch*. Yeah, they showed that Channel Seven had cut off the . . . had misquoted the person. The Muslim fellow had said, 'I don't want to assimilate into the way Australians drink and drink and drink'. What went to air was, 'I don't want to assimilate'.

He notes that most of the boys, prior to this activity, had viewed and 'were swayed by' the *Today Tonight* report:

> . . . they're saying, 'Let's get rid of Muslims'. I said, 'Oh, hang on, who's telling you? Why are they telling you? Who owns the media?' and to sort of process it [in] that sort of way.

Ross says that this activity was important because it made transparent how anti-Muslim sentiment is 'beaten up' by the media and how such reports legitimise our reasons to dismiss minority groups. Certainly—and aligning with the productive pedagogies framework we detailed in Chapter 2—this activity can be seen as particularly significant in that it connects with real-world issues that are relevant and meaningful to these boys in ways that provoke critical interrogation of how knowledge is fabricated and how inequities are constructed. Such a focus, as we pointed out earlier, enables a valuing of difference that supports students to become critically aware of the inequitable power relations of our social world that marginalise and oppress groups unfairly.

In trying to teach for cultural acceptance and diversity, Ross is mindful of the limited resources to which he has access at the school. He finds that much of the textbook, video and material resources he uses are 'either Catholic or white Anglo-based

because they're the people that publish them'. He tries, nevertheless, to present material that is culturally, gender, ethnically
and religiously 'balanced'. Ross finds that drawing on other
sources through community work and fieldwork is an effective
way to challenge narrow views and stereotypes. He describes
how he, and the school, engage students with 'different ethnic
groups and people of different faiths':

> . . . we try to get out into the community and do fieldwork
> as much as possible to get boys to, you know, come up with a
> hypothesis which is usually a generalised stereotype about
> a religious group or a community, and then to go and explore
> that. Our community service program . . . has been a really
> good way of getting the boys out into the world and seeing
> that, for example, the Aboriginal people that live under the
> bridge are just normal people. Or the people with mental
> illness who are living in the parks and things are people and
> they can have, build friendships with those people. That's been
> effective in terms of challenging narrow views or stereotypes.
> The only way you can do it is to meet the people rather than
> just relying on what they think is the reality.

This approach is clearly tied to the religious component of
the educational program at the school. Ross says that the school
is 'trying to put structures in place that allow more kids to have
opportunities, to get involved in such 'ethical experiential' activities—which he describes as far preferable to 'just hitting them in
the head with a Bible'. To some extent, such an approach can
have limitations if it works within a paternalistic framework that
involves either a studying, or a fixing up, of the 'other'. Furthermore, unless explicitly located within a commitment to engaging
students with active citizenship imperatives, this form of community service can reinforce deficit models of those who have been
marginalised by various forms of discrimination. However,
this program appears to be closely tied to the citizenship goals

advocated in more secular schools. It also highlights the importance of students from privileged backgrounds being exposed to
difference and developing a social conscience. Notwithstanding,
and as we noted in Chapter 2, such forms of consciousness-
raising can be particularly productive in moving beyond a
superficial engagement with 'otherness' to an experiential challenging of narrow views and stereotypes—drawing on a sense of
community and group identity to mobilise boys' care and
responsibility for the welfare of others.

Ross argues that the boys' experiences in such social justice
and community service programs, as well as their participation
in other cultural programs like music and performing arts,
contribute to the school's inclusive tenor. He attributes this to
the school's valuing of these pursuits, and says that this inclusive
tenor is counter to the typical 'Rugby school' environment
that characterises many elite boys' schools. In this respect, he
says that his school does not support all the 'negative things that
go along with the "ra-ra" tradition'—'there's no, "Oh you have
to play Rugby to be a real man" sort of thing. That's not, like
it's acceptable to do lots of different things.' He goes on to say:

> . . . this place, while they do play Rugby, it's more, the focus is
> on participating and having a go. Like the school culture itself
> doesn't put Rugby at the top of the pile, it's just one of the
> many activities in the school. But the culture of winning and
> achieving and participating is a long historical part of the
> college, but I don't think the leadership or the staff go: 'you
> know, this is who we are' . . . some schools I worked in, the
> only people who get attention in assembly are the First Fifteen
> or the First Thirteen sort of thing, whereas here it's just part of
> the culture not the dominant culture . . . I think that's differ-
> ent from five/ten years ago in boys' schools where your
> masculinity was identified through what sport you played so
> you had to do it to fit in sort of thing.

The mention of Rugby football here is interesting. There has been much written about the ways in which football, of various codes in a variety of school locations, is a powerful influence on the construction of masculinities. This relates to boys who both engage with and disengage from football. Many working in the area of gender and education (see, for example, Mills, 2001; Fitzclarence & Hickey, 1998; Gilbert & Gilbert, 1998) have argued that any reform agenda which seeks to provide boys with a greater range of masculinities that are less harmful to themselves and others has to problematise boys' relationship with football. Ross indicates here that this has to happen at the school level, not just at the individual level. However, even in situations where the school valorises those boys who excel at football—as is the case in many elite private schools—individual teachers like Ross are able to challenge conventional wisdoms about boys and football. This, of course, requires intellectual engagement with theories of gender—and, in this case, theories of masculinities.

What becomes clear from our conversations with Ross is that, for him, there is a close correlation between stretching students intellectually and challenging dominant cultural knowledges. In particular, he sees that his efforts to encourage his students to 'think from another angle', and to understand that there are 'no absolutes', are important in terms of equipping boys with the skills to make informed and just decisions in their relations with others. He explains the importance of being:

> . . . able to get students to think from another angle on an issue, whether it's, you know, a minority group or another cultural group, just, you know . . . there's more than one way, of, there's no absolute sort of thing, and what one person considers to be right may not be for somebody else and to look at the circumstances . . . and, you know, I really think if boys can think that way then in terms of the way they relate with their girlfriends or their partners or their wives or kids

or whatever, that they won't just operate out of the dominant alpha male sort of 'I'm right, I'm a male' sort of thing.

Ross's gender analysis is located within his broader critical awareness of how our social world produces multiple dominant and marginal realities. He can see that challenging dominant knowledges involves challenging students' notions of what it means to be male. Here we are reminded of the Jane Kenway comment about how important the feminist problematising of masculinity is for women and men:

> Most feminists want boys and men to change so that they cause less trouble for girls and women and themselves, so the sexes can live alongside each other in a safe, secure, stable, respectful, harmonious way and in relationships of mutual life-enhancing respect (Kenway, 1996, p. 447).

This challenging of students, Ross suggests, has to be accompanied by an approach that is supportive of and respectful towards students. In stressing the difference between this school and Catholic schools grounded in other traditions, he points out that 'they control through fear and we control through love'. This 'love' is demonstrated through the ways in which the teachers are expected to treat students by nurturing the boys' learning and by not focusing on punishment as a means of control. This focus—which, as we have noted in earlier chapters, is imperative in improving the hostile relationship many disengaged boys have with 'official' and invariably authoritarian school cultures—has been evolving at the school over the last ten to fifteen years. Ross told us of a key female teacher, alongside other new teachers, who since joining the staff:

> . . . has systematically introduced an approach to teaching that is based on respect and building a relationship and rapport . . . and I think good teachers have always done it. But to actually

name it as a good pedagogy—I think they got rid of lots of teachers—or teachers moved on that didn't fit into those newer philosophies . . . And employing nurturing teachers that are good role models for that—and this school I think has done a really good job at getting most of our staff fitting in with that philosophy . . .

Developing respectful and nurturing relationships, which are based on conciliation rather than control, is a key part of Ross's teaching philosophy. He understands this as a gender issue. Acknowledging the broader masculinity politics that intersect with the processes of schooling to amplify many boys' disruptive and resistance behaviours, Ross argues that such conciliatory teacher–student relations are particularly important for boys, 'otherwise they just won't connect with whatever you're trying to teach'. Such ways of thinking highlight Ross's strong commitment to student-centred learning—a philosophy that he sees as aligning with that of the school's discipline structure set up around the 'heads of house' and 'deputies who deal with kids in terms of misbehaviour', where he claims that:

> The way they deal with them I think is very affirming of the kids' identity and who they are. It's not a fear-driven thing; it's not a power-driven thing. It's what's best for the kid sort of thing.

Ross attributes the school's inclusive tenor to the broader collective efforts of staff to 'strongly promote a discipline structure that's based on quality relationships and mutual respect between the teachers and students rather than the fear/authoritarian model'. This focus, as we mentioned before, has been a key emphasis in the school for some time, framing the discipline and pastoral care structures. Ross talks about how this emphasis has impacted on other areas such as classroom practice; the researching of 'boys' issues' (where a group of teachers interviews boys about issues of significance and concern to them at the school); and the adoption of strategies such as the Responsible Thinking Process (RTP). He describes some of these practices:

> . . . things like the whole shift of curriculum structure to focus on best practice teaching and learning rather than the teacher up the front being the expert sort of thing . . . and the boys' committee—they have been looking at boys' issues, researching every six months on a bullying issue, and those sorts of things. But just a really clear expectation . . . to respect the kids and not to use fear and coercion to get them to do things, and I think the RTP thing, it's the student's choice whether they're gonna engage or not, and you can't force them.

Ross says that one of the things he 'likes about' the RTP is that he is able to draw on it 'to challenge any statement, stereotype or racist comment or bigoted comment . . . [any] paying out on kids because they're effeminate or, you know, from India or Black whatever it is. That's not acceptable.' He says that he never 'allows things like that to go unchallenged' and, through the RTP, encourages students to take responsibility for their behaviour by asking them to 'explain what they mean'. He uses this process to teach students 'non-confronting' ways of interacting, and he finds that generally, in relation to abusive behaviours, the kids that he deals with 'won't tolerate that sort of thing'. Importantly—and as we argued in Chapter 2—Ross seems to adopt this approach in non-authoritarian and non-clinical ways that are cognisant of and sensitive to the broader social context within which his students' behaviours are located.

It is against this backdrop that Ross brings up the issue of boys and role modelling. This issue, as we detailed in Chapter 2, is one that has permeated the literature on boys' education and raised important questions about the sex of the teacher and essentialised constructions of male and female teachers. Significantly, while much of the formal initiatives around this issue—such as those focused on increasing the number of male teachers in boys' school-lives—are inherently problematic, the debate has foregrounded the issue that Ross raises around teacher quality, and more specifically the types of male teachers that would be most positive for boys.

Role models

Ross talks about the importance of schools providing positive male (and also female) role models for boys: 'of a whole variety of styles; gentle people and assertive and confident—you know—the whole range of types of people'. He points out, however, that there can be negative male role models for boys: 'The worst one would probably be the stereotype Phys Ed, Manual Arts, big strong Rugby rant and rave [because] they're relying on fear to control kids rather than wanting kids to learn for their own wanting and desire.' He says that the deputy head of the school, as a role model, is in stark contrast to this image of control and fear, and is therefore very positive for the boys:

> Like our deputy of the school is the most laidback, not passive, but anti-authority figure, and every kid would respect him because he talks with them and spends time with them and he . . . if there's a problem they go and see him . . .

Ross talks in positive ways about how his school seems to reflect a diversity of 'really good' male and female role models, particularly since the recent 'deliberate' push to 'get females into the school . . . as fewer brothers (members of the school's founding religious order) have been around and the males have moved on'. He does, however, also engage with the current trend to stress the importance of male teachers. For instance, he states:

I think—like we're very lucky that we have a lot of male staff in the Primary School—the junior school. Most—you know we've got probably five, six, seven, footballer clone sort of types that love their sport and in this school and most schools that's a good way to connect with boys, but it's not the only way.

Significantly, he does note that this is 'not the only way'. He goes on to suggest that it is important for boys to be exposed to men who do not reflect dominant masculine characteristics:

In our Music department, drama club there's all the—you know it's not a rough blokey [place]—like sport doesn't run this school even though it has a section of the place. It's a way of relating but it's not a testosterone-filled environment.

This diversity is, of course, important in a staff. While not subscribing to role theory, and recognising that young people do not have the freedom to take up any role, and that gender is constructed in complex ways that involve the policing of dominant ways of being male or female, we do acknowledge that it is important for students to be exposed to a variety of gender performances. Such exposure to non-dominant ways of being—especially when such behaviours are performed by people students respect—can serve to disrupt the legitimacy of, for instance, hegemonic constructions of masculinity.

However, subscribing to role theory can have its problems, as indicated by some of the concerns Ross raises about the staffing of the English Department at the school. He states that the English Department is probably the 'most high-profile' department in the school, and is at the 'cutting edge' in terms of curriculum and in particular critical literacy; and as a consequence, he says, English is the 'most highly regarded subject in the school'. He tells us in one interview that the teachers in this department are 'passionate' and 'professional' about their work and really 'know their stuff' but that:

. . . they're all, most of them . . . young or middle-aged female teachers who are of a certain teaching style and something the boys, just in conversation, they think, that must be the way all women are . . .

In a follow-up interview he goes on to say that:

I think is a bit of an issue for some of the boys because specific subjects have become female dominated. Like the English [Department] has a lot of strong females who are very competent teachers but who are probably—I don't know, a bit more operating out of their dominate–control model.

He regards the predominance of female teachers within the English Department as a problem because he claims that what can happen is that the boys 'type and categorise' teachers. For instance, he suggests that in Religion they categorise the teachers as the 'nice holy people' and then 'wipe them off as an entity'. In English, he sees the same typecasting and discarding where, he suggests, 'male egos' tend to be 'threatened' by the predominance of 'young blonde upwardly mobile professional female teachers who are strong and confident and can manage boys well'. As he explains:

. . . if a boy has problems with females in terms of taking authority from them as often confident young men do, they may ignore the whole message because of the medium sort of thing . . . if they sort of don't like females or they struggle with a female telling them what to do, does that mean then English as a subject is therefore ignored, or not valued?

While Ross is concerned about the number of female teachers in English, he does not cast these concerns in the same framework as many within the boys' lobby. For him, it is often a question of balance. For, as he says in relation to the lack of female teachers in his own department:

So like I've got the opposite problem, I don't have the female side especially with relational stuff, marriage, morality, sexuality—all that sort of stuff. They're only getting one version—which is a male version.

Thus there is not the presumption that male teachers are better at connecting with the boys than female teachers. He suggests instead that there are both male and female perspectives on the world and that it is good for the boys to be exposed to both of these. This could be interpreted in essentialist ways—that is, that he perceives there to be a natural way of being a man or a woman. However, his understanding of difference outlined in another interview would also seem to suggest that this is not the case. At the same time, there is a danger of slipping into treating men and women as homogeneous groups, divorced from power relations, by looking for a simple balance of males and females in various subject areas.

For instance, in the case of English, there needs to be a problematising of why it is that men have avoided working in the field of English teaching and why English has been constructed as a 'feminised' subject (see Martino, 2000), rather than simply seeking to employ more male teachers in these areas. It is important that boys learn to work with, and for, women, and gender equity is not likely to be furthered in situations where boys are denied the opportunity to work for and with women. However, while for many boys the construction of English as a 'feminised' subject is perpetuated by the lack of men working in the field, a colonisation of the English teaching field by men, or a remasculinisation of the curriculum content, would be unlikely to change this view. Instead, we would argue, based on our experiences, that an approach such as Ross's which encourages boys to value diverse ways of being male and to challenge those dominant constructions of masculinities that inhibit diversity and that are harmful to boys and others is much more likely to have long-term benefits for boys. However, the issue of role models, as we acknowledged in Chapter 2, is a complex one, and we consider the importance of role models in the following section.

Examining Ross's philosophies, practices and understandings about gender

Ross brings a brand of liberation theological politics to his teaching. When we sat in his office for one of our interviews with him, he was passionate about his desire to 'comfort the afflicted and afflict the comfortable'. Indeed, he saw this as his purpose at the school, indicating that he had been brought from a less affluent school in a low socioeconomic area, belonging to the same Catholic order, for the purpose of ruffling the complacency of both the students and teachers at the current school. Underpinning this politics was a broad theorising of social justice that helped shape Ross's understandings about gender. This theorising recognises the hierarchical constructions of masculinity associated with class, religion and race (Connell, 1995). Ross's concern about the relations of power and privilege connected with being a particular kind of boy highlights his understanding of masculinity as it is constructed and endorsed through inequitable social relations that privilege some ways of being male while marginalising others. Here Ross recognises, in particular, the power and privilege associated with being an Anglo boy from an affluent background in terms of generating, in many of the boys he teaches, a sense of entitlement and a view that 'the world owes me a living'. In this context, Ross expresses concern about the dangers associated with his school's mono-cultural and elite environment, and his students' narrow family backgrounds. In particular, he sees these contexts both as providing his students with access to power and authority and as promoting a materialistic elitism that engenders self-interest and a lack of acceptance and appreciation of difference and diversity.

Ross's social justice lenses 'act against the grain' (Giroux, 2003) in problematising these dominant cultural understandings. Such lenses inform his commitment to the imperative of critical thinking in terms of facilitating his students' capacities to 'question and reason through' issues of identity and power in ways that broaden their understandings of difference. He sees such skills as particularly important in a 'day and age' where dominant cultural views distort political and religious issues in ways that endorse inequitable understandings of marginalised groups, such as Muslims. Ross's focus on how such issues are shaped by social interactions and contexts enables him to argue that more positive and just ways of being are possible through boys 'thinking from a different angle' and understanding that there are 'no absolutes' in terms of how different issues might be understood. In terms of gender justice, Ross positions such ways of thinking and being as central to his students developing respectful personal relationships with females, where 'they won't just operate out of the dominant alpha male sort of "I'm right, I'm a male" sort of thing'.

Consistent with his promotion of difference and diversity, Ross recognises the importance of multiple male and female role models in boys' lives. However, and aligning with principles of gender justice, he acknowledges how certain male role models—in particular, those that ascribe to dominant notions of masculinity—are harmful in terms of shaping boys' behaviours (see, for example, Roulston & Mills, 2000). As he says, 'the worst [male role model] would probably be the stereotype Phys Ed, Manual Arts, big strong Rugby rant and rave' who relies on fear to control kids. Ross suggests that his school's deputy principal, an 'anti-authority figure' who demonstrates care for his students, is a far better role model for boys. Such problematising of constructions of masculinity that valorise exertions of power, control and domination highlight Ross's understanding of how inequitable relations of gender and power can be reproduced, but also disrupted and transformed (Salisbury & Jackson, 1996; Mills, 2001).

In some of Ross's discussions, he demonstrates how gender issues can become complex when seeking to challenge these constructions of masculinity. This is evident in his comments about the female teachers in the school's English Department. Ross talks positively about the school's 'recent deliberate push' to attract more female teachers, but notes an over-representation of females in English. While he describes these predominantly female teachers as passionate and professional about their work in this 'cutting edge' and 'high-profile' department, he also raises concern about the messages this gender balance sends to the boys. His comments here, of course, reflect many of the current debates about male teachers, in particular those relating to why there are so few male teachers in certain areas of schooling—for example, early childhood and languages (see Roulston & Mills, 2000; Mills et al., 2004).

Understanding gender as constructed through inequitable binary relations that ascribe power and value to the masculine side of the binary, Ross suggests here that boys' general marginalising of females and 'the feminine' can enable them to typecast these teachers and 'wipe them off as an entity'. In this respect, Ross expresses concern about how boys draw on this binary to devalue the subject of English and to dismiss or discard these teachers' attempts to engage them in important (and potentially socially transformative) critical literacy work. We would, in this instance, argue—contrary to Ross—that, rather than considering altering the composition of the English staff because the boys devalue English, it would be helpful to confront the reasons—for example, misogynous and homophobic attitudes—that boys devalue things associated with femininity. Notwithstanding this, and significant in pursuing the goals of gender justice, Ross recognises how inequitable gender relations are installed by school structures and processes through the value assigned to extra-curricula activities (Connell, 1995). He talks here about the importance of disrupting the high status generally assigned to Rugby in many elite boys' schools (and all the 'negative things that go along with the "ra-ra" tradition') by ensuring that other more socially responsible and inclusive pursuits like the boys' participation in social justice and community service activities are promoted and valued in forums such as school assemblies.

However, Ross's philosophies about social justice inform a practice that seeks to broaden his students' narrow and restrictive understandings of identity to be more inclusive of difference and diversity (Lingard et al., 2002). Like the attempts made by Jennifer (see Chapter 3) to provide her students with a 'fresh look' at taken-for-granted ways of knowing, Ross supports his students to think from a different angle through the practices of critical literacy. Ross challenges his students to understand knowledge construction as problematic through foregrounding the 'missing voice'. Here he encourages debate and dialogue about 'real-world' social issues to support students to 'think from the unspoken person'. For example, Ross taps into a contentious but highly significant contemporary issue regarding race and religion to explore issues of power and the representation of Muslims in the media. In this activity, Ross makes transparent the non-innocent and politically driven way that dominant cultural products such as commercial media (re)present minority groups in ways that affirm and reinscribe the 'status quo' of inequitable race and religious relations. Importantly, in engaging the space of schooling as a site of contestation, resistance and possibility, Ross connects this critical learning to the experiences and histories that students bring to the classroom in terms of the anti-Muslim sentiment expressed by his students (Giroux, 2003).

Ross also attempts to broaden his students' narrow views through scaffolding critical learning experiences beyond the school setting. In 'real-world' community contexts, Ross supports his students to examine and question particular stereotypical assumptions about minority groups (for example, Indigenous people and individuals with mental illness) through 'getting the boys out into the world' so that they know and understand members of these marginalised groups, rather than seeing them as largely different and 'other'. These critical learning exercises—or, as Ross describes them, 'ethical experiential' activities—facilitate boys' recognition of multiple ways of being, thinking and acting. Importantly, they provide a context for boys to listen to voices from the margins—those positioned as 'other' to the masculinity seen as culturally superior, those existing at the borders. Recognising and legitimising these 'borderland' identities is politically generative because it demonstrates how individuals construct and negotiate alternative masculinities (Martino & Pallotta-Chiarolli, 2003).

Ross further troubles and seeks to transform the dominant cultural views that subsume difference and diversity in his examination of curriculum materials. Similar to Jennifer's recognition of the 'unremittingly Western male' perspective of the Philosophy curriculum that she teaches to, Ross recognises the cultural biases in the curriculum materials available to him. He problematises these Catholic or Anglo-based resources as 'limited' and, in teaching for cultural acceptance and diversity, draws on materials and contexts that are more culturally, gender, ethnically and religiously 'balanced' and inclusive.

Ross's talk about the broader structures and processes that support his practice highlights the importance of a whole-school approach to issues of boys and schooling. Ross attributes his school's inclusive tenor to the broader collective efforts of staff within a whole-school philosophy that focuses on quality teaching and positive relationships. Ross argues that this whole-school philosophy has impacted positively on classroom practices (in relation to a move away from direct 'teacher as expert' models of instruction) and the school's discipline and pastoral care systems (in terms of a rejection of authoritarian and power-driven models of behaviour management). These broader philosophies seem to inform the way

Ross draws on the whole-school RTP disciplinary strategy in terms of resolving conflict through non-confrontational ways that model alternatives to dominant and dominating constructions of masculinity. Importantly, Ross draws on this model in ways that challenge discriminatory (sexist, homophobic and racist) behaviours and encourage boys to take responsibility for their behaviours.

We have foregrounded Ross's story for a number of reasons. We found him passionate about the students he teaches and committed to creating a more socially just world through his teaching and the programs he has introduced into the school. In many ways, he reflects the qualities of a teacher leader outlined in Lingard et al. (2003). He is someone who has high expectations of students, he has a commitment to students beyond his own classroom and he is convinced that he can make a difference to his students' worlds and beyond. In our research—or indeed any other research with which we have been involved—we do not come across many men who are prepared to state that they support feminist principles and that these principles can help frame up approaches to boys' education. While we are not convinced that there is a need for more male role models in schools, even of a particular type, we do contend that men like Ross can make a difference to boys and the various ways in which they come to construct their masculinities.

Learning from Ross

Ross troubles the inequitable relations of power in his teaching context that he sees as constraining social justice. He recognises how these relations construct narrow and hierarchical understandings that privilege some ways of being a boy while marginalising others. For Ross, the problematising of class and cultural privilege informs how he teaches for and about social justice. Such thinking frames a pedagogy that supports his students' exploration of marginalised identities. In this section, we draw on these ways of knowing as a framework to stimulate your thinking about issues of masculinity, power and privilege in your schooling context and how such issues might inform how, like Ross, you might disrupt gender inequities through teaching that 'afflicts the comfortable' and 'comforts the afflicted'.

MASCULINE HIERARCHIES

Not all boys are the same. The broad social justice lenses that Ross uses to understand the boys he teaches, and boys in general, help to highlight the domination and oppression that invariably result from the multiple ways in which forms of masculinity interplay. This interplay works to construct hierarchical understandings of gender. Here particular versions of (generally white, middle-class, heterosexual and able-bodied) masculinity work to mark prestige or difference from other versions of masculinity and femininity, through positioning these groups as subordinate and somehow inferior. In Ross's schooling context, it is the power differentials based upon social class and culture that are foremost in his considerations about justice and equity.

Ross understands the elitism, materialism and ethno-centrism of many of the boys he teaches as constraining in terms of perpetuating hierarchical understandings of masculinity. We might refer to such ways of being as 'social baggage' that, as we detailed in Chapter 2, delimits how these boys represent and interpret their worlds. Certainly, Ross sees such social baggage as promoting a sense of privilege ('the world owes me a living') that works to endorse narrow views about what is important in life (good matriculation results and a high-paying job) and restrictive ideas about issues of cultural diversity (the denigration of Muslims, for example).

Moreover, Ross refers to this social baggage as constraining in terms of his students' tendencies to be compliant and play the game rather than express their own opinions and constructively critique church teaching or school policy.

While Ross acknowledges the broader factors such as family background and parental influence that contribute to the social baggage the boys bring to school, importantly he is aware of how the structures and practices in his school can work in ways that endorse but also serve to disrupt this version of privileged masculinity. Here he talks about the school's mono-cultural environment as hindering boys' capacities to appreciate cultural diversity. And, in terms of broadening understandings of difference and diversity, he talks about issues such as the school's valuing of extra-curricula activities (beyond the Rugby 'ra-ra' tradition), the importance of inclusive curriculum materials and resources, the importance of positive counter-stereotypical role models—particularly in relation to non-authoritarian male role models—and the significance of conciliatory and respectful approaches to behaviour management.

RELATIONS OF POWER, MASCULINITY AND IDENTITY: EXPLORING CONSTRUCTIONS OF PRIVILEGE AND MARGINALISATION IN YOUR SCHOOLING CONTEXT

The purpose of this exercise is to explore how male students in your schooling context enact different versions of masculinity in relation to issues of femininity, class, race, sexuality, ability and so on. Such exploration will support a critical analysis of how relations of power operate in your school to position groups hierarchically, but also how such positionings, far from being fixed, can shift over time and depending on context.

- Think about the different groups of boys at your school (or in your class). See if you can give each of these groups a different name. For instance, Wayne Martino (1999), in one of his studies, describes the different groups of boys in one school, drawing upon their own language, as the 'cool boys', 'party animals', 'squids' and 'poofters'. In Chapter 2, Alexandra (who teaches at Ross's school) names distinctive groups of boys at her school—the football boys are called the 'jocks' or the 'boyos', while the 'dead-heads' are called the 'undercross' group.
- What are the qualities that make each of these groups 'a group'. What behaviours are considered appropriate/inappropriate to a particular group?
- Try to rank these groups hierarchically from most popular to least popular. With this in mind, consider the interplay of power between groups in relation to issues such as gender, class, race, ethnicity and sexuality. How does this interplay produce dominant and marginalised identities? Think here about the ways in which each group defines itself in relation to other groups (for example, in Martino's study the 'party animals' and the 'cool boys' tended to define themselves as anti-intellectual and hyper-masculine and in opposition to the more studious, artistic and 'feminine' 'squids' and 'poofters'). What are some of the behaviours that work to maintain and police— or indeed, disrupt—these hierarchical constructions of masculinity?
- Comment on the social baggage that might be associated with each group. How might this social baggage perpetuate narrow ideas about identity, and particularly gender? How might this social baggage constrain learning?
- Reflect on Ross's schooling context or your own school experience as a student. How would your observations and categorisations of gender hierarchies in your

current context differ from these contexts? What does this indicate about the contextual and historically contingent nature of gender relations?

LOCATING HIERARCHICAL CONSTRUCTIONS OF MASCULINITY WITHIN BROADER STRUCTURES AND PRACTICES AT YOUR SCHOOL

The exercise supports an identification of particular structures and practices in your school that might on the one hand endorse, but on the other disrupt, students' hierarchical understandings of masculinity and femininity.

- Drawing on Ross's story, think about your school's cultural landscape (is cultural diversity represented in inclusive ways?); the value your school places on extra-curricula activities (are cultural pursuits valued in similar ways to sporting pursuits, for example?); and the tenor of teacher–student relationships (is discipline administered in overly authoritarian, clinical or rational ways?). What messages do these practices send to students about gender? How might these messages reinforce or disrupt the hierarchical masculinities you identified earlier?
- In terms of the tenor of teacher–student relationships and picking up on one of the key issues in Ross's story—male role models—consider the following teachers, Alexandra and Brad, whose voices feature in Chapter 2. These teacher voices illustrate Ross's point about how particular role models can be problematic in the teaching of boys. Both teachers talk about how they have attempted to connect with and develop a respectful rapport with the boys they teach. While Alexandra talks about how she felt that she had to be

excessively strict to develop some 'street cred' with her male students, Brad tries to tap into the interests of the boys he teaches:

I think I've gone from being a really strict nasty disciplinarian, you know, Miss Witch in the classroom, from the beginning stages, 'cause I felt I had to do that, to get my street cred with them. I really felt as a female that was the hard yards. I would be very strict and very firm, and, you know, 'don't smile till Easter'. (Alexandra)

Y'know if we spend fifteen minutes in some lessons talking about cars or y'know bull riding or pig chasing then I don't see it as fifteen minutes wasted . . . a couple of years ago, I had a Year 12 student—he was pretty awful for most people but he took me on my first pig chasing trip like said y'know 'Come out pig chasing' and I said, 'Oh all right, OK, I'll go out' and he sort of saw that I was willing to get in there and have a go and that had a massive transfer into the classroom. He certainly toed the line for me a lot better than what he was doing in a lot of other classrooms. (Brad)

These data snippets highlight different ways of relating that can similarly endorse a particular version of masculinity. On the one hand, Alexandra's excessively strict approach, as we pointed out in Chapter 2, is likely to affirm—and indeed, exacerbate—boys' take-up of dominant constructions of masculinity. On the other hand, while Brad's approach clearly contrasts with Alexandra's, his collusion in the hyper-masculine interests of some boys similarly works to endorse investments in dominant constructions of masculinity. With this in mind, reflect on the premise that only males can 'do masculinity' and only females 'femininity'—a premise that seems to undergird the simplistic take-up of the male role model issue. Consider how and why the gender of these teachers shapes their ways of relating to the boys they teach. Think of a time when your actions might have been interpreted as endorsing or colluding with inequitable understandings of masculinity. How was your gender implicated in this endorsing/colluding? How might you have behaved in more gender-just ways?

Disrupting the hierarchy: Afflicting the comfortable and comforting the afflicted

Ross recognises how the boys he teaches tap into their positions of privilege and power to legitimise their masculinity. In attempting to broaden their narrow views in relation to issues of class, race and religion—specifically their sense of entitlement, elitism and ethnocentrism—Ross encourages his male students to think from a different angle by foregrounding the 'missing voice'. In this respect, his efforts to afflict the comfortable and comfort the afflicted involve facilitating boys' recognition and valuing of those who are socially marginalised, such as the poor and homeless, or those who subscribe to a 'different' culture. Here Ross scaffolds real-world and connected learning experiences that encourage boys' critical analysis of texts (for example, the challenging of the anti-Muslim sentiment in *Today Tonight*) and 'ethical experiential' activities (where the boys' stereotypical assumptions are challenged through their experience with marginalised groups within the broader community).

These activities are informed by Ross's attempts to problematise some of the class- and culture-related social baggage that he sees constrains his students' identity and learning. Importantly, such pedagogies can work to highlight for the boys how their class and cultural privilege, rather than being a 'given', is socially constructed by non-innocent and often inequitable power relations that should be questioned and challenged.

CHALLENGING OPPRESSIVE RELATIONS

This exercise encourages consideration of ways in which you might support students to challenge the issues of oppression relevant to your context. Drawing on your understandings of how privilege, power and identity are constructed and negotiated in your school, the exercise provokes thought about how narrow and inequitable views might be broadened through a pedagogy that supports thinking from another angle.

- Drawing on the insights developed from the series of activities in the earlier exercise that identified the social baggage associated with particular versions of masculinity at your school, identify the positions of privilege that you believe should be problematised in pursuing the goals of social justice. Such positions of privilege might relate, as with Ross, to class and cultural issues or, as the data we presented in Chapter 1 highlighted, to issues of sexuality and homophobia (e.g. the privileging of heterosexuality and marginalising of homosexuality). Certainly these positions of privilege may not be so neatly categorised, but may well relate to multiple oppressions and issues relevant to your context and beyond.

- How, like Ross, would you go about constructing real-world 'ethical experiential' activities that tap into and challenge the issues of oppression relevant to your context? How will these activities enable a valuing of difference that foregrounds marginalised voices and supports students to think from another angle? How will such activities mobilise students' care and responsibility for the welfare of others? How will you ensure that these activities move beyond a superficial engagement with 'otherness' to facilitate students' genuine critical awareness of the inequitable power relations of our social world that marginalise and oppress unfairly on the basis of a particular group identity?

5 RACHEL: CHALLENGING 'POWER-DRIVEN' NOTIONS OF BEING MALE

Introduction

Rachel teaches at Magnolia State High School. It is a co-educational school located on the outskirts of a regional Australian city. It is not an easy school to teach at. It serves a population that is sometimes troubled by racial and ethnic conflict, there are high levels of poverty and welfare dependency within the community, and it is a city that is often constructed by outsiders as a violent place. Schools within this city often have to battle with ensuring that their students are not stigmatised as a result of coming from the area. It is also a city that has a number of private schools which draw many students from higher socio-economic backgrounds away from the local government schools. According to its 2005 Annual Report, the school only manages to retain through to Year 12 approximately 55 per cent of its Year 8 (the first year of high school in Queensland) cohort. However, the image that outsiders often have of such schools is belied by the commitment that many teachers in these schools have towards the welfare of their students.

We are telling Rachel's story because she is one such teacher. She is committed to working with students in her care to improve their lives by challenging those discourses and practices that restrict their ways of engaging with their various worlds. She is particularly concerned with the well-being of boys at her school. However, this concern is constructed within a gender justice framework which recognises that certain improvements in the lives of boys will have a positive impact upon their relationships with girls and women, as well as with other males. As we have made clear throughout this book, there is a significant amount of literature that reflects a 'competing victim syndrome' (Cox, 1995) when it comes to boys' education. Much of the literature that seeks to improve the lives of boys often claims that it does not want to do so at the expense of girls (see Mills, 2003, for a critique of such literature). However, implicit within much of this work is an anti-feminist rhetoric which suggests that developments in girls' education over the last 30 years or so have come at the expense of boys. Rachel's story indicates that it is possible to work towards improving boys' education without taking such a stance.

Rachel's gender justice work is centrally concerned with the way some boys' masculinities have negative impacts upon their own learning as well as that of others. Various research has indicated that some boys regard a positive engagement with schooling as not being 'cool' (see, for example, Martino, 1999, 2000; Francis & Skelton, 2005; Connolly, 2004; Mills, 2001; Jackson, 2002; Renold, 2001; Epstein, 1998). This attitude clearly has to be addressed in order for those boys who are failing, and being failed by, the education system to achieve a more positive outcome from their schooling experiences. Rachel's story provides some indications about how this might be achieved without resorting to simplistic behaviour-management tech- niques. She utilises a sophisticated gender-theory to develop programs that seek to challenge boys' dominant understandings of what it means to be male. This same understanding of gender also infuses all of her other teaching. Her highly effective work with the boys in her care provides a wonderful example of the work that female teachers can do with boys to promote gender equity. It thus provides a strong counter to the claims that boys respond better to male teachers.

Like other teachers whose stories we have chosen to foreground in this book, Rachel's pedagogy is one that rejects deficit models of students. She has high expectations of her students. She is convinced that they can rise to meet the challenges that she puts in front of them both intellectually and socially. This is evident in the program described later in this chapter, where she works with a difficult group of Year 8 boys on issues of masculinity for the purposes of them later mentoring younger boys. She is aware that, for students to rise to the challenges she lays before them, they will need to see how her expectations are connected with their worlds, and that for the confrontational work—and there is no doubt that some of the material she covers in her class is confrontational to those who have very set ideas about gender—they will have to be heavily supported in their learning. Like the other teachers, a valuing of difference also permeates her gender work. In her lessons in all curriculum areas, Rachel seeks to ensure that students consider the multiple ways in which boys and girls can perform their gender and why it is that some are valued and others not.

Rachel's story also addresses two different approaches to working with boys on issues of masculinity. In the first instance, she works with a specific boys' program in a boys-only class. This is a method consistent with those employed within many schools where issues of masculinity are problematised. It is an important approach in that it provides a focus on masculinity within a context that is specifically designed to disrupt normalised constructions of masculinity. However, it can suffer from being treated as an add-on to the formal curriculum and as a result be marginalised (see, for example, Mills, 1998, 2001).

Rachel is aware of this and therefore, in tandem with this approach, she works gender issues into lessons in all areas of the curriculum. The material in this chapter covers her pedagogical practices in both contexts. The lessons that can be taken away from her story are that, regardless of the curriculum area concerned, effective ways of addressing change for boys—and girls—require the development of a respectful pedagogy. Furthermore, the textual analyses she conducts with students in her class have pertinence for multiple curriculum areas.

Rachel's story

On the day we meet Rachel for the first time, we arrive just before morning recess and wait for her in the school foyer. The somewhat clinical and corporate tenor of this room does little to disguise the unrest beyond the front reception area. Amid the usual students waiting to see the office staff about various requests, Rachel and some other senior staff are dealing with a particular boy who 'just doesn't want to be here' and is 'determined to be suspended'. Rachel takes a brief time out of this situation to greet us and we follow her as she prepares for her morning recess duty. Armed with a bucket of plastic bags, several pairs of tongs, three litter 'pick up' tools, sun hat, glasses and mobile phone, Rachel begins her tour around the school yard. On the way out she sympathetically attends to one boy in the foyer who is feeling sick. We follow Rachel as she strides through the disorder and chaos that is recess—at every turn she is confronted with an issue or conflict to resolve. To name just a few, today's problems involve dealing with a flying water bomb, a conflict between a group of boys, a boy who insists on throwing a ball in a thoroughfare/non-play area, a group of boys playing football who just miss hitting a group of girls sitting on the periphery of the oval, and a sobbing girl who had just experienced a 'dacking' by some older girls.

Rachel is intermittently on her mobile phone talking to the office about how she is dealing with these issues. As all of this is happening, she makes her way around the school grounds, handing out her stash of plastic bags and litter tools to groups of students. She explains that litter is a real problem at Magnolia High School. Her manner is firm, assertive and confident, while also being friendly, cheerful, funny and respectful with the students. Three girls run up to her and volunteer to pick up rubbish with the tools, which seem to be something of a novelty—at other times, Rachel nominates particular groups of students to clean their area. One of the volunteer girls has a non-uniform pink fleecy jacket on—Rachel reminds the girl that, when wearing non-uniform clothing, students must stay in a particular area (a school rule so that teachers, if need be, can easily and quickly detect non-school intruders—an infrequent but nevertheless worrying situation at Magnolia). As the girl starts to shrug the jacket off, she informs Rachel that she was wearing it to protect her from stones that a boy was throwing at her earlier.

Rachel has been deputy principal of this large suburban working-class state high school for about a year. She is in her early forties and has been teaching for 20 years across several subject areas including English, History and Media Studies. As a substantial part of her current position involves dealing with behaviour-management issues, she comes into contact with many boys—indeed, she estimates that about 90 per cent of the students referred to her are boys. Rachel's passion for gender justice is clearly articulated throughout her story. In her personal and professional lives, she is committed to fighting against the gender stereotypes that she sees as constraining boys' lifeworlds. She wants a life for her young son that sees no limits in terms of how gender is viewed, and she wants futures for her students that 'break out of the box' of restrictive gender stereotypes. She is particularly concerned with challenging and broadening boys' 'power-driven' notions of being male. To these ends, her one-on-one interactions with boys and her pedagogy in the classroom seek to problematise and disrupt these notions. In both, she tries to offer alternative ways of thinking and acting through a conciliatory approach that scaffolds boys' examinations of being male and a transformative practice that explores issues such as homophobia and sexism.

Developing a respectful pedagogy

Within Rachel's school, boys' behaviours are a problem—though, of course, behavioural problems are not restricted to boys. But, as she indicates, the vast majority—around 90 per cent—of the behavioural issues at her school stem from boys' disengagement with schooling. In many schools, the methods adopted to address such behaviours often exacerbate boys' behaviours and can be used to blame boys. In the first instance, confrontational approaches to addressing boys' behaviours can often result in boys feeling like their masculinity has been challenged, and they can respond by asserting dominant masculine behaviours that escalate into a test of masculinity—indeed, Rachel makes mention of one particular boy who regularly clashed with male teachers in this regard. In the second, there can be a tendency to divorce the behaviours of some boys from the broader social context where certain masculine behaviours are valorised; such an approach, as both McLean (1997) and Denborough (1996) have indicated, diverts responsibilities from adults to young people for the current unjust set of gender relations. Rachel actively seeks to avoid both of these effects of seeking to improve boys' behaviours by adopting what could be referred to as a 'respectful pedagogy' (Mills, 2001; Martino & Pallotta-Chiarolli, 2005).

In 'helping boys to adopt more positive behaviours', Rachel sees it as imperative that she model the skills of respect, negotiation and compromise in her relations with boys. She argues that such skills are often lacking in boys' interactions with others, and notes that this model of relations is far preferable to the 'deadly habits' of 'punishing, threatening, complaining, criticising or nagging'—external forms of control with which she suggests many boys are familiar:

> . . . like at first when I started with them, they're used to the whole external control thing—you know, threaten, punish, punish, punish, blah, blah blah—and that does nothing to make anything different.

Rachel reflects that this external control approach does very little to teach the skills of negotiation and compromise and, importantly, does not encourage the boys to take responsibility for their own behaviours. And for her this is a gender issue. For instance, she suggests that a lot of boys' problematic behaviours 'are very power driven.' She says that many boys' 'standover power stuff' is 'really, really central to their notion of being male'. She sees this as 'typified' in oppositional and resistant behaviours where boys are determined to 'stand up' and 'not back down' in conflict situations:

> . . . that whole idea—if you back down you're weak, you're a cookie—you know, you can't back down! Not even with teachers and you certainly don't back down near the playground.

Hence, in her behaviour-management and teaching roles, Rachel feels that, in 'facilitating any kind of change', positive teacher–student relationships are imperative. For her, this means being 'very respectful' of boys' cultures in terms of understanding 'where they're coming from [and] what is important to them'. As she points out, 'they've got to perceive me as someone who cares about them and someone who's going to go that extra bit for them'. In terms of addressing behaviour-management issues,

Rachel finds that Glasser's choice theory (see, for example, Glasser, 1992, 1998), and in particular the notion of 'quality world' (things of personal importance in an individual's life), provides a useful frame for exploring boys' understandings of themselves and gently challenging oppositional and resistant behaviours:

> I find that the whole idea—notion of 'quality world' is really really integral to being able to get kids to think differently, behave differently—the whole notion of, you know, in your quality world you've got pictures that are of things that are very important to you and in boys' quality world their picture of how they are and how they are being a boy is very important, it's the most important picture that, that anyone can have in their quality world—is the picture of yourself—it's the most important thing . . .

With this in mind, Rachel scaffolds boys' exploration and understanding of the 'pictures they have of (or want for) themselves' as well as 'what they want in the bigger picture' in terms of their personal desires for future success. Here, in trying to change the 'restrictive' notions of masculinity boys have in their 'quality world', she encourages thinking about how these two pictures might better 'marry up'. Rachel finds that such a process involves 'a lot of discussion about gender and what is expected of them as far as being boys'. In illustrating her point, she talks about a particular boy whose quality world involves 'being the cool guy':

> He sees himself as being the tough guy, you know, the cool guy—the guy who stands up to teachers and is really, really sort of into power and things like that. And he's a powerful person in that way. He's into football and he's really into motors and all of that kind of stuff. And, you know there's a very, very strong picture of himself, as a male and when I talk to him, I try

to tap into those pictures I know in his quality world and, and the biggest picture that I'm challenging with him and getting him, trying to get him to address, is this notion of men as being—you know because he really has a lot of trouble with male teachers—[he] stands up to them and gets in their face. And he's really really problematic in lots of ways, and one of things that I am trying to address with him is why he needs to do that. You know, why—what is he gaining out of it? He gets into trouble out of it and is that what he wants? And you know in the long term if he keeps doing that, what is that going to get him? Because he wants to be out in the world of work— so in the world of work—as the male employee—what happens if you stand up to your boss? What happens? You know, so—being male doesn't necessarily mean you have to do that sort of standover power stuff—and I get that a lot with the boys I deal with.

Rachel's conciliatory and respectful Glasser-informed approach thus involves her listening to and acknowledging these boys' quality worlds, exploring with them why they are thinking, acting and feeling in particular ways, and identifying with them alternative ways that might be more effective in getting them what they want. Rachel believes that this approach, while sometimes taking 'a long time' to establish with particular boys who are used to reverting to oppositional behaviours, works to defuse 'power over' relations and provides a structure for boys to 'rethink some of their behaviours' and accept responsibility for their actions.

Consequently, in talking about what is important in teaching boys, Rachel is principally concerned with their 'very narrow view of the world and of the self in the world'. As she says, 'the bottom line is that I think they have very, very restricted notions of what it means to be male and I think that they act them out'. Thus, in her interactions with boys, Rachel thinks that it 'is really important [to] try to give them different perspectives . . . and different ways of looking at and thinking about things'. While Rachel understands girls' behaviours as generally more open and accepting than that of boys in terms of gender difference, she also believes that this approach is important in teaching girls.

Rachel associates her concerns about boys with her personal experiences as a woman, wife, and mother of a young boy. As she explains:

> . . . if I thought that we couldn't change the way that people viewed gender, I would just be devastated. Because I don't want my son growing up in a world which says 'You can't do this and this and this and this if you are a man'. And I just don't accept that, I don't accept it and I won't accept it and I will keep fighting against it.

The rationale behind Rachel's resolve to 'fight against' gender stereotyping and 'make a society in which it's not such a problem' becomes clear in her following comment about restrictive masculinity: 'It's a huge issue—it just sometimes becomes so frustrating, because I can see that it's at the bottom of so many of our problems—domestic violence, suicide, you know—just discontented, unhappy people.' Rachel also associates gender stereotyping with getting in the way of boys' success at school:

> . . . it really does get in their way of success because—on the one hand they don't want to be successful because it's you know part of, of a feminine feminised sort of thing—that education is a feminine thing . . . so if you're successful in that then you're—well what's that saying about you? . . . but then on the other hand, they don't like failing either. So what they do is they just don't try . . . 'cause if they try and they don't do well then that's just you know bad, because y'know men are powerful and when you fail you're not powerful so—so you know and they make sure that everyone knows that they're

not trying so that when they get the crap mark, 'Oh well big deal, it doesn't bother me—I didn't try, blah, blah, blah'. Or they just don't even engage at all—don't hand it in at all.

With this in mind, Rachel sees that 'a lot more opportunities' and 'options' would be available for boys if they were 'brave enough' to 'break out of the box' of stereotypes. She believes that this is possible because she thinks of gender as a construction:

> I've tried to get through to the boys that it is a construction. And it's—it's you know it's not something that just is because you're [a boy]—y'know 'that's just the way boys are'. And you know, sometimes I think yeah maybe, but I still think that y'know we can do something about it—change it and I try to address that in boys. So, it's the way that people interact with you that you learn about how to be male or female—so, if it can be built, it can be dismantled and rebuilt, can't it? I always say to kids build up a Lego tower, then un-build it and change it. And that's the way that masculinity is. It's not something that's set in stone. It's something that is a construction—it's been developed and it has been built over the years. So we need to start, you know, maybe dismantling it and rebuilding it.

While Rachel is confident of the effectiveness of her approach in terms of its potential to shape boys' behaviours in positive ways, she also acknowledges its limitations. Here she talks about the strong impact broader contexts and cultures, such as the peer group, have on 'policing' boys' behaviours:

> I think peers are probably the most, the most I suppose dominant policemen of this whole notion of masculinity . . . you know, this one-on-one stuff is so important but we've got to start like looking at the notions of the wider, you know the wider population of kids.

However, it is of course not just peer groups that police gender boundaries, as Rachel notes in relation to her role as a deputy principal:

> And I've had so many dads in here saying 'I've told him he has to hit back. I've told him if anyone says anything about his mother—he has to do this, this and this.' And so then [laughing] you have to whack the parents.

It is such an understanding of the ways in which gender is policed as well as constructed that underpins Rachel's gender work with her students. Hence her philosophies and understandings about gender undergird a practice that is 'gently' but insistently 'challenging' of boys' restrictive behaviours. Here Rachel says that she has to sometimes 'ask the hard questions' and be 'challenging' to 'plant that seed', but then 'you've got to back off'. She adds:

> . . . gently challenging is really important when you're dealing with gender stuff with boys because a lot of it is so entrenched and so part of who they are and their pictures of themselves that if you go at it like a bull at a gate y'know you just are going to have no progress at all and you're going to get them offside . . .

In attempting to address this issue, Rachel has designed a program for a core group of Year 11 boys based on 'the whole concept of being male' and set up to support the processes of peer tutoring and mentoring of the school's Year 8 boys. Recognising the power of peers to shape boys' understandings of masculinity, the program—consistent with the research we detailed in Chapter 2—positions the peer context as a potentially productive space for identifying and exploring positive alternatives to narrow constructions of gender. Within an all-boys environment, Rachel attempts to facilitate the exploration and critical self-analysis of gender construction and ideas about masculinity. Against this backdrop, these older boys, through specific activities, are groomed to work with the younger boys to critically explore issues of masculinity and what it means to be male.

Deconstructing masculinity

One of the classes that we observe whilst visiting Rachel involves a group of fourteen Year 8 boys from a variety of cultural backgrounds working on a project called 'Boys' Stuff', related to what it means to be a boy. Structured along the lines of the program mentioned above, it is an eight-week course that covers the following topics: 'What it means to be a male'; 'Producing and policing masculinity'; 'Developing communication and social skills'; and 'Mentoring planning'. An extremely detailed unit plan constructed by Rachel outlines how each lesson runs through an 'Orientation', 'Enhancing' and 'Synthesising' phase. The objectives of the unit are set:

- to explore the idea of masculinity as a social construction;
- to raise the notion that there are many ways of being male;
- to promote acceptance of these different ways of being male;
- to challenge negative, restrictive masculinities;
- to offer alternative ways of thinking and behaving; and
- to develop a lesson that shares some of these ideas with boys at a primary school level.

In the lesson, we observe that the students are in the early stages of this program and would have had little to do with Rachel up until this point, unless it had been coming into contact with her through her role as deputy principal. The lesson is billed as 'Being a boy can be a risky business' and links with a concurrent unit in Health and Physical Education (HPE) called 'Risky Business'. We present this lesson in some depth, as it is indicative of a gender-just theory informing classroom practices designed to challenge boys' understandings of masculinity. In particular, and aligned with the pedagogical framework detailed in Chapter 2, the lesson illustrates how Rachel connects to her students' lifeworlds to problematise gendered knowledge in ways that promote a critical awareness of the self, others and broader social contexts and discourses.

The class starts with Rachel displaying on the wall large butcher's paper posters done in an earlier session consisting of the outline of a boy. Within and around these outlines, boys have brainstormed words that describe what it means to be a boy. These words include 'strong', 'porn', 'smoking', 'drugs', 'girlfriends', 'skydiving', 'killing', 'football', 'speed', 'cars' and so on. 'Porn' appears on each of the posters, and its presence is made obvious by the students. However, as one watches the boys talk about their various posters, it is hard to avoid the impression that this has been included for the sole purpose of testing Rachel's reaction to it as a word. Rachel does not seek to make an issue of it, apart from one brief aside to the effect that it is interesting that they are so obsessed with it—unlike other groups of boys she has worked with.

Rachel begins the lesson by revisiting these posters and, intermingled with a few personal stories, explores the extent to which such behaviours and attitudes are expected of boys and how these promote risk-taking on the part of boys. For instance, the notion that 'drink driving comes from [boys'] risk-taking' is raised by some students. Rachel then poses the question that will frame the analyses of texts that are to follow: 'Who makes up the rules about being a boy?' The students pose a range of possibilities: 'peers', 'friends', 'Dad', 'family', 'TV', 'videos', 'magazines', 'coaches' and, interestingly, 'girls'. As the students suggest these answers, Rachel makes the odd comment, but in the main transcribes the answers on to the board. She then tells the students that they will be looking at some advertisements. She has selected several from magazines and television.

Rachel starts with a series of print advertisements to explore the messages they contain about being male. The first advertisement is for a men's hair gel. It adopts a *Mission Impossible* image where a leather-jacketed Tom Cruise look-alike is saving a provocatively dressed 'damsel in distress' from a flaming disaster. The students and teacher discuss several things about this advertisement. They talk about the regularity with which they see men 'rescuing' women, about how it is important for a man to retain his composure—even to the extent of not raising a sweat or, importantly for the advertisement, not having one's hair out of place. Discussion also focuses on the young woman and her appearance as weak, as a 'good-looking chick' and as vulnerable. Throughout, Rachel prods with a series of questions—for example: 'What messages do you get?' 'Who else is in the picture?' 'What's he doing with her?' 'Does being a boy mean being a hero?' 'Why not a "saint"?' and 'How many "chicks" have you saved?'

A similar process is followed with another two magazine advertisements. One is for an American motorbike, which includes a motorcycle rider in full black-leather gear above a caption reading 'You want nice, go pick mommy a flower', with the bike described as the 'ultimate naked bike'. The other is for tobacco and contains a picture of the torso of a young muscular man who has a tattoo on his upper arm of a scantily clad young woman; the advertisement's caption reads: 'You're looking at my feminine side.' In the discussions that follow, Rachel again provokes with a range of questions: 'Should you only be nice to your mummy?' 'Is it a positive or negative thing to pick flowers for your mother?' 'What would an alien coming to this planet think about men if all they had were these advertisements to go on?' and 'What info do these ads give you about being male?'

In the selection of television advertisements that follow, some similar themes emerge—although in one beer commercial there is reference to 'male intelligence', almost treating it as an oxymoron, where men seek to avoid their wives (or female partners) in order to drink beer with their male 'mates' in masculinised spaces. When this is playing on the television, one of the boys calls out: 'I love this ad.' Rachel then asks the boys if there are a lot of television ads that portray men as stupid. The boys come up with several examples. She asks them if the kinds of messages that are being portrayed in these commercials along with the magazines will help them 'in the long run'. There is then some discussion of video games and the similarity between them and the advertisements. There is one interesting moment in this section when one boy tells of this game where the female character has to rescue the male one—there is general laughter from the boys, thereby making Rachel's point about how the dominant messages about being male have become normalised for the boys.

At the conclusion of this activity, Rachel goes back to the question posed at the start of the class: 'Who makes the rules?' To this she adds: 'Who polices the rules?' Organising the earlier brainstorm into groupings, the students decide to explore the extent to which 'family', 'friends' and 'girls' help to make and police the rules of being a boy. The students are then organised into three groupings and each of these headings is put on a piece of butcher's paper. Using a 'hot potato' activity, students are expected to write for two minutes as many instances as they can think of where someone from one of these categories of people has taught them how to be male. At the conclusion of that time, the papers are circulated to the next group for another two minutes and the process is then repeated for a third and last time.

As each group of students presents their poster, they indicate that in families, fathers and brothers put a lot of pressure on them. They inform us that, amongst other things, they have been told: 'don't cry', 'don't show emotions', 'be masculine', 'don't be a pussy', 'be more aggressive', 'don't smoke/don't drink', 'have sex' and 'read porn'. Apparently their friends tell them: 'don't be a baby', 'have a smoke/don't smoke', 'have a girlfriend', 'win' and 'fight back'. And girls have supposedly told them to: 'be strong', 'don't be gay', 'don't be an idiot', 'be cool not gay', 'be a homophobe' and 'you've got to hate gay people'. During the course of the conversations, it becomes apparent that, whilst these messages are clearly present in their lives, there has been some gender stereotyping going on—for instance, they indicate that some fathers clearly challenge dominant ways of being a boy. Homophobia is clearly an issue for this group, and it seems that Rachel has raised it with them before, as the 'be a homophobe' comment would seem to indicate. Previous exposure is also apparent in Rachel's off-the-cuff comment as the boys talk about sex: 'Let's not just assume that boys want to have sex with girls.' The relationship between misogyny and homophobia also raises its head in this discussion when one boy tells her that it is an insult for a boy to be called a 'girl'. Rachel asks: 'Why's that an insult? What's so bad about being a girl?' The student replies: 'Because being a girl is like being gay!'

What we find particularly productive about this unit and Rachel's pedagogy are their capacities to highlight the relationship between the boys' construction of themselves and their construction of knowledge and 'truth' (Davies, 1998). As we noted in Chapter 2, such critical self-reflection is central to enabling 'the capacity to read against the grain of dominant discourses, and against the grain of the privileged positions constructed within them' (Davies, 1998, pp. 12–13). The unit's activities, and Rachel's questioning, provide a framework for her students to begin to see how particular 'truths' about gender speak us and others into being, and how conventional and constraining ways of being male or female might be challenged and rethought.

In observing this lesson, it was not difficult to be overwhelmed by the enormous weight of the gender messages that were coming through the lesson materials *and* from the boys' comments. Here was evidence of the reproductive power of normalised constructions of gender at work. (And indeed, students expressed the importance of 'fitting in' as being more important than 'doing the right thing'.) Within the constructions of masculinity with which the students were working, the importance of compulsory heterosexuality, as well as the denigration of girls and women, and of other boys' 'difference', were amplified by some boys' behaviours. However, the respectful ways in which Rachel dealt with these behaviours were consistent with the Glasser-inspired behaviour-management work she had described to us in an earlier interview, and which she had displayed on our walk around the school with her during lunch. For instance, when one boy was being particularly obnoxious and challenging, she asked three simple questions in a lowered voice: 'Are you helping?' 'Do you want to help?' and 'How can you help?' This seemed to break the cycle of behaviour in a way that enabled the student to change without losing face. It is quite likely that a more confrontational approach could have escalated into a far less satisfactory conclusion.

Whilst the unit we observed was directly related to gender—in this case, masculinities—Rachel raises gender at any opportunity with students. Indeed, we have seen a Year 8 Media Studies class of hers that covers the topic of fairy tales. The students in this class discussed issues of homophobia, heterosexism, and dominant constructions of masculinity and femininity. During the lesson, students challenged and transformed storylines within fairy tales. Rachel tells us that her commitment to gender justice frames all of her classroom practice—as she says: 'I waste no opportunity to address gender issues . . . I don't care if I go off the subject or whatever. Some of the best work I've done has been right off the track.' She sees such opportunities 'everywhere': 'Gender is everywhere and there're opportunities in every curriculum area all the time to be challenging dominant notions of gender and it's not a hard thing to do.' In such endeavours, she wants students to become their own 'challengers and inquirers about things'—not 'just settling' for the gendered status quo. However, she also notes the imperative of always trying to connect with 'what the students are going to get out of this . . . there's got to be something in it for them. They've got to see, you know, some benefit for them or some effect on them, otherwise they're not interested.' Rachel finds many explicit ways to explore gender issues with her students through her roles as English teacher and Media Studies teacher. In English, as a response to what she describes as some 'very problematic homophobic stuff' in her classroom, Rachel has shown her students edited snippets of the film *American Beauty* that highlight the homophobic interactions between the father character and his son. She tries here to scaffold students' empathy for others:

> I contextualised it for them and explained . . . and they were just looking at it and really, they felt it was really unfair the way he was treating this boy, thinking he was gay. So I said well what's the difference then between the way you're talking in class? How do you know there are not people around you who are grappling with this stuff?

She also talks about a video games unit where the students explore issues of gender and power. The unit, which attracts a predomination of male students, involves playing and analysing different video games. Rachel describes the culminating activity for this unit, which involves the students constructing a game that would be applicable for a specific audience. For this activity, she deliberately sets groups of boys the task of designing a game for a particular female audience such as a 40-year-old woman or a thirteen-year-old girl. She says that while some of what the boys produce draws on gender stereotypes, at other times the boys are 'quite on the mark because the girls in the class say, "Yeah, that would be cool."'

Rachel finds it interesting that the girls in her classes, in terms of their assertiveness and willingness to engage with these issues, have a very positive impact on the boys' thoughts and behaviours:

> Because here are these girls that are just not taking their crap and not, you know, not accepting what they're saying. And getting right to the heart of it—one girl said something absolutely perceptive about—when we were talking about these notions of being a boy . . . we talk about what it's like to be a boy, what it's like to be girl . . . and we were talking about this policing of it—and who actually, you know polices these ideals about being male? and . . . you know I said to them— 'How many of you have fallen over and your father's saying, "Just take it like a man"'—all this—and you know and boys put their hand up and say, 'My mother said it too' and I said, 'Ahhhh bingo!' It's not just men who are policing it, it's women as well! Not just your dad. It's your mum; it's your sisters sometimes. And it's a cultural and a social thing . . . and then I said, 'Well why, why do you think they're doing it?' and one girl said, 'The fathers are afraid of what their boys might be.'

What is also interesting here, as with the listing that the boys came up with in terms of 'Who makes up the rules about being a boy?' in the boys' program, is the recognition that girls and women can also become complicit in policing dominant constructions of masculinity as well as boys and men. However, contrary to the claims made by many within the boys' lobby, female policing of such masculinities does not tend to work in the interests of girls and women. The reasons for such policing can be manifold, and can include such things as wanting to ensure sons are not bullied, having a social investment in being associated with hegemonic versions of masculinity, and acquiring a particular form of power and pleasure by being valued and accepted within the dominant patriarchal framework. As Rachel recognises, such policing has costs for both boys and girls, however, for girls it means subsuming their interests to those of men and boys (see Levy, 2005).

Examining Rachel's philosophies and practice

Like Jennifer, Rachel's philosophies and understandings about gender reflect the principles of social justice. She expresses particular concern about the potential costs for boys and girls arising from boys understanding successful masculinity as synonymous with power, control and domination, but also notes how such behaviours are central to many boys' notions of being male and their access to positions of agency and autonomy (Davies & Laws, 2000; Skelton, 2001). She associates males' ascription to narrow versions of masculinity with poor school performance and anti-school behaviours, and more broadly with social problems such as domestic violence and suicide. In this sense, she highlights how such ascriptions have deleterious consequences for males, but also for females and broader communities. Rachel's recognition of how narrow versions of masculinity involve an aversion to 'the feminine' illustrates her understanding of gender as a system of inequitable and unjust power relations within which many boys define themselves in opposition to females and femininity (Alloway, 1995; Connell, 1995, 2000; Davies, 1993; Lingard & Douglas, 1999; Francis & Skelton, 2005).

Along similar lines to Jennifer, Rachel talks about how her personal experiences as a woman have shaped her philosophies about gender. Rachel explains how her social positioning as a mother of a young son and a wife has impacted on her desire (and action) for gender change. In particular, she does not want narrow versions of maleness to restrict her son's options and choices, and thus she works in ways that attempt to counteract such restrictions. Underpinning Rachel's strong sense of gender justice is her recognition of the possibilities that arise when we understand maleness and femaleness as social constructions rather than ways of being that are 'set in stone' (Alloway, 1995; Davies, 1993). As she says: 'It's [through] the way that people interact with you that you learn about how to be male or female.' To illustrate her thinking, Rachel describes this construction as a Lego tower that can be built but also dismantled and rebuilt. Such thinking is evident in how Rachel understands particular boys' poor school performance and anti-school behaviours. Here she talks about boys who 'don't want to be successful [at school] because it's part of a feminine thing' and observes behaviours such as boys 'making sure that everyone knows that they're not trying'. Such observations, of course, are commonplace within the masculinities and schooling literature (see, for example, Connolly, 2004; Francis & Skelton, 2005). Importantly in terms of gender justice, Rachel's presentation of this issue indicates an understanding of these versions of masculinity as fabrications or social performances for an audience rather than innate or pre-determined behaviours (Alloway, 1995; Butler, 1999). Such thinking informs her strong belief that gender change, particularly in terms of harmful constructions of masculinity, is possible through alternative ways of understanding and relating.

Rachel's philosophies and understandings about gender frame a practice that 'gently but persistently' works for social change. Like Jennifer, Rachel recognises the political nature of her teaching and 'engages the space of schooling as a site of contestation, resistance and possibility' (Giroux, 2003, p. 6). This is clearly evident in terms of her interactions with particular boys in relation to issues of behaviour management and in her pedagogy. Here Rachel thinks and acts against the grain of normalised understandings of gender and masculinity in the hope of broadening particular boys' restrictive ways of being male (Giroux, 2003; Lingard & Douglas, 1999; Lingard et al., 2002; Alloway et al., 2002; Martino & Pallotta-Chiarolli, 2003, 2005).

Rachel's one-on-one interactions with boys (who she describes as exhibiting 'problematic' behaviours) are particularly instructive here in terms of illustrating connected and supportive ways that explorations of masculinity might be facilitated. As discussed earlier, it is well established that the excessive relations of hyper-rationality and control that often characterise teacher practice and school structures normalise gendered relations of power and boys' investments in hegemonic masculinity. Rachel recognises the futility of excessive relations of external control (such as punishing, threatening, criticising or nagging) in her interactions with students—referring to these as 'deadly habits' that 'boys are used to'. In challenging and seeking to transform boys' controlling behaviours, she models relations of negotiation, conciliation and compromise as alternative ways to resolve conflict. In this sense, Rachel—like Jennifer—disrupts the traditional power relations of the teacher–student binary and offers these boys a sense of agency and autonomy in their everyday school lives. Key research tells us that boys' social and behavioural outcomes are enhanced through such democratic disciplinary approaches, and are central to developing positive student–teacher relationships of mutual respect (Alloway et al., 2002; Lingard et al., 2002; Martino & Pallotta-Chiarolli, 2003). This is, of course, facilitated through teachers' active interest in and concern for students. As Rachel says: 'They've got to perceive me as someone who cares about them and someone who's going to go that extra bit for them.' Developing such relationships is a clear imperative for Rachel, and would certainly be a necessary prerequisite in terms of constructing an environment conducive to challenging issues of masculinity in ways that might generate positive responses.

Importantly, in modelling relations of negotiation and conciliation through a Glasser (1992, 1998) framework (a framework informed by theories of psychology and, as we detailed earlier, sometimes criticised as ignoring or sidelining the significance broader social contexts represent in shaping behaviour),

Rachel recognises and attempts to address how issues of gender and masculinity are associated with these boys' problematic behaviours. In this respect, she draws on Glasser's work in ways that support her to facilitate boys' explorations of masculinity. Here, Rachel's emphasis on knowing and understanding, rather than controlling and punishing, acknowledges boys' enactments of masculinity as located within broader cultural and social contexts (Gilbert & Gilbert, 1998; Lingard et al., 2002; Martino & Pallotta-Chiarolli, 2003). This acknowledgement is most important in terms of moving beyond blame discourses (recently ascendant in gender debates) that individualise and/or pathologise boys' behaviours. Such discourses tend to promote conventional manifestations of 'boyness', and generate an understanding of 'boys as victims' in need of special treatment (Francis & Skelton, 2005).

Rachel's experience with one particular boy (who she describes as 'really into power') provides an example of how she enacts this framework. Here she begins by trying to understand where this boy is 'coming from' in terms of what is important to him. Rachel articulates this boy's quality world as a world where being 'tough', 'cool' and standing up to the male teachers are all very important. She tries to tap into these pictures to 'discuss gender and what is expected of [him] as far as being a boy' in order to challenge notions that associate successful maleness with domination, control and 'standover power stuff'. In this case, she does this by exploring with this boy why he feels compelled to behave in such ways, identifying in particular the negative implications associated with his behaviours—especially in terms of constraining his long-term goals to be 'out in the world of work'. Such explorations provide a meaningful and connected platform for Rachel to begin encouraging this boy to behave in alternative and less destructive ways—ways of being male that are more likely to 'get him what he wants'.

Importantly, Rachel's ways of relating to boys in this one-on-one environment are consistent with the gender messages conveyed through her classroom practice. In the classroom, Rachel encourages boys to think and behave in less gendered ways through her pedagogy. Here, as the Boys' Stuff unit exemplifies, she draws on a variety of real-world contexts and textual resources to provoke students' questioning of normalised understandings of masculinity and femininity. Through scaffolding the students' examination of the many dominant discourses and contexts that 'speak them into existence' and police their ways of being particular kinds of boys, Rachel highlights the relationship between the construction of the self and the construction of knowledge, and promotes boys' capacities to see such knowledge as amenable to challenge and transformation (Davies, 1998).

Such analysis highlights for students how gender is constructed in multiple ways for particular contexts and for specific purposes, and how such constructions—far from being neutral or just—can contribute and reinforce inequitable or binary understandings of gender as difference and opposition (Alloway, 1995). Rachel's use of popular culture such as *American Beauty* that has currency with her adolescent audience is especially productive in her illumination of such injustices. Additionally, the culminating activity in the video games unit that involves students constructing a game that would appeal to a particular audience is evidence of Rachel's further scaffolding of her students' challenging of taken-for-granted assumptions about gender. Rachel's aim here is for her students to draw on what they have learnt throughout the unit to move beyond stereotypical understandings of what an audience target group might be attracted to in a video game. In particular, she challenges the boys to construct a game that would appeal to an identity group that they would see as unfamiliar, such as 40-year-old women or thirteen-year-old girls. Along similar lines to Rachel's Boys' Stuff unit, this activity has the transformative potential to broaden these boys' understanding of gender to be more inclusive of difference and diversity (Lingard et al., 2002).

We selected Rachel's story to tell because she is someone who has long been committed to gender justice. Whilst her work with boys has grown out of her experiences of working in schools and theorising about those experiences, she also has a personal reason for her commitment to creating a better environment for boys: her son. Rachel does want boys' lives to improve so that their life opportunities and experiences are not limited by restrictive forms of masculinity. She sees that such improvements in the lives of boys will benefit many. However, for Rachel there is a recognition that, in contemporary Western societies (as in most others), men's interests are privileged over those of women, and that work with boys has to be conducted within that context. Hence she—like the other teachers whose stories we have told here—seeks to trouble boys' understandings of themselves and to provide them with the tools to dismantle some of the building blocks of valorised masculinities. She does this through a critical textual analysis that supports the boys' critical analysis of themselves. In order to undertake this process effectively, she contends that it is only possible to effect such changes in a respectful and supportive environment. We agree.

Learning from Rachel

Rachel's respectful pedagogy aims to broaden boys' restrictive notions of being male. In her disciplinary interactions, such a pedagogy is supported by the theories of Glasser (1992, 1998) and frames her discussions about masculinity with boys. In her classroom practice, and particularly her Boys' Stuff unit, this respectful pedagogy underpins a gentle but insistent challenging of boys' restrictive behaviours through critical textual analysis and critical self-analysis. In this section, we draw on Rachel's story to examine how such issues play out in your schooling context. Specifically, we draw on her insights into issues of discipline, masculinity and critical literacy to stimulate discussion about behaviour management and the critical deconstruction of gender in texts and contexts, including looking at constructions of femininity and gender justice, and issues associated with how gender justice can be constrained and enabled by our personal 'social baggage' (see Lemon, 1995; Davies, 1998).

Developing a respectful pedagogy

Rachel's respectful pedagogy with boys draws significantly on Glasser's (1998) choice theory. This framework supports her to understand boys' behaviours and to make explicit the expectations and boundaries associated with such behaviours. There are concerns associated with these sorts of frameworks, as we outlined in Chapter 2. For example, their invariably rationalist ways of managing behaviour can be overly prescriptive and clinical. Such rationalist paradigms tend to ignore the broader social context, and tend not to be sensitive to the dynamic nature of human social relationships—particularly in relation to the domain of the affective (Kenway & Fitzclarence, 1997). If taken up in controlling ways, they can perpetuate, rather than disrupt, problematic behaviours. In Chapter 2, we argued the importance of these approaches being taken up in ways that recognise (and problematise) how boys' behaviours are situated and invested within broader gendered/raced/classed (and so on) power relations and discourses, and in ways that respect student agency and autonomy. Rachel's take-up of Glasser seems to address the potential limitations that may be associated with this model. In her disciplinary interactions with particular boys, she uses Glasser's theories to support discussions about issues of masculinity and power in connected and conciliatory ways. For example, she draws on Glasser's notion of the 'quality world' to frame her insights into 'where boys are coming from and what is important to them', and draws on this knowledge as a way of connecting with and broadening boys' restrictive notions of masculinity. Such respectful pedagogies also seem to underpin how she has structured her Boys' Stuff unit. Importantly, this unit's focus on peer tutoring and mentoring on issues associated with masculinity aligns with these tenets and sits within the school's broader disciplinary framework.

EXAMINING YOUR SCHOOL'S DISCIPLINARY FRAMEWORK

Drawing on Rachel's story, this activity seeks to promote critical reflection on the behaviour-management policies/systems operating in your school context. Such reflection will scaffold analysis of how such policies/systems address issues of gender justice in theory, but also in practice.

- How do your school's disciplinary programs (including, for example, behaviour-management plans, bullying policies, equity guidelines) support a critical exploration of issues of gender, power and identity?
- In what ways do the broader disciplinary frameworks at your school move beyond a prescriptive set of rules and sanctions for behaviour to a consideration of social issues associated with student identity (for example, a consideration of the dynamics of context and in particular contextual expectations that shape problematic behaviour, or an exploration of multiple identities and multiple perspectives relating to problematic behaviours)? Comment on how your practice reflects these considerations.
- How does your school disciplinary program support respectful pedagogies? For example, does the program position students with little or no agency and autonomy? Have students been included in writing this program? Are they included in maintaining/

administering the program? How might these considerations be implicated in facilitating students accepting responsibility for their behaviour?

- Considering how Rachel draws on Glasser (1992, 1998), in what ways might your school's disciplinary framework, or your enactment of this framework, be modified to support a broadening of boys' understandings of masculinity to be more inclusive of difference and diversity?

- Consider the peer mentoring focus of Rachel's Boys' Stuff unit and how it sits within the broader Glasser-informed disciplinary framework at her school to facilitate boys' explorations of masculinity. How might the disciplinary framework at your school support such a unit?

Critical textual analysis and deconstruction

Like Jennifer, Rachel tries to broaden her students' narrow ideas about gender through scaffolding their critical textual analysis of cultural products such as the media and advertising. Particularly with boys, she tries to scaffold learning experiences in ways that highlight 'different ways of looking and thinking about things'. Rachel sees opportunities to address gender issues 'everywhere'—she sees opportunities to challenge dominant notions of gender in every curriculum area. Drawing on her experiences as a Media Studies, English and History teacher, she scaffolds gender deconstruction activities that challenge students to examine and question the stereotypical representations of masculinity and femininity in magazine and television advertisements, and in films and video games. Her aim here is to connect with students in ways that encourage them to become their own 'challengers and inquirers about things' so that they don't just 'settle for the gendered status quo'.

CHALLENGING DOMINANT NOTIONS OF MASCULINITY AND FEMININITY

The purpose of this exercise is to identify a range of ways that gender issues can be taken up and critically examined in your school/classroom context. This process supports consideration of how such issues might be addressed with students in gender-just, connected and meaningful ways.

- How might your classroom teaching explicitly facilitate students' critical explorations of gender? How might you support students to recognise gendered knowledge as problematic through an examination of power and issues of representation? Such explorations, as reflected in Rachel's teaching, might examine how and why gender is (inequitably) represented and performed in different texts (such as magazines and films).

- How (as Rachel does in her use of *American Beauty* to encourage student empathy for a character marginalised by homophobia) might you appeal to students' sense of social commitment and their capacities to appreciate injustice (Gilbert & Gilbert, 1998) in your scaffolding of these explorations?

- How, like Rachel, would you ensure that these learnings are connected to students' lifeworlds (their interests, preferences and opinions, and specifically their experiences of domination, marginalisation and surveillance in terms of dominant expectations associated with 'being a girl' and 'being a boy')?

- In what ways will this scaffolding support students' understandings of how gender injustice is constructed, policed and regulated and facilitate a broadening of particularly boys' understandings of masculinity?

Examining issues of gender identity

Rachel's deconstruction of masculinity is explicit in its focus on encouraging boys to critically analyse themselves. Rachel's Boys' Stuff unit, in particular, scaffolds students' identification and examination of the many discourses and contexts that 'speak them into existence' and police their ways of being particular kinds of boys. Subsequent to a brainstorm session that identifies 'rules' associated with what it means to be a boy, for example, Rachel explores with boys the ways in which particular versions of masculinity are variously endorsed by the expectations of others, such as family, friends and female peers. Such examination can make transparent how particular 'truths' about gender speak us and others into being, and how conventional and constraining ways of being male or female might be resisted and transformed. Of significance, this process—which is apparent in Rachel's story more broadly, and also in Jennifer's story—brings to light ways in which female students endorse but also challenge boys' restrictive masculinities.

The normative masculinist frameworks within which girls continue to define their femininities are familiar. Anne Summers's 1975 book *Damned Whores and God's Police* perhaps best crystallises the key binary that supports these frameworks. Such binaries continue to shape girls' hierarchical constructions of femininity as Martino and Pallotta-Chiarolli's recent work (2005) illustrates. Their work, and that of others (see also Levy, 2005), explores the harmful impacts associated with these constructions of femininity, and in particular how such constructions are regulated through popular understandings about beauty, appearance and the performance of an appropriate (hetero)sexualised femininity. Here issues such as body image, body weight and sexuality—issues that these authors locate within a Madonna/whore binary driven by boys—regulate many girls' ways of being. Such binary understandings of femininity have clearly negative implications in terms of constraining the schooling performance, confidence and well-being of many girls. They also serve to reinforce inequitable understandings of gender and dominant constructions of masculinity.

CONSTRUCTIONS OF FEMININITY: EXAMINING HOW PARTICULAR VERSIONS OF MASCULINITY ARE ENDORSED

The aims of this exercise are to identify how female students in your schooling context take up constructions of femininity, and to explore how these constructions might be circumscribed by the normative masculinist frameworks that perpetuate gender inequities. The exercise will provoke critical discussion about issues of gender and power, and more specifically look at how the Madonna/whore binary is enforced in your school by students and teachers, the implications of this binary and how it might be challenged and transformed.

- Think about the different groups of girls at your school (or in your class). See if you can give each of these groups a different name. For example, Diane Reay's (2001) exploration of girl cultures at a particular UK primary school generated the following group identities: the 'spice girls', the 'nice girls', the 'girlies' and the 'tomboys'.
- What are the qualities that make each of these groups 'a group'? What behaviours are considered appropriate/inappropriate to a particular group?
- Try to rank these groups hierarchically from most popular to least popular. Consider how the different groups construct their identities in relation to other femininities and in relation to dominant versions of masculinity and heterosexuality. Consider issues of beauty and appearance, such as body image, body weight and sexuality. How do these issues interplay in

girls' performances of appropriate (hetero)sexualised femininity?

- How does the Madonna/whore binary inform hierarchical constructions of femininity? How is this binary supported or endorsed by girls and boys? How, for example, do some of the boys (and girls) at your school draw on this binary to police girls' ways of being?

- How do such behaviours contribute to inequitable understandings of gender in your school? For instance, what are the implications of these constructions and surveillance in terms of popularity/power for girls and boys? What are some of the costs? For example, while girls' heterosexualised identities might gain them popularity, they may also render them powerless and open to objectification, trivialisation and denigration. Boys' heterosexualised identities, on the other hand, invariably position them as powerful.

- Identify the ways that such constructions are challenged and disrupted by boys and girls at your school. In Rachel's story, for instance, she talks about the positive impact assertive and critically reflective girls have on boys. These girls are able to offer thoughtful insight and alternative perspectives on what it means to be male or female. How do the broader policy frameworks, teacher practices and culture at your school support such challenging?

Knowledge as problematic: Multiple interpretive possibilities

Such interrogation of the social processes that both endorse and challenge normative gender frameworks is central in highlighting the relationship between the construction of the self and the construction of knowledge (Davies, 1998). Rachel's work with students, to these ends, can support their capacities 'to read against the grain of dominant discourses and against the grain of the privileged positions constructed within them' (Davies, 1998, pp. 12–13). Within a context where knowledge is viewed as problematic—as constructed and maintained by social, political and cultural forces—such capacities, as the previous activities bring to light, are developed through the critical examination of multiple identities and perspectives. With this in mind, and to pick up on an important point that we explored in Ross's story, such critical examination also necessitates an exploration of our personal 'social baggage' because this baggage shapes how we represent and interpret things, and more particularly our capacities to take up the invited readings within particular texts and contexts (Lemon, 1995; Davies, 1998). In terms of finding ways to enable gender justice, understanding the social baggage that we bring to our readings of texts and contexts is central.

EXAMINING SOCIAL BAGGAGE

This exercise seeks to highlight how an individual's social baggage shapes how texts and contexts are interpreted. In so doing, the exercise will also bring to light the implications of social baggage in terms of gender justice, and particularly how such baggage can both delimit but also enable capacities for recognising and taking up spaces of gender justice.

Consider the following script written by Year 11 boys. Along similar lines to the one we presented in Chapter 2, this snippet was generated from a drama activity that supported boys' exploration of male identity. In small groups, the boys were required to write a script around the focus question 'What is masculinity?' This particular snippet is an interchange between two thirteen-year-old boys, Tim and Tom, and is set in a schoolyard.

Tim: Hey Tom.

Tom: Hey Tim, what are you doing? I thought you were going to do weights this morning?

Tim: Yeah, I was going to but I don't really think I'm up to it; some of those other guys are a bit intimidating.

Tom: Ah, come on, can't be that bad. I did weights a few times and I'm more of a twig than you. That's no excuse!

Tim: Maybe, but it's not just that, it's also a question of . . . you know . . .

Tom: No . . . what?

Tim: You know, being a 'man'.

Tom: What about it? Just because you can't lift a few weights you think you're not a man? What kind of crap is that?

Tim: It sounds stupid, I know, but that's the message everyone is getting from those guys.

Tom: Look, the only reason they flaunt the 'macho' thing is because they don't have enough of a brain to excel anywhere else. Don't be hard on yourself just because of that.

Tim: Maybe. (*looks unsatisfied*)

Tom: You don't seem very convinced. Sit here, let's talk.

Tim: What?!

Tom: Dude, you're so immature, I'm not getting all gay on you . . . just sit down.

Tim: No, I didn't mean that, just the 'let's talk' thing makes me a little uncomfortable.

(*Tom stares at Tim, in an awkward silence*)

Tom: You're shitting me, right?

Tim: No, I'm being serious. Guys don't sit down and talk, that's what girls do . . .

Tom: You are so full of it. Listen idiot, I'm trying to help you. If you're so insecure that you can't even sit down and talk to a mate, you have issues. Come back when you have some sense about you.

- Working individually, identify the different readings about masculinity we are invited to take up in this text. What assumptions about gender inform these readings? What do you see as the gender/social justice issues?
- Identify the spaces of social/gender injustice and justice—that is, identify how inequitable understandings of gender and masculinity are both endorsed and challenged.
- Comment on how you think elements of your personal social baggage have shaped your interpretation of gender issues in this exercise. How might this baggage be implicated in constraining or enabling social justice in your classroom? In Rachel's story, for example, she talks about how her experiences as a woman and mother of a young son compel her to challenge restrictive and limited notions of gender. She sees restrictive masculinity as a 'huge issue' that is 'at the bottom of so many of our problems' such as domestic violence and suicide.
- Having identified how inequitable understandings of gender and masculinity are endorsed and challenged in the script, how might you draw on your social baggage or other real-world experiences of marginalisation, like Rachel, to problematise these inequities? For example, how might you present these experiences to students in ways that legitimate alternatives to hegemonic constructions of masculinity? How will you ensure that such scaffolding connects with students' lifeworlds to promote critical self-awareness?
- Share your interpretations with a colleague and explore in particular how different social baggage can variously shape how this script is interpreted and understood in terms of gender/social justice issues and how these issues might be presented to students.

6 MONICA: SCHOOLING CHILDREN FOR LIFE BEYOND SCHOOL

Introduction

The 60-minute flight and one-hour drive to visit Monica at Warilda State Primary School is quite the expedition. After some difficulty locating Warilda on the map, we begin the drive to this tiny country town, population 138, from the airport of a large regional town. On the main highway, we can't help but notice a massive shop sign that reads: 'A Man's Toy Shop'. While tempted, we nonetheless contain our desire to stop and browse through the various blokey artefacts on display—mainly agricultural/earthmoving equipment, power tools and the like. The shop epitomises the town's farming heritage which, along with mining in this district, produces both the highest incomes, but lowest tertiary standard of education, per head of population, in the country.

On the hour's drive to Warilda, we are struck by the isolation of this part of the world—the endless dry and arid expanse is broken up only every now and then by tiny 'if-you-blink-you-will-miss-it' communities. Indeed, we nearly miss the turn-off to Warilda—the sign is so small—but nevertheless arrive on time to meet Monica at her school. As we arrive, we get a sense of what Monica means when she says that coming here eighteen months earlier was like stepping back 50 years. We notice that the town has only one shop, that also doubles as the petrol station. Monica's Year 5/6/7 classroom, however, seems largely to reflect a typical Western-style contemporary primary school environment. The desks, complete with plastic storage tubs and bucket chairs, are arranged in a horseshoe shape facing the teacher's desk. Half a dozen or so computers of various models and years are located around the periphery of the classroom, attached to a printer that doesn't seem to work. Cluttered plastic tubs of books are stacked in various places and a tattered lace curtain covers the storage space underneath the large whiteboard. In the 'wet area', a thick plastic sheet covers the art table—assorted tubes of coloured paint sit on the shelves over the sink adjacent to a small derelict portable oven on an adjoining bench. The walls are cluttered with student information and work. A list of 'student goals', including 'accepting responsibility for one's own actions' and 'listening and respecting others', is displayed on the back wall amongst several assorted charts that detail student achievements and awards. Also on the back wall are A5-sized photo portraits of each child arranged in a large wheel and backed on bright coloured cardboard. Next to eighteen smiling faces (eleven boys and seven girls) there is a sentence that tells us about each child's interests. We notice that several boys like 'riding motorbikes' and 'playing sport', one boy 'loves hunting and riding horses', another 'loves dogs and motor cross', one girl 'loves animals and English', while another 'loves playing sport and the piano'.

The children's portraits tell us something of the town's demographics. The school and broader community are sustained by the surrounding crop and cattle farms. Many of the more privileged children live on these farms while a minority live in the town where, although there are no services or employment, the housing is cheap. The town's designation by the federal government as a 'disadvantaged' area has generated much-needed financial support for the school in the past. Notwithstanding this, Monica tells us that issues of class, rurality and isolation, as well as the large Christian fundamentalist population and lack of cultural diversity within the school and surrounding areas, circumscribe and constrain what the children see as being possible in their lives. She talks here about the children's expectations being 'very local', their worlds 'very small'. For this reason, it seems, the school sometimes 'loses' students to private boarding schools in the somewhat more cosmopolitan town 70 kilometres away. A parent of one such 'loss' moved her daughter from Warilda because she 'wanted less' to do with the people of this tiny town. Within this context, Monica expresses concern about the conventional assumptions about gender that permeate the community. She describes the area as 'very male-dominated' and links such views with the masculine stereotypes associated with work on the land.

Monica's story provides an important reminder that, in undertaking any form of school reform—in this case, gender reform—the broader social context and community relations have to be taken into account. In many of the books on boys' education that provide a 'tips for teachers' approach, there is a failure to acknowledge this. However, what has become very apparent to us in our various research is that such a decontextualised approach rarely works as it fails to take into account the different ways in which boys learn to construct their masculinities within their local environments. At the same time, of course, wider gender representations of ideal masculinities still impact upon these constructions. Monica recognises this, and has had to address issues relating to the 'gender regime' of the school and the broader 'gender order' (Connell, 1987) of the local community. For Connell, the gender regime relates to the ways in which gender relationships are organised within an institution such as a school. These relationships, whilst not divorced from the broader gender order—that is, the ways in which gender relationships are organised within society—can be constructed in opposition to those broader sets of politics.

In Monica's story, her efforts to challenge the gendered regime of the school and to work at changing the gendered assumptions in the local community are detailed. Hers is also a story that demonstrates the possibilities of providing a forum that has enabled girls in her class to 'be heard' and a variety of non-dominant masculinities to be performed. In so doing, she has had to take into consideration her teaching situation, where there is a predominance of boys in her class, and the broader gendered assumptions and understandings of the rural community that have tended to amplify issues of masculine dominance at her school. The following story highlights some of the broader social factors that constrain her efforts to teach in socially just ways and shows how, through her pedagogy—which works 'against the grain' of these factors—she seeks to broaden students' 'horizons' and challenge limited notions of masculinity and femininity through teaching for and about active citizenship. This version of active citizenship sees students engaged in their local community in ways that bring the community into the school with the effect of exposing its members to the alternative gender discourses that shape Monica's practice.

Monica's story

Monica has been teaching in the upper primary area for approximately nineteen years. When we first met her she was eighteen months into her appointment as a teacher-principal at Warilda primary, a school of 50 students. Prior to this, she had taught for about sixteen years at another government primary school of 200 students in a small, low socio-economic area north of a large city. During the morning session on the day of our visit to Monica's classroom, the students are working independently on an integrated unit called 'Students Making It Happen at Warilda'. This unit is designed to encourage student awareness and their sense of responsibility towards caring for their health and their local environment. As we wander around the classroom, we get a sense of the key concern facing this community: environmental sustainability, and particularly the implications of drought. Today, some of the students are Google re/searching an aspect of their environment on the internet while others are working on the health care and physical activity element of this unit. Regarding the latter, several of the boys are engrossed in constructing a set of rules and deciding players for a whole-school football competition between representative teams—nominally Australia, France, Germany and England. We later watch the energetic scramble that is France versus Germany in the school's dust bowl 'oval'. We are not sure who wins, but there seems to be a problem with the effectiveness of the 'rules' that the boys have written up. Apparently, according to a small girl who complains to Monica, an episode of swearing failed to be sanctioned appropriately by the issue of a yellow card—a warning for minor transgressions.

In working for gender justice, while Monica takes into account the specific social and cultural issues and factors of inequity relevant to her particular context, she also deals with the typical day-to-day gender issues with which many of us are very familiar. For example, it seems that with Monica's class, as with many of the classes we have observed, there is at least one boy's name that we can recall at the end of our visit. Today it is Jason—an excessively fidgety Year 6 boy with a mischievous grin who insists on writing on his arms and gently stabbing himself with his pen—disruptive behaviours that cause Monica to separate him from others. During our visit, we also note a few girls' equally distracted but far less disruptive behaviours—one girl, during a reading activity, spends about five minutes of transfixed effort sharpening most of her HB pencil into her tub while another girl expends an inordinate amount of time and concentration carefully picking a scab off her left knee. In observing this class, it is apparent that Monica's concern with the well-being of both boys and girls is well justified.

Problematising the gender regime of the school

Monica says that one of the 'major hurdles' that she had to overcome before she could be accepted as being 'worth anything' in her new role as teacher-principal at Warilda was that she was female. She explains that 'it's a disadvantage being female' within the 'male culture' of her school's broader farming community, where women are devalued and 'men are just generally regarded as more useful'. Monica describes this small rural environment as 'very predictable' in terms of the endorsing of gender stereotypes, even though 'a lot of the women work alongside the men as well as doing other work'. When Monica arrived at the school, she felt 'covert' and 'overt' resistance 'not just from the kids', but also the parents (both male and female) who made their thoughts about her clear through what she describes as some 'very blunt' comments like 'The kids really like to have a man as principal'. Monica talks about feeling diminished by and angry about these views. She notes that:

> . . . it's that whole thing of women having to work harder to gain respect. It doesn't always come as easily—like I have been here—like this is my second year and I would say that I've overcome most of that as far as the community and kids have gone, but they would still be really happy if when I leave that it's a bloke that comes in. You know—that really is how it goes.

It is apparent here, as Robinson (2000) points out, that the broader discourses of gender and power in Monica's community that authorise 'maleness' work to delegitimise her authority. Mindful of how issues of rurality tend to amplify conventional gender inequities, it appears that some of the parents and students at Monica's school draw on discourses—which privilege the male body, and masculinised knowledge and practice—to dismiss or 'diminish' her (Jones, 1993; Robinson, 2000). As key authors argue, where parents and students (and indeed other teachers) associate legitimate authority with the hegemonic masculine body and dominant masculine characteristics, and conversely, illegitimacy with the female body and femininity, the professionalism of female teachers is frequently undermined (Davies, 1988; Clark, 1993; Robinson, 2000). And, as Monica argues, such understandings seem to be enduring for, despite her efforts to gain the respect of her broader schooling community, they would still be really happy when she leaves for a 'bloke' to take her place. Unfortunately, as Robinson's work (2000) points out, such perceptions about female teachers— which result in many having to work much harder than their male counterparts—are far from uncommon.

In comparing her current teaching environment with her previous school's location in a less isolated (low socioeconomic) area on the coast, Monica relays her concern about issues of gender. While she notes that in both contexts 'the boys generally try to dominate most of the areas', she observes a 'big cultural difference' between the coastal and rural girls' behaviours. Whereas Monica has had to work hard to promote the self-esteem of many of the rural girls 'in relation to the boys because they're just used to taking the backseat', this was not the case with the coastal girls:

> . . . with the coastal girls you really didn't have to work anywhere near as hard in that area as you do here. The girls were much more likely to take a chance—to want to be seen, to want to be doing things and have some control.

Exacerbating Monica's efforts to raise her female students' self-esteem and confidence in her current teaching environment

is the preponderance of boys in her class of eighteen students.
As she says, 'it's an issue I have to be aware of because the boys
will dominate. I have to be careful to make sure that the girls get
a say.' Such observations of course—as we pointed out in
Chapter 1—are far from uncommon and reflect the gendered
dimensions of classroom/school interactions in relation to boys'
tendencies to colonise the educational space. Notwithstanding
this—and a key issue here—Monica's comments indicate her
sensitivity to the nuances of context in shaping her gender
equity concerns. Considering how the different (coastal and
rural) contexts shape issues of power and marginalisation in ways
that are particularly marginalising for the rural girls, such sensitivity is clearly imperative.

Monica's ways of teaching are mindful of equity factors
relevant to her context, such as the over-representation of boys
in her class; boys' tendencies to dominate; girls' tendencies to
lack confidence and self-esteem; and the school's broader
gendered climate. Aligned with our discussion about diversity
and equality in Chapter 2—in relation to deciding whose diversities are worthy of support—Monica tries here to model an
understanding of difference that enables students to become
critically aware of the inequitable power relations in her school
and broader community that marginalise females. For example,
while boys comprise two-thirds of her class, Monica ensures that
there is a female student to represent the girls on the student
council, despite some reluctance from the girls and some resistance from the boys:

> . . . when I first came here, the student representative council
> was being filled for positions and only boys put their hands up,
> you know only boys were nominated. And I said, 'Oh come on
> girls we can't just sit back here and let all the boys do all the
> talking'—just in what I thought was a light-hearted way. And
> eventually one of them was the treasurer but some of the boys
> got very offended and that one incident took a long time for

me to counterbalance because that to them was favouring the girls. It really took a while to get over that and it went home to the families, you know? It took a while to win back credibility that I didn't favour girls. That was it. That was seen as the way I wanted them to be heard.

To these ends, Monica acknowledges that the broader gendered world of the community means that she has to 'work within what's acceptable by the people who live and work around and in the school'. She indicates that she has to be 'gentle' and 'tread cautiously' because she is trying to change familiar, comfortable and very deep-seated ways of being—indeed, as she says: 'You can be challenging things without even knowing you're challenging them!' While she will not compromise her focus on gender justice, and admits that as a younger woman she would never have been able to 'tread so cautiously', Monica says that such experiences have meant adjusting her expectations. She describes this as still 'making a difference' and still 'putting something in place that will self-perpetuate', but in a 'milder way'. In terms of the broader structures and cultures that she sees as particularly constraining for the girls at her school, Monica's attempts to make a difference are evident in her consistent efforts to encourage girls' confidence and self-esteem—particularly in relation to taking on leadership roles—in the hope of 'broadening their horizons'.

Reflecting on boys' tendencies to 'try and control what happens in the classroom', regardless of their broader environments, Monica talks about the various contexts such as family, sport and the military that send messages to children about 'rightful male dominance' and what is valued in terms of being male. Regarding some boys' tendencies to be disruptive in her classroom, Monica remarks on how powerful family assumptions about gender are in shaping boys' behaviour in ways that endorse a particular masculine stereotype. For instance, and associated more generally with the tenor of broader community views at

Warilda, she finds that many parents understand and condone rebellious or aggressive behaviours in boys as harmless—as just 'boys being boys'. Monica's observations here, as Connolly's work (2004) indicates, bring to light the key challenges that teachers face when there are significant mismatches between the values and attitudes of students' home and school lives—mismatches that often occur in low socio-economic and rural areas that, when mixed with dominant masculinity politics, tend to exacerbate many boys' disengagement and alienation from school.

Challenging this relationship between dominant constructions of masculinity and some boys' disengagement and alienation from schooling will thus require an analysis and problematisation of those aspects of a school's gender regime that reinforce valorised forms of masculinity. These aspects might include behaviour-management processes, curriculum offerings, use of playground space, and gendered roles and responsibilities within the school. Important within the gender regime of a school is the role of sport. Commenting on the issue of masculinity and domination, Monica expresses particular concern about some of the messages associated with competitive sport in terms of its impact on what children—and especially boys—see as important in their lives. She sees this as 'a real issue', particularly in this rural context. As she says: 'It doesn't matter how you go when it comes to school work, but if you are a good sportsperson then you have everybody's respect and friendship and that is what's admired.' With her concern about the high status associated with male-dominated sport in mind, Monica tells of a particular instance where she clashed with her principal at her former school over the introduction of a female cheer squad:

> . . . he wanted to let this particular group of girls start a cheer squad for the boys' football team. And I mean like—he could not understand—especially in a low socio-economic area when you're struggling all of the time with all of that stereo-

type stuff you know, and he just could not understand how offensive that was. Like this was right in the middle of those—whichever football club it was—multiple rape charges—you know all that stuff and he couldn't understand the gender issues that were involved in that.

Monica expresses concern here about some of the behaviours that seem to be embedded in football culture. Such concern is certainly reflected in research that highlights the significance of football in the social construction and negotiation of hegemonic masculinities (Renold, 1997; Skelton, 2000; Swain, 2000; Mills, 2001). We do not want to detract from the positive elements of football in terms of developing fitness, physical strength, discipline and teamwork—indeed, these elements are promoted in the sporting program that comprises a significant element of Monica's unit 'Students Making It Happen at Warilda' to which we refer later.

However, we—like Monica—do want to highlight our concern that football encapsulates opportunities for exercising many negative elements of hegemonic masculinity (Skelton, 1997). In particular, as Monica's concerns indicate, football can act as a legitimate arena for the denigration and oppression of girls (and, of course, other boys who don't measure up). We certainly share Monica's concerns that allowing a girls' cheer squad for the boys at her school—especially within the context of the rape charges associated with a particular major football club at the time—would mean endorsing the inequitable and oppressive gender relations embedded in football culture. And as research in this area has established, even very young boys take up these power relations to legitimise their identities and denigrate and subordinate girls and women (Renold, 1997; Skelton, 1997; Keddie, 2003). Of course, the image of the cheerleader is far from an empowering one for females, and plays into such inequitable relations—she is the object of the male gaze, a mascot; her body is scrutinised; she is decorative, sexualised, peripheral and dependent. Given these circumstances and issues, we would see the formation of a cheer squad as sanctioning the femiphobia and sexual harassment endemic in football culture. Here we agree with Monica when she says that, in relation to football culture, 'the behaviour that is rewarded in boys as being masculine is the behaviour that is not necessarily what we want to encourage in our citizens'. More broadly, and consistent with the tenor of research in this area that understands male-dominated competitive sport as the 'last bastion of masculinity' (see Fitzclarence & Hickey, 1998), Monica criticises the adulation our society bestows on (mostly male) sporting heroes:

> The main recognition from society—well look at it. Who are our heroes? Who can we afford to put the money into to create these superstars? It's our sportsmen. It isn't our thinkers—it's sportspeople who are focused on.

In this context, where academic success for boys is often not expected—and indeed has the potential to be constructed as 'feminine'—it becomes important for boys to demonstrate their adherence to particular constructions of masculinity that are perceived to have currency in the local community. Hence, challenging the ways in which sports have a downside as well as a positive impact also has to be canvassed with students and the broader community in general.

In a similar vein, Monica is also critical of the masculinising effect that valorising a militaristic society has on boys. Within the context of the Australian federal government's recent $29.7 million national values education framework for schools, Monica makes particular reference to the military image featured on the poster distributed to schools as part of this initiative. (It is a condition of federal government financial assistance that this poster be displayed prominently in every Australian school: Department of Education, Science and Training, 2005b.) With the Australian flag used as a header, the poster displays the phrase 'Character is destiny' and features an image of 'Simpson and his donkey', an image of a wounded World War I Anzac (Australian and New Zealand Army Corps) soldier being carried by a donkey and led by Simpson, a medical orderly. While Monica says that the values framework is generally 'really good stuff', she finds this example of 'character' 'quite offensive':

> . . . well once again the absolute militarism is there—all male by the way of course. And that's the type of stuff that is being reflected on—and I don't for a minute want to take away from the importance of our military history but it's not the only history we have and they're not the only heroes. The soldiers and the sportsmen are not the only Australians that kids should look up to—in my opinion—they're the ones that are admired and in the wider society, and that's what masculinity is about. It's about the action and the wang-bang, and there's no valuing of the other—you know the creative side—the intellect. It's just not valued in the same way, in my opinion.

Along similar lines, in terms of broader discourses and institutions promoting particular—and generally limited—versions of gender, Monica talks about the current attention and status associated with the military in terms of sending children particular messages about what is and is not valued in our society:

> . . . the focus on conflict and violence—you know the whole admiration of the military—it's very, very prevalent and that is being really pumped up by the federal government. You would not believe the amount of resources that come into our schools which cover the area of war and Australia's war history . . . it's massive, and what's more—it's the best financed part of the whole curriculum.

Monica raises several issues about the gender regime of the school and the broader gender order that impacts upon the school. There is the community that struggles with the notion of a woman being 'in charge', where a 'boys will be boys' attitude is apparently prevalent amongst parents, where there is an expectation that boys occupy the role of leaders within the school and that girls are happy to be 'cared for' by the boys, where sport is a valorised institution, and where the curriculum that the school is expected to work with is highly masculinised. These aspects of the school's gender regime have to be disrupted in order for the creation of an environment in which boys' and girls' life opportunities can be expanded in ways that are not restricted by limited understandings of gender. Whilst Monica seeks to disrupt these aspects of the school's gender regime as the school principal, she also makes their disruption a focus of her classroom practice.

Active citizenship: Working with and changing the community

In Monica's classroom practice, an awareness of how broader social discourses can perpetuate limited understandings of gender and identity informs her attempts to broaden students' perspectives and choices. Through civics-type problem-based activities, she aims to provide opportunities for students to develop 'the skills to be active citizens within a community'. Such opportunities focus on engendering in children a sense that they can affect how their school and broader community operate through particular decision-making structures and processes. Monica says that her main aim here is to prevent kids from feeling alienated within their various lifeworlds—to prevent them from feeling that they do not have any power. To these ends, she attempts to provide both a classroom that gives students a voice and a sense that they can make a difference, but also one that builds an ongoing critical awareness about social and environmental consciousness, care and responsibility.

For Monica, much of the work she undertakes with students has to have purchase beyond the classroom.

Along these lines, Monica talks about her teacher role as schooling children for life beyond school. This philosophy seems to shape Monica's relationships with students, as well as her pedagogy and curriculum choices. At Warilda, there is currently a strong emphasis on strengthening the agency and autonomy of the student representative council (SRC). Indeed, it is the basis on which the ongoing unit 'Students Making It Happen at Warilda' is based. Key elements of this unit are about ensuring that students have more say and responsibility in the decision-making processes within the school. As mentioned earlier, the primary areas of focus tap into the concerns of the students and their broader community, and relate to health care, nutrition and fitness, and environmental care and sustainability within the context of prolonged drought. A participatory and inclusive focus that attempts to promote independent learning characterises the activities within these areas. In relation to health care, nutrition and fitness, for example, the students—for this term—have elected to organise and compete in a whole-school lunchtime football tournament. Apparently football (soccer) is very popular with both girls and boys. This has involved researching (including school-wide surveying of students); diet and exercise routines to maximise fitness at various age levels; constructing, modifying and implementing a set of procedures, rules and regulations for play; organising teams; and planning and timetabling the tournament. As far as the participation in and running of this tournament goes, Monica promotes the children's independence and self-regulation—as she says, 'they're in charge'. In relation to the environmental care and sustainability component of the unit, the children have been involved in researching and writing about issues to do with water conservation, recycling and land care within the school and broader community. Such a context, consistent with some of the issues we foregrounded in

Chapter 2, can be seen as particularly productive in terms of pedagogy, in that it provides real-world connectedness that centres the student voice in ways that promote a sense of community and responsibility for the welfare of others.

For Monica, exploring these topics has provided a backdrop for teaching about issues concerning equity and democratic process, as these are associated with access to power and agency. For instance, this unit sits within the responsibilities of the SRC, and as such has involved the election of a team of leaders who are responsible for coordinating particular activities within the two focus areas. This team was elected following a values session about local community, school and student concerns, the construction of two political parties and a school-wide democratic election campaign that involved the articulation (through the genre of persuasive speech) of a set of goals for action in and around the school. Such processes, and ·the unit's activities which have involved substantial multi-age peer mentoring and collaboration, have, according to Monica, worked to build a sense of group cohesion, identity and agency amongst students. For boys, she sees these collaborative processes as particularly important because they disrupt and provide alternatives to the masculine stereotypes dominant in the area. She talks here about how these processes have helped to legitimise, for example, boys' interest in and care for the younger children in the school. Monica mentions here several 'cool' boys who, despite regularly 'playing with the preps'— something that would generally be seen as 'uncool' or 'what girls do'—have managed to maintain their peer status and 'coolness' with the older children. Monica says, in this respect, that the small size of the school can be very positive in terms of its potential to offer genuine opportunities for student leadership and responsibility.

In terms of broadening boys' horizons, Monica sees that it is imperative to establish connected relationships. As she says: 'You need to be able to connect with their world—if you can't connect with them you end up having to manage a lot of behaviour issues.' In this respect, Monica tries to make her teaching as 'varied and engaging as possible'. She finds the integrated and communities-focused approach most useful here—particularly because, in facilitating a sense of active citizenship, it promotes student awareness of different and diverse perspectives, as she explains:

> . . . for instance, investigating an environmental or social issue within the community where the school is placed and working with various groups. So the kids are actually doing things that have an importance for the society and the community as well as the environment often and they're relating with people from various age groups and various backgrounds while they're doing their measuring or their science or SOSE [Study of Society and the Environment] or whatever. That or doing history projects in a group in the community which means they are actively interacting with other people and investigating—you know what I mean—so really, really trying to get them to act outside of the school environment that broadens their minds and brings them into contact with lots of different types of issues and people and attitudes.

While Monica notes that the size of the school community can hinder this process, she nevertheless scaffolds student contact with authorities such as the local council and environmental organisations such as Landcare. Forging links with these community groups, as well as 'getting kids to act outside the school environment', to refer back to our earlier point, can be seen as particularly useful in going some of the way towards reconciling the mismatches between the values and attitudes of students' home/community and school lives at Warilda (Connolly, 2004). Monica understands this process also as promoting active citizenship through alerting children to the appropriate avenues for accessing power and making a difference:

I try to channel them to, OK if there's an issue then there's always a body that they can approach to attempt to resolve that issue—so it gives them a sense of power in that way. I try to develop their sense of power in a legitimate way to get things done. So that they know that—OK this is an issue, so what I can do is write to the local council, you know we can do a petition, we can do this and try and—try approaches in that way.

Monica sees that the capacities of this approach—to provide students with legitimate social pathways for action and agency—also serve to promote alternative and less gender-stereotypical behaviours in her students, and especially those boys in her class who tend to want to dominate and control what happens. This kind of process also teaches boys how to negotiate, how to work with girls and each other in equitable ways, and how to make a difference to their and others' lives. As we indicated in Chapter 2, these skills and knowledges do not come naturally—they have to be taught specifically. This Monica seeks to do in non-threatening and engaging ways. Student voice is valued, but boys' voices are tempered by understandings of gender equity—although we could perhaps question the extent to which girls 'freely' agreed to the football tournament—and by the need to listen to others.

Examining Monica's philosophies, understandings and practices

Like Jennifer and Rachel, Monica thinks of gender as a system of interdependent relations. Such a focus, for her, highlights issues of gender, power and inequity in her teaching context. In particular, she suggests that the expectations and assumptions within her school's broader farming community construct narrow understandings of gender as difference and opposition. Monica, for example, attributes her experience of being marginalised as a female principal/teacher to these views (as she says, being female was a 'major hurdle' for her to 'overcome' because 'men are just generally regarded as more useful')—here she recognises how being male (especially within this rural context) brings with it social power and privilege that being female does not (Davies, 1993; Robinson, 2000; Kenway et al., 1998; Reid, 1999; Epstein & Johnson, 1994).

Monica understands her position as female principal/teacher through lenses that recognise how issues of context and, in this case, issues of community rurality and isolation work to endorse conventional and inequitable notions of gender (see, for example, Yates & McLeod, 1994). Such lenses also inform how she sees her students' behaviour. Monica acknowledges how these broader dynamics impact on particular groups of girls. She notes, in this regard, how issues of rurality and low socio-economic status can exacerbate gender stereotypes with especially negative consequences for girls (for example, girls' poor self-esteem and lack of confidence). From a relational understanding of gender, Monica talks about how notions of 'rightful male dominance', endorsed by broader social contexts/institutions such as family, sport and the military, are associated with boys' tendencies to 'try and control what happens in the classroom'. She refers here to a particular kind of tough, strong, belligerent and competitive maleness (epitomised in sporting heroes and soldiers) that is promoted—even celebrated—in these contexts/institutions; it is one that she sees as endorsing 'action' and 'wang-bang' rather than 'creativity and intellect'.

For gender justice, such awareness is imperative, as institutions are highly gendered and gendering (Connell, 2000; Weedon, 1999). Through the circulation of definitions of masculinity and femininity, institutions produce particular understandings of gender, and regulate and normalise particular behaviours, promoting some ways of being and not others. Consistent with Monica's observations, Connell (2000) talks of particular kinds of masculinity as being embedded in institutions such as the army, corporations, schools and sporting clubs. These institutions are seen as shaping and regulating masculinities and femininities through constructing and calling into existence 'specific conditions for social practice' (2000, p. 45). In particular, such institutions tend to be underpinned and governed by the subordination of the sphere of femininities, and thus work to promote particular, limited understandings of masculinity at the expense and marginalisation of other ways of being.

Monica's reference to the values education poster and the girls' cheerleading squad illustrates her awareness of how she sees such marginalisation and brings to light the way institutionalised understandings of gender as difference and opposition are taken for granted as the way things are or ought to be (Alloway, 1995; Davies, 1993). With regard to the poster that Monica must display in her school as a condition of federal funding, she finds the representation of character (a 'masculine' image of two white male soldiers) 'quite offensive' in terms of its 'absolute militarism' and limited in terms of what 'kids should look up to' and 'what masculinity is all about'. Certainly such imagery can be seen as subordinating the sphere of femininities, but it can also be seen as subordinating a range of masculinities—particularly in terms of ethnicity and race, and particularly if considered in light of the broader contexts of global terrorism, anti-Muslim sentiment and resurgent nationalism within which this initiative was spawned. Similarly, Monica's clash with a former male principal over the introduction of a girls' cheer squad for the boys highlights the institutionalisation of gender inequities. It seems here that taken-for-granted understandings of females and femininity as subordinate to males and masculinity frame the principal's view that it is appropriate to introduce cheerleading for the girls despite, as Monica points out, broader issues and contexts that amplify gender inequities and injustice, such as the school's low socio-economic status and the highly masculinised and anti-'feminine' (at times misogynous) space of competitive sport.

Monica's understanding of gender as a product of social processes that are fluid and situational allows her to see inequitable relations as amenable to change rather than as fixed, predetermined or inevitable (Davies, 1993; MacNaughton, 2000). This, alongside her sense of social justice, frames a practice that works in contextually specific ways to 'act against the grain' of gender stereotyping within a broader framework that promotes active citizenship. This paradigm supports Monica in her attempts to redress boys' tendencies to dominate (amplified by the broader gendered discourses in her rural community and the over-representation of boys in her classroom) in terms of, for example, encouraging girls' self-esteem and confidence, and ensuring that girls are represented equitably on the school's student council. This is despite resistance from the girls (and boys)—a resistance that might prompt another teacher to individualise such behaviours (i.e. boys as active/girls as passive) as natural or inevitable rather than as located within and shaped by the gendered context within and beyond the broader school community. In this respect, it seems that Monica acknowledges, but works to redress, the mismatches between the official equity and justice values espoused by her and instituted within her school and the values of the broader community (Connolly, 2004).

Monica's efforts to redress these mismatches (between the values of her school and the values of the broader community) are further evidenced in her general teaching approach. Here, like Ross, she attempts to build connections between these two environments in ways that seek to broaden her students' horizons as well as their sense of agency and legitimacy. Through activities that are real-world/community-focused in terms of investigating specific issues that are relevant and meaningful to students' immediate community and the broader society, Monica finds ways to 'get them to act outside of the school environment' to facilitate 'active interaction' and 'engagement' with 'people from various age groups and backgrounds'. Her aim here is to broaden students' minds through exposure to 'lots of different types of issues and attitudes'. Engaging her students in ways that highlight issues of difference and diversity within their own community, and working with—rather than in isolation from—the community, would seem to be particularly constructive, and certainly is mindful of Monica's observation that she must 'work within what's acceptable by the people who live and work around and in the school' because she is trying to change 'familiar, comfortable and very deep-seated ways of being'. Such an approach represents the potential to connect with students to mobilise their sense of responsibility for the welfare of others in ways that foster their capacity to appreciate injustices (Gilbert & Gilbert, 1998).

Importantly, Monica encourages her students' sense of autonomy and active citizenship in her setting up of leadership teams within the school and in her scaffolding of 'legitimate' avenues beyond the school for problem-solving or conflict-resolution. From a gender justice perspective, such strategies—in promoting students' sense of responsibility and community—can be seen as positive because they provide alternatives to (in particular) dominant and restrictive enact-ments of masculinity. Most importantly, perhaps, Monica's endeavours here seem to reflect genuine attempts to position her students with agency and legitimacy within a democratic framework. As we pointed out in Chapter 2, such attempts can work in very positive ways in terms of disrupting the traditional inequitable teacher–student power relations that invariably exacerbate the hostile relationship that many disengaged boys have with the adult-centric cultures of 'official' schooling. Certainly Monica's attempts to strengthen the SRC's say and responsibility in the decision-making processes within the school align with the gender justice imperatives of other work. Martino and Pallotta-Chiarolli (2003), for example, point out that many student representative and leadership positions in schools have a token input in school decision-making rather than having a genuine role in terms of making a difference for students in schools. To illustrate, the boys in their study describe these leadership roles as students being the 'principal's puppets'. They argue that such token student leadership does little to challenge or disrupt the adult-centric cultures in schools that amplify students' sense of powerlessness. Monica's approach, conversely, seems to promote genuine student input into school decision-making, and thus constitutes a shift in the hierarchical power relations that are seen as perpetuating some boys' investments in dominant and dominating behaviours.

Learning from Monica

Monica's story indicates that tackling issues of boys' education at school requires an analysis of the gender regime of the school alongside the broader gender order. Individual teachers can make *a* difference to student values and attitudes towards learning, student behaviours and student outcomes. However, they do not make *the* difference. Broader societal discourses that run through school communities and the communities they support also impact upon students. For instance, students—both boys and girls—would be getting very mixed messages in a school that has a female cheer squad for a boys' football team whilst also having teachers who were trying to problematise dominant constructions of masculinity and femininity. Likewise, schools that are trying to open up the range of possible masculinities (and femininities) for their students are likely to have their efforts inhibited by community attitudes that restrict and devalue non-traditional gendered performances. Thus, in opening up possibilities for students, schools will often need to make structural rearrangements as well as working closely with the local community. In this section, we draw stimulus from Monica's story, and especially her efforts to redress inequities through pedagogies of connectedness and active citizenship, as described in Chapter 2, to facilitate such work. In providing a scaffold for examining issues of context and equity within your school and local community, we frame the following exercises around the principles of action research.

Understanding the school and local community

We have been very critical in this book, and elsewhere (Keddie, 2005; 2006b; Martino, Lingard & Mills, 2004; Mills, 2003), of approaches to boys' education which provide a simplistic 'tips for teachers' approach and which fail to take account of the uniqueness of each school. 'Tips for teachers' usually treat all boys and all girls as the same, often drawing on biological discourses to make such claims. As by far the majority of teachers know, this is not the case. Generalising about boys is hugely problematic—for instance, not all boys like sport; not all boys assume it is 'nerdy' to study; not all boys are homophobic; and not all boys are unable to concentrate for extended periods of time. However, there are powerful gendered discourses that do impact upon all boys, albeit in very different ways and often with very different consequences. For instance, by far the majority of boys in countries such as Australia, New Zealand, the United States and the United Kingdom (from where many of these 'tips for teachers' works originate) are affected by the expectation that boys *should* like sport. In many contexts, boys who are good at sport are highly valued—and more so if they excel in particular sports, such as the version of the locally valorised form of football—and those boys who actively resist its allure are marginalised. Many boys who are not good at sport and who have sometimes felt marginalised by their lack of sporting prowess have been able to compensate for this by supporting those who are. It is very hard for most boys to be completely unaffected by sport and the gendered discourses that surround it. Likewise, there are other highly gendered discourses that surround the ways in which boys are supposed to engage with the school curriculum, with aspirations about work, with their relationships with females and other males, and with authority. Boys will engage with these differently, but nonetheless they will have to engage.

Boys' different engagement with the various pressures impacting upon them will be shaped by such things as class, race/ethnicity, physical abilities and sexuality. For instance, in low socio-economic areas where boys—and girls—have very little social privilege and where there are certain work expectations that discount the possibility of supposedly middle-class occupations, there are often misogynous attitudes displayed towards women and reflected in the feminisation of middle-class men. A recent meat pie advertisement on Australian television captures this as two very working-class men discuss the merits of a meat pie whilst observing two 'well-dressed' men eating in a fancy restaurant. Violence also appears to be a greater problem amongst low socio-economic and marginalised ethnic communities experiencing high levels of poverty, although it would be foolish to assume that violence was restricted to such communities (see, for example, Scutt, 1990; Saltmarsh, 2005). Thus it is important to acknowledge the different ways in which men, and boys, demonstrate their power over each other and over women in different social contexts. Complicating understandings of gender as affected by other factors is the fact that, even with taking into account all these factors, not all boys and men respond equally to dominant discourses about gender—hence, for example, not all gay, white, middle-class boys respond in the same ways to various discourses about sport. These different responses are, of course, important in any gender work undertaken in schools in that they demonstrate that gendered identities are not fixed, and that there are possibilities for boys to take up gendered positions that are not oppressive of women and girls, or each other, and that do not have negative consequences for themselves.

The 'tips for teachers' approaches also fail to acknowledge that not all schools are the same. Most schools are recognisable as such and have very common characteristics, and various constructions of appropriate schooling. What is expected of teachers, students and administrators is usually consistent across schools, and school curricula are remarkably similar. However, whilst there are more things common to schools than there are differences, differences do exist. These differences might stem from their location, their histories, their positioning within a particular sector (government, private, independent, systemic religious, etc.), curriculum offerings, and so on. These differences often give schools a uniqueness, and understanding this is also important for introducing gender work in schools. Monica, for instance, notes how at her school there is a local resistance to a female principal that is grounded in the local 'blokey' culture. Again we would note that schools do undergo change, and that school structures and procedures are not fixed by their histories and are always open to transformation. However, such transformations require a knowledge of and engagement with the local community. Action research can be an important means of doing both things (see, for example, Atweh et al., 1998). The following activities detail the action research model and provide some suggestions for undertaking an analysis of the school's gender regime and the broader gender order of the local community.

Undertaking action research

The articulation by schools of a common vision or policy about gender equity and boys' education that engenders broad staff support and commitment is central to supporting teacher practice in this regard (Lingard et al., 2000; Lingard et al., 2001; Martino & Pallotta-Chiarolli, 2003, 2005). In effectively addressing the educational needs of boys, research outlines the importance of schools articulating a coherent set of programs and practices, framed within a common vision. This will ensure that student-centred and whole-school approaches are coordinated and integrated to be aligned with broader school policy and practice in other areas (such as discipline, bullying, harassment, and curriculum choice and content) (Gilbert & Gilbert, 1998; Lingard et al., 2002). This process will necessarily involve schools conducting sustained research concerning issues specific to their context. For example, programs and practices will be shaped by data collected to identify specific areas of educational disadvantage within the school, and will be enriched through the consideration of students' views as well as the views expressed by the broader school community (Lingard et al., 2002; Martino & Pallotta-Chiarolli, 2003).

Action research recognises the uniqueness of each school and seeks to understand the local context in order that policies informed by theory can be created to tackle perceived problems. The research can be undertaken by school staff or students—we have, for instance, seen students undertaking action research on student behaviour as part of a unit of work. In some instances, critical friends can be employed to help facilitate this process. In beginning this work it is best to start with a small, interested group. Once the group has been formed, there are several steps to undertake in the development of school gender policies:

- Form the research question(s) by first considering what the gender issues are at this school—for example, behaviour, under-achievement, retention, homophobic bullying and so on. Consider the variety of viewpoints on this issue. What are the different views?

- Once the research question has been developed—for instance, 'How can we address the high suspension rate of boys in this school?'—a range of sub-questions need to be developed. These might include, for example, 'What are community attitudes towards boys' behaviours?' 'What kinds of offences are boys suspended for?' 'Is there a common pattern to these?' 'Are issues of class and race/ethnicity relevant in considering which boys tend to be suspended?' 'Is there a particular year level that is more susceptible to suspension?' 'How do these boys' behaviours impact upon girls, other boys and teachers in the school?' 'Are there some boys who have been suspended more than once?' and 'What strategies are in place to help students reintegrate back into school after suspension?'

• In order to answer some of these questions, data need to be gathered. At every school there will be recorded data that can be analysed—on, for example, suspensions, unexplained absences, and report data indicating not only achievement but usually also homework and industry. However, these data should also be supported by such things as interviews, surveys, observations, mapping playground usage, examining student work and, in some cases, through class-based activities designed to elicit student values and opinions—as well, such data should be supported by consultation with the relevant research literature. In the construction of surveys and other forms of data-gathering, there has to be a consideration of gathering information on the ways in which traditional forms of gender are supported, rearticulated and reinscribed by various community attitudes, school practices and peer groups. Issues such as curriculum and pedagogy need to be explored alongside teacher relationships with students and teacher commitments to notions of gender justice.

• These data can be used as evidence of the 'problem', and also to devise strategies for addressing the problem. For instance, consideration might be given to the ways in which all aspects of schooling can be informed by anti-homophobic, anti-racist and anti-sexist principles. Once these strategies have been set in place and some time has passed, they should then also be scrutinised through the action research process to determine their effectiveness in relation to the original problem and to consider ways in which they may need to be modified.

- The developed strategies will constitute the school-based policies on gender. However, the action research process is dynamic and recognises that times change, that school populations change (both in terms of school personnel and students), and that gendered identities are not fixed. Hence policies are never completed, and action research should be part of an ever-changing school culture that helps to provide evidence to ensure that students receive a quality education and that school policies are appropriately aligned with this.

Engaging students with the community

Like all of the teachers we have foregrounded in the stories in this book, Monica's pedagogy coincides with the productive pedagogies model. She challenges students intellectually. For instance, in one class we observed, after reading a section of a novel to the students, she picked out a phrase used in the book and asked students how it was possible to be 'happily horrified'. Here the students were required to examine the language effects of this apparent oxymoron. There are no right answers, but students drew upon the text as they hypothesised about and analysed the effects of this phrase. Monica is also cognisant of the need for students to see the relevance and connectedness of the work undertaken in class with the world beyond the classroom. This is clearly evident in her 'Students Making It Happen at Warilda' unit, where the activities in the unit have real-world applicability and are connected to the concerns of students. In her interviews, she demonstrates a concern with broader issues of social justice; this concern is also evident in her pedagogy as she seeks to address issues of discrimination based on a devaluing of difference. For instance, we witness an engaging lesson formed around a novel detailing the persecution of Jews in Nazi Germany. Monica encourages the students to question the effects of 'separating people because they are different'. Students are expected to detail on a 'Y chart' what such practices might 'look like', 'feel like' and 'sound like'. For her, there is also the need to provide students with appropriate social supports. These include scaffolding the learning of students and the ways in which she encourages students to monitor their own behaviours. For example, throughout this lesson there are very few behavioural problems, apart from two boys who are easily brought back to task with a few words of encouragement from Monica. The attention she gives to providing students with a voice also coincides with the productive pedagogies concern with social support and students having a say in the direction of their studies.

However, what we want to foreground here are aspects of the connectedness dimension, and the student voice and active citizenship components of the productive pedagogies model. Monica's work with the 'Students Making It Happen at Warilda' unit gives students a sense that they can make a difference in their worlds and encourages them to engage with the unit because of its real-world implications. Implicit within this unit are a number of gender issues. Monica's concerns about boys' behaviours and inabilities to work together are built into this unit. Hence, whilst working with students from low socio-economic backgrounds who often have little say over their worlds, she is also trying to teach the boys in her class how to cooperate and how to negotiate rather than impose their will on others in highly masculinised ways. At the same time, this engagement with the community has an educative effect on that community. Having her students working out in the community serves to publicise what is going on in the school, demonstrates the effectiveness of Monica's pedagogy, foregrounds the value that the school extends to the community, and helps to shape the valuing of particular characteristics in both boys and girls. We do not want to be naive by suggesting that this form of work is likely to lead to a radical transformation of the local community or of attitudes within it. However, we do remain hopeful that change is possible, and that such work on the part of teachers can make *a* difference to the local community—thereby strengthening community–school relations and extending the possible range of masculinities and femininities open to students.

Developing active citizenship

Drawing on the lessons from Monica, we want to suggest ways in which students can be encouraged to work with the community to help open up the range of possibilities for boys and girls in those communities. Here we are attracted to one of Education Queensland's 'Rich Tasks' that was part of its 'New Basics' program. 'Improving the wellbeing of the local community' (see <http://education.qld.gov.au/corporate/newbasics/html/rich tasks/year9/year9.html>) resonates with 'Making It Happen at Warilda'. In this task, there is an expectation that students will utilise the action research process to improve their community. This community might be internal or external to the school. We make some suggestions here about how that might be developed with students with a gender focus in ways that are intellectually challenging, connected to their world, involve students in the decision-making aspects of the process and are grounded in principles of social justice. It is a task that we structure as a unit that can be undertaken by groups within a class, or even by a whole class, in order to make a difference to their local community. As with Monica's work, the unit is designed to encourage students—particularly boys—to negotiate and to learn to work cooperatively with each other, and at the same time develop their knowledge of the community and to have the community develop a knowledge of the school. The gender focus of the unit can be utilised in ways that encourage boys to question some of the costs of those aspects of traditional masculinity that are harmful to them and to others. It should also raise the ways in which the range of femininities for girls are restricted by boys' attitudes and behaviours which are grounded in normalised understandings of femininity. Hence it can be designed in ways that encourage boys to question their own privileges.

We do not provide specifics here; rather, we present an outline of ideas that we think can be used to scaffold an action research project with students that engages them with their community. We do not specify an age range, and assume that teachers are able to modify these ideas according to their needs. We also do not locate it within a particular discipline area, as a number of disciplinary practices and content can be integrated—for example, Social Science, Maths, English, Health and Science—depending upon the various problems that are constructed with the unit. In planning for this unit, teachers may wish to identify the various curriculum content and outcomes that would be incorporated in the delivery of this unit—for example, survey design might pick up on certain Social Science outcomes; the tabulation and analysis of the data gathered might draw on various Maths knowledges; the interview data might require certain communication skills being developed as part of the English curriculum; and attempts to address physical health in the community might involve Health and Physical Education subjects in conjunction with Science.

- We suggest that this unit begin with a question that serves to frame the problem to be solved—for example, 'How can we make our community a better place to live?' This will require students to determine the key issues in their community.
- These issues can be determined through surveys, interviews, their own experiences, scans of local newspapers, and so on. In order to give the unit a gender focus, or to ensure that gender issues surface that enable the problematising of those traditional forms of gender that have negative consequences for boys and girls in the school, some teacher direction will be necessary. However, students will need to be given the sense that this is a 'real' task that grows out of

their research, and that has the potential to make a 'real' difference to their community. Issues that could surface might be: single-vehicle accidents involving young drivers; sexual health; unemployment or casualised employment for young people; young women's safety; local crime; homophobic bullying; sport and violence; peer, family or community relationships; and/or youth boredom.

- Data to inform the unit can be gathered by students from a diverse range of sources. Depending upon the nature of the local community, these could include, in addition to parents and other students, employment agencies, neighbourhood centres, sporting groups, local politicians, women's refuges, police officers, Indigenous organisations, refugee centres, arts groups, health centres and various youth groups.

- As with the action research model referred to above, these data can be used to demonstrate that a problem does exist and to inform strategies for addressing the problem. In order to engage students in active citizenship, it is important that these strategies are advocated for by the students. This might involve preparing a written report for the local council, organising a news story with the local newspaper that details the students' recommendations, engaging in an awareness-raising campaign, speaking on assembly or at another venue, fundraising to put a particular strategy into place, and so on. Some of this may, of course, necessitate a 'behind the scenes' involvement on the part of the teacher.

- The follow-up aspect of this project can be undertaken by the class involved, or it may become part of a longitudinal study that involves classes from future years. However, it is important that at some stage there is an evaluation for the students of the impact that their work has had on the community, and an attempt to understand the effects—both intended and unintended—of their strategies, or at least of their attempt to engage with their community.

7 PRACTICES OF PERSISTENCE AND HOPE

Introduction

Many books have been written about boys in education. Much of this literature focuses on the issue of academic outcomes and positions boys' supposed under-achievement against that of girls. In so doing, it often locates boys as victims and provides teachers, and schools, with sets of instructions on how to improve the quality of boys' education. We have several problems with this approach. In the first instance, there is a failure to acknowledge the ways in which broader sets of social relations privilege men and boys in relation to women and girls. In so doing, there is also a lack of acknowledgement of how some boys' behaviours in schools are oppressive to girls, other boys and sometimes teachers. Furthermore, this approach also treats boys and girls as essentially the same, regardless of their social and geographical background, and hence what works in one location with one set of boys is supposedly transferable to boys in all other locations.

We treat claims that all boys are being failed by the school system and that schools meet the needs of all girls as foolish;

however, we do recognise that some boys are not performing well at school and that some are at risk of failing to reap many benefits from their schooling experiences. We are concerned about these students, but want to acknowledge that—as for girls—academic achievement is affected heavily by factors other than gender, such as class and race. However, while students—boys and girls—from low socio-economic and various marginalised cultural backgrounds regularly under-achieve at school, gender is not unimportant. Rather than locating concerns about boys with a supposedly feminised school system, or with a supposedly feminist captured state, as some would imply, we have suggested in this book that the problem lies with particular constructions of masculinity that devalue learning as 'effeminate', that valorise the physical over the emotional—and in some cases also over the intellectual—and that encourage boys to define themselves according to their ability to dominate and compete against others. Hence we have strongly suggested that those boys whose outcomes from schooling are affected negatively by their identification with such forms of masculinity will benefit from schooling processes that problematise these constructions.

However, it is not only the boys themselves whose experiences of schooling are affected negatively by a valorisation of traditional forms of masculinity. This is particularly evident when behavioural issues are taken into account. Our book is replete with teacher accounts of such issues, from the masculinity politics associated with many boys' disruption of the learning of others to issues associated with homophobia and the sexual harassment of female teachers. In presenting a case for why it is necessary to take boys' education seriously, we have also sought to provide an account of pedagogical practices that are respectful to boys who are under-achieving. For instance, we think those approaches that encourage the 'dumbing down' of the curriculum to meet boys' supposed limited abilities to engage in extended writing or complex forms of communication are disrespectful to boys. They construct boys as deficit. We reject such a construction. Thus we have been drawn to a pedagogical model—productive pedagogies—that is grounded in the presumption that all students—boys and girls—can achieve and that, as a matter of social justice, all students should be provided with quality pedagogies that stretch them intellectually.

At the same time, we have wanted to acknowledge the harm that some boys do to others. This requires boys from all backgrounds being placed in situations where they are confronted with problematising dominant constructions of masculinity *and* being provided with the space to safely perform less harmful forms of masculinity. Again, we have found the productive pedagogies model useful. Its emphasis on working with and valuing difference, and its concern with providing students with a supportive learning environment, are both important for providing such situations. Thus, throughout this book, we have highlighted productive pedagogies as a framework through which issues in boys' education can be addressed. We are also attracted to productive pedagogies as a framework for considering issues in the education of boys rather than providing a detailed set of instructions on how to teach boys. We are wary of books that provide such instructions.

Schools in various locations serve very different school populations, and have their own sets of values, issues and priorities. For instance, what is required for addressing boys' educational needs in the Australian context would be very different in schools in remote areas serving Indigenous students from that required for boys in urban areas in major cities. Furthermore, different areas of, say, Sydney or London would also require different approaches to boys' education depending upon local issues. Hence there can be no one-size-fits-all model for teaching boys. However, there are enough commonalities in relation to dominant constructions of gender to suggest some key issues that do need to be addressed, especially in relation to the ways in which certain knowledges about gender have become hegemonised. Productive pedagogies is a pedagogical approach that enables these considerations of gender to be foregrounded whilst also having enough inbuilt flexibility to ensure that the peculiarities of each location can be taken into account.

Productive pedagogies

We have both worked with teachers and the productive pedagogies framework in a variety of locations, and the principles which underpin the model have purchase in these different locations. Regardless of the context, the improvement of student outcomes requires the delivery of work that stretches students intellectually—and this is the case for all students, but especially those who are under-achieving. Improving the social outcomes of all students, especially in relation to expanding gender knowledges, is facilitated by a commitment to valuing and working with non-dominant knowledges and encouraging active citizenship activities. The productive pedagogies emphasis on supporting students' learning by giving them voice, by scaffolding their learning and by providing a context for encouraging risk-taking in the learning process also applies in the majority of locations and classrooms. The notion that learning has to be connected to have meaning to under-achieving and disengaged students is also significant in all environments. The four teachers we have foregrounded in this book all demonstrated significant aspects of the productive pedagogies model when we observed them in their classrooms.

However, this does not mean that the take-up of productive pedagogies in the education of boys occurs unproblematically. For instance, the emphasis on connectedness within this model resonates with those claims which have suggested that schools need to be more connected to boys' interest. We reject this notion to the extent that such concerns suggest there is a universal way of being a boy and fail to recognise that some of the traditional ways of being a boy might have harmful consequences for boys, girls and others around boys in schools. This under-standing of connectedness was represented in some of the interview data presented in Chapter 4, where a teacher spoke of his attempt to engage with boys by connecting with their inter-ests in bull riding and pig chasing. However, whilst rejecting this form of connectedness, for disengaged students—including boys—school work has to be made meaningful. We saw this with Monica, who encouraged her students to address real-life problems in the local community; with Ross, who encouraged the boys in his class to engage with current debates about repre-sentations of young Muslim men; and with Jennifer and Rachel's use of popular visual texts to explore issues of gender. This form of connectedness does interest students and makes them open to tackling work of high intellectual quality that is critical for improving the academic and social outcomes of all students.

That all students are provided with work of high intellectual quality is an important aspect of a socially just teaching approach, and is grounded in the presumption that all students can achieve academically. As with the productive pedagogies research, we emphasise that this is especially important for students who are under-achieving at school, and in those cases where boys are not achieving academically, a focus on providing them with intellectually challenging work will help them to improve their academic outcomes. It is often assumed that it is only students who are perceived as high flyers who are capable of work that stretches their thinking. For example, it would have been no surprise to many to see the students in Ross's class-rooms rising to the challenges he presented them with. However, we also saw work of high intellectual quality being undertaken in Rachel's classrooms, with a group of boys who regularly do not achieve well at school. Rachel's work with this group of boys engaged students in intellectual inquiry that inter-rogated the 'normality' of traditional forms of masculinity. This was quite challenging for some of these boys at an emotional as well as an intellectual level. However, as with all the other teachers whose stories we have foregrounded, Rachel's respectful relationships with her students supported boys' engagement with this confronting work.

In observing all four teachers whose stories we have told in this book, we were impressed with the quality of relationships that they had with their students. However, the quality of these relationships was not based on a form of paternalism, but appeared to be genuine in its concern to ensure that students' voices were heard in the classroom. Each of the teachers sought to provide a democratic classroom that encouraged students to take risks with their learning. For instance, Jennifer provided a space where boys (and girls) could be different, and free from the forms of harassment that often work against the academic interests of some boys and contribute towards some boys becoming a behavioural problem for others. Monica, too, was concerned with students' relationships and emphasised boys learning particular forms of negotiating skills that were in contrast to some of their attitudes grounded in domination and competition. This aspect of building positive relationships with students also surfaced in some of the teachers' commitment to working with and valuing difference amongst their students.

It is the productive pedagogies model's commitment to working with and valuing difference that we think is especially important in the education of boys. The dimension of intellectual quality is important in that all students, including under-achieving boys, need to be challenged intellectually in order to ensure high-quality academic outcomes. The connectedness dimension gives meaning to the work carried out in class to attract the interests of disengaged students, and the socially supportive environment dimension ensures that those students whose cultural backgrounds do not 'fit' with those of the school are provided with explicit instructions on how to achieve and provides a space for student voices to be heard. However, within a gender justice framework that problematises traditionally valorised (and often harmful) gender performances, it is the working with and valuing difference dimension that can contribute to the legitimation of non-stereotypic and less-harmful behaviours.

This disruption of dominant knowledges is especially important for boys who invest in and take up restrictive versions of masculinity. We are convinced that boys who are under-achieving will have their academic outcomes improved by rejecting those forms of masculinity that are dismissive of partic-ular ways of learning—for example, those related to literacy—as being non-masculine. We are likewise convinced that boys who are a problem to each other and to girls—and sometimes to teachers—are likely to be less so when alternative and less destructive masculinities are legitimated. In Rachel's work with a specific boys' program and Jennifer's whole-class work, we saw teachers who were committed to providing boys with a range of masculinities that would prove less harmful to each other, to girls and to others. We also saw such commitment in Ross's classroom. What was significant here was that, for many teachers, the boys in his classroom would not have presented as a problem. However, for Ross, valuing difference is not just about managing boys' behaviours but also about addressing their privilege. Ross noted that this was especially important with boys who came from middle-class backgrounds. Hence Ross—with his commitment to 'comforting the afflicted and afflicting the comfortable'—works to ensure that middle-class boys come to question their own privilege. This is consistent with the productive pedagogies commitment to presenting non-dominant cultural knowledges and engaging students in active citizenship activities.

When we have conducted in-services for teachers on a variety of issues, we have often made the point that sometimes the best in-service available to teachers can be found within the school. By far the majority of schools have high-quality staff who have thought through key issues in education on a range of topics, including boys' education, and put this into practice in their own classrooms. In this book, we have sought to capture this sentiment by providing four stories from teachers who have thought about issues of gender and education and who integrate their theorising about gender into their teaching. We were impressed by each of these teachers, and our observations of their classroom practice demonstrated to us that—while not necessarily familiar with productive pedagogies—their practice was consistent with that represented by this framework. These were not the only teachers we observed whose stories we could have told. However, we felt that each offered something different from which we as researchers and others as teachers could learn. It was our intention to use these teacher narratives in ways that are not prescriptive, but rather can stimulate thought and action in other school contexts. At the conclusion of each story, we have provided a series of activities that draw heavily upon what it is possible to learn from these teachers.

The teacher narratives

As we indicated in the Introduction, much has been written about boys' education. Much of this literature, as well as working with deficit models of boys, has treated teachers as deficit by presenting an approach free of gender theory, as if teachers simply want to be told what to do on Monday mornings. This is not our experience of teachers in classrooms who strive to make a difference with their students. These teachers recognise that teaching is intellectual labour, and they engage in complex theorising about their content areas, their pedagogies and a range of other educational matters. The teachers whose narratives we have provided in this book use such theorising about gender, alongside other educational theories, to inform their practice. They do not see such theorising as an add-on to their work, but regard it as being integral to providing care to their students. These four teachers care whether their students' grades are down; they care if their behaviours disrupt others; they care about their students' futures; and they care about the present. They also hope that their students will come to make a difference to the world. However, whilst this care is evident in their classroom practices, they each raise different issues for the enactment of such care. In telling each story, we highlight those aspects of their practice that have the potential to inform practice elsewhere.

Jennifer's story foregrounds a pedagogical approach that makes the problematising of gender central in her everyday work. She is concerned about the sense of entitlement that many boys display, and how they are committed to particular constructions of masculinity that pose a problem to themselves and to others. She is constantly on the alert for ways to use the everyday to disrupt gender norms in order for her students to see the world from a different perspective, and consequently to broaden their understandings of gender. She does this through the various texts that she uses in class, and through her teacher–student relationships. What we found particularly inspiring about Jennifer was the way in which she constantly scrutinises her own actions to consider how she might be reinforcing student perceptions of the world in traditional, and harmful, ways. Jennifer's story reminds us to keep in mind the understanding that gendering processes are everywhere, and that many of the actions we perform and attitudes that we hold can seem so 'natural' and 'normal' that we often simply take them for granted. Hence, as with Jennifer's approach to teaching boys, there is a need to be constantly reflexive about our own practices as well as problematising those of students.

When we were selecting the stories to tell in this book, we particularly wanted to tell that of Ross. The boys that Ross was working with were from very different social backgrounds to the vast majority of boys in, for example, Rachel's and Monica's classes. These were boys who were from very privileged, comfortable, middle–class backgrounds, from which students are normally very successful at school. Furthermore—and this was borne out by our observations at the school—these boys rarely pose obvious behavioural issues. However, Ross saw that there were issues of masculinity to confront with these boys. Whilst the issues were, on one level, quite different from those of Rachel's school, they also required boys to consider issues of power and privilege. The need for this work was supported by some of the female teachers' comments to us about the ways in which some boys at the school would harass them and police their behaviours. For Ross, encouraging boys to consider their own privileges was grounded in his Christian principle of 'comforting the afflicted and afflicting the comfortable'. However, we would argue that understanding boys' privileges and power has to be a cornerstone of any work conducted with boys from all backgrounds. This, of course, does not only relate to gender. Thus, in Ross's story, we suggested that teachers consider the complex ways in which masculinities are formed into various hierarchies within schools. This means that issues of class, ethnicity, sexuality and physical abilities would all have to be considered—along with, of course, how hierarchies of masculinity might be supported and reinscribed by particular structures and practices in schools like those that might be associated with the male role model issue.

Rachel has a very similar pedagogical approach to Jennifer: she wants boys to have a greater range of possibilities in their lives than those allowed by restrictive constructions of masculinity. She encourages this broadening of students' understandings of gender through the everyday curriculum, and she uses textual resources to do this. However, her story has also indicated the ways in which special programs for boys might take up issues of masculinity. In her role as deputy principal at a school in a low socio-economic area, Rachel is reflexive about the disproportionate numbers of boys who are sent to her for behavioural issues. Rachel's concern about these boys being at risk of becoming the source of serious behavioural problems at the school, and of the likelihood of them either failing to complete their schooling or at least under-achieving academically, has compelled her to give considerable thought to issues in boys' education. She attributes many of these boys' problems to their restrictive understandings of masculinity. Hence she has been instrumental in setting up a special program for boys who are sometimes a behavioural problem, where space is provided for them to engage in activities that problematise harmful constructions of masculinity. Within this program, Rachel is incredibly respectful towards the boys. This respect serves to recognise that boys cannot be held wholly responsible for adopting those forms of masculine identity that are valorised through everyday culture. Thus we see her seeking to demonstrate to the boys that a lot of cultural work goes into creating such a valorisation. That she respects and trusts these boys is evident in the ways in which she sees them as potential mentors for younger boys. Rachel's respectful pedagogy—like Jennifer's—reminds us that we also need to consider the ways in which such things as behaviour-management strategies and structures can contribute to the dominant cultural knowledges about gender; and that, as teachers, we should not make sweeping generalisations about boys and girls, but rather explore the differences amongst girls and amongst boys as well as between girls and boys.

Monica's story draws attention to the importance of working with the local community, and also to the ways in which the local community both shapes and is shaped by gendered relationships. Monica indicated to us the difficulties of being a woman teacher, and principal, in a highly masculinised community. This presented several problems for Monica. For instance, her story demonstrates how a female principal's practices and authority with students can be undermined if she cannot command the respect within the community that a male principal would in such circumstances. However, it would be treating the community as deficit if Monica refused to engage with them in positive ways. She does this rather subtly by having the students in her classes undertake projects that take them out into the community. This works on the one hand to value the community and on the other by giving the community an opportunity to understand the value of the work that Monica is conducting in the school with her students. Whilst we are supportive of Monica's struggles with a highly masculinised local community, we are also cognisant of those situations where local schools that reflect an Anglo middle-class culture do not resonate with the concerns of the local community. Again we would stress the importance of working with those communities in order to create two-way conversations with them. Learning from Monica's desire to understand her local context, we have stressed in her story the importance of undertaking action research in schools in order to understand the local context and the local issues that will inform gender policies at the school. We also suggest, as does Monica, that the kind of group work involved in the active citizenship activities that take students out into the community also subtly works to encourage boys' development of negotiating and cooperating skills rather than the competitive and dominating behaviours that seem to be expected by the local context.

When we selected these four stories to tell, we took many factors into consideration. We wanted to highlight some differences in contexts. For instance, we wanted to show teachers working with boys who were struggling with academic achievement and we also wanted to show what teachers were doing with boys where this was not the case. We wanted to highlight constructive ways in which teachers were addressing behavioural issues, both as part of their regular classroom practice and as part of special programs. We wanted to find situations where students—both boys and girls—were engaged in their classrooms and were valued by their teachers. We wanted to see high-quality pedagogies that were inclusive of diversity and were intellectually challenging. We also wanted to get a spread of schools across government and private sectors, rural and urban, primary and secondary, coeducational and single-sex, multicultural and monocultural. We did not expect any of these schools, or the teachers in them, to 'speak' for all like schools and their teachers. But we did want to illustrate the positive work that was being done with boys in schools, and to show that some teachers are working against the anti-feminist approach to boys' education that is prevalent, and that such work can have academic and social benefits for all students. These illustrations, we believe, in the hands of teachers who are committed to social justice, enjoy the challenge of theorising their practice and/or are engaged in gender reform in their schools, can be used to stimulate new solutions to local issues in boys' education.

Conclusion

In the Introduction to this book, we repeated the question that Becky Francis (2000, p. 129) asked: 'Do we want boys to change?' We do want some boys to change. Many misbehaving boys are conforming to a particular construction of masculinity that limits their possibilities in life, both educationally and socially, and also harms others. We do want these boys to change so that they, as Kenway (1996) indicates, can have richer lives and will present less of a problem to girls, women and each other. In addition, we do want *all* boys to consider the privileges they have as boys; we do want them to be committed to contributing to a better world; and we do want them to con-sider how their behaviours and attitudes might be harmful to themselves and to others. This is not, however, because we have deficit models of boys. Nor is it because we have failed to acknowledge how they might be oppressed by their class, ethnicity, religion, sexuality and physical abilities.

In this book, we have outlined a number of concerns that some teachers have about boys. Many of these teachers have been concerned with boys' behaviours. However, most of these teachers—like the four teachers we have foregrounded—do not work with deficit models of boys. They do not expect boys to behave badly—to the contrary, they expect boys to behave well. In situations where boys are a problem, they attribute these problems to the boys' restrictive versions of masculinity. In order to address some boys' negative behaviours towards others, disengagement from schooling, rejection of school learning and a masculine sense of entitlement, these teachers seek to broaden boys' (and girls') understandings of what it means to be male and female. However, these teachers recognise that structural arrangements and broader societal discourses impact heavily upon boys' identification and rejection of particular forms of masculinity. To these ends, they are reflexive about their own practices, seek to make structural rearrangements and create classroom contexts that provide support to students who reject harmful forms of masculinity and that challenge, in respectful ways, students' identification with those forms of masculinity.

This respect for the boys also extends to an understanding of how most boys experience some form of oppression, not as males, but because of their age, and their social and economic backgrounds. Most of these teachers recognise that issues of privilege that arise from particular forms of, for example, racism, ethnocentricism, classism and ageism also have to be confronted alongside issues of sexism and homophobia. These issues affect both girls' and boys' social and academic well-being, and without them being addressed, schools are unlikely to provide a socially just educational environment. Addressing boys' behaviours, then, is not simply about encouraging boys to change, but also about addressing and changing the ways in which schools and their practices reinscribe and reproduce particular forms of oppression based upon the intersections of gender, class, race, ethnicity and physical abilities. We thus also contend that, as well as some boys needing to change, some schools also have to change. Respectful pedagogies require it.

This has been a book about boys' education. However, we hope that the time for writing about boys as boys is coming to an end. We hope that this is especially the case where boys are being treated as 'victims', as such approaches are not helpful to boys, girls or teachers. What we do hope is that schools, and the broader community, will continue to value the contribution that teachers such as Jennifer, Rachel, Ross and Monica make to the lives of the students in their care. These teachers recognise that students do not come to them unaffected by gender, class, ethnicity and so on. They seek to understand and theorise these differences in ways that can contribute meaningfully to their students and to the broader community. In so doing, they understand that, as teachers, they play an important role in the lives of young people and that they make a difference to the community. They are teachers who are not prepared to give up on gender justice, and their practices of persistence and hope make a difference. Both boys and girls deserve to be taught by such teachers.

REFERENCES

Allan, J. (2003) Productive pedagogies and the challenge of inclusion, *British Journal of Special Education* 30(4), pp. 175–79.

Alloway, N. (1995) *Foundation stones: The construction of gender in early childhood*, Melbourne: Curriculum Corporation.

Alloway, N., Dalley-Trim, L., Gilbert, R. & Trist, S. (2006) *Success for boys: Planning guide and core module*, Canberra: Commonwealth of Australia.

Alloway, N., Freebody, P., Gilbert, P. & Muspratt, S. (2002) *Boys, literacy and schooling: Expanding the repertoires of practice*, Canberra: Commonwealth Department of Education, Science and Training.

Apple, M. (2001) *Educating the 'right' way: Markets, standards, god and inequality*, New York: Routledge Falmer.

Apple, M. & Beane, J. (1999a) Lessons from democratic schools, in M. Apple & J. Beane (eds), *Democratic schools: Lessons from the chalkface*, Buckingham: Open University Press, pp. 118–23.

——(eds) (1999b) *Democratic schools: Lessons from the chalkface*, Buckingham: Open University Press.

Archer, L. (2003) *Race, masculinity and schooling: Muslim boys and education*, Maidenhead: Open University Press.

Ashman, A. & Conway, R. (1993) *Using cognitive methods in the classroom*, London: Routledge.

——(1997) *An introduction to cognitive education: Theory and applications*, London: Routledge.

Atweh, B., Kemmis, S. & Weeks, P. (eds) (1998) *Action research in practice: Partnership for social justice in education*, London: Routledge.

Biddulph, S. (1995) *Manhood: an action plan for changing men's lives*, 2nd edn, Sydney: Finch.

——(1997) *Raising Boys*, Sydney: Finch.

Boaler, J. (2002) *Experiencing school mathematics: Traditional and reform approaches to teaching and their impact on student learning*, Mahwah, NJ: Lawrence Erlbaum.

Bourdieu, P. (1993) *The field of cultural production*, Columbia: Columbia University Press.

Bourdieu, P. & Passeron, J. (1977) *Reproduction in education, society and culture*, London: Sage.

Burstyn, V. (1999) *The rites of men: Manhood, politics, and the culture of sport*, Toronto: University of Toronto Press.

Butler, J. (1999) *Gender trouble: Feminism and the subversion of identity*, New York: Routledge.

Charlton, E., Mills, M., Martino, W. & Beckett, L. (2007) Sacrificial girls: A case study of the impact of streaming and setting on gender reform, *British Education Research Journal*, 33(4).

Clark, M. (1993) *The great divide*, Melbourne: Curriculum Corporation.

Collins, C., Kenway, J. & McLeod, J. (2000) *Factors influencing the educational performance of males and females in school and their initial destinations after leaving school*, Canberra: DEETYA.

Connell, R. (1987) *Gender and power*, Cambridge: Polity Press.

——(1995) *Masculinities*, Sydney: Allen & Unwin.

——(2000) *The men and the boys*, Sydney: Allen & Unwin.

Connolly, P. (1998) *Racism, gender identities and young children*, London: Routledge.

——(2004) *Boys and schooling in the early years*, London: Routledge Falmer.

Cooper, D. (2004) *Challenging diversity: Rethinking equality and the value of difference*, Cambridge: Cambridge University Press.

Cope, B. & Kalantzis, M. (eds) (1995) *The power of literacy*, London: Falmer.

Cox, E. (1995) *A truly civil society*, Sydney: ABC.

Darling-Hammond, L. (1997) *The right to learn: A blueprint for creating schools that work*, San Francisco: Jossey-Bass.

Davies, B. (1988) *Gender equity and early childhood*, Canberra: Curriculum Development Centre.

——(1993) *Shards of glass: Children reading and writing beyond gendered identities*, Sydney: Allen & Unwin.

——(1997) Constructing and deconstructing masculinities through critical literacy, *Gender & Education* 9(1), pp. 9–31.

——(1998) Critical literacy in practice: Language lessons for and about boys, *Opinion* 27(2), pp. 12–22.

——(2000) *A body of writing 1990–1999*, New York: Alta Mira Press.

Davies, B. & Hunt, R. (2000) Classroom competencies and marginal positionings, in B. Davies (ed.), *A body of writing 1990–1999*, New York: AltaMira Press, pp. 107–31.

Davies, B. & Laws, C. (2000) Poststructuralist theory in practice: working with 'behaviourally disturbed' children, in B. Davies, (ed.), *A body of writing*, New York: AltaMira Press, pp. 145–64.

Denborough, D. (1996) Step by step: Developing respectful and effective ways of working with young men to reduce violence, in C. McLean, M. Carey & C. White (eds), *Men's ways of being*, Colorado: Westview Press, pp. 91–115.

Department for Education and Skills (DfES) (2003) *Using the national healthy school standard to raise boys' achievement*, Wetherby: Health Development Agency.

Department of Education, Science and Training (2003) *Meeting the Challenge: Guiding principles for success from the Boys'*

Education Lighthouse Programme Stage One 2003, Canberra: DEST.

——(2005a) *Success for boys*, retrieved 1 April 2005 from http://www.successforboys.edu.au/background.asp.

——(2005b) *Values for Australian schooling*, retrieved 22 September 2005 from http://www.valueseducation.edu.au/values/.

Donnelly, K. (2004) *Why our schools are failing: What parents need to know about Australian education*, Kingston: Duffy and Snelgrove.

Education Queensland (2007) *New Basics Project: Third Suite: Years 7–10*, http://education.qld.gov.au/corporate/new basics/html/richtasks/year9/year9.html.

——(2002) *Male teachers strategy: Strategic plan for the attraction, recruitment and retention of male teachers in Queensland State Schools 2002–2005*, Brisbane: Queensland Government.

Ellsworth, E. (1989) Why doesn't this feel empowering? Working through the repressive myths of critical pedagogy, *Harvard Educational Review* 59(3), pp. 297–324.

Epstein, D. (1998) Real boys don't work: 'Underachievement', masculinity and the harassment of 'sissies', in D. Epstein, J. Elwood, V. Hey & J. Maw (eds), *Failing boys? Issues in gender and achievement*, Buckingham: Open University Press, pp. 96–108.

Epstein, D., Elwood, J., Hey, V. & Maw, J. (eds) (1998) *Failing boys? Issues in gender and achievement*, Buckingham: Open University Press.

Epstein, D. & Johnson, R. (1994) On the straight and narrow, in D. Epstein (ed.), *Challenging lesbian and gay inequalities in education*, Buckingham: Open University Press, pp. 197–230.

Faludi, S. (1992) *Backlash: The undeclared war against women*, London: Chatto & Windus.

Fitzclarence, L. (2000) Learning and teaching in education's shadowland: Violence, gender relations and pedagogic possibilities, *The Review of Education/Pedagogy/Cultural Studies* 22(2), pp. 147–73.

Fitzclarence, L. & Hickey, C. (1998) Learning to rationalise abusive behaviour through football, in C. Hickey, L. Fitzclarence & R. Matthews (eds), *Where the boys are*, Geelong: Deakin University, pp. 67–81.

Francis, B. (1999) Lads, lasses and (New) Labour: 14–16-year-old students' responses to the 'laddish behaviour and boys' underachievement' debate, *British Journal of Sociology of Education* 20(3), pp. 355–71.

——(2000) *Boys, girls and achievement: Addressing the classroom issues*, London: Routledge.

——(2006) Heroes or zeroes? The discursive positioning of 'underachieving boys' in English neo-liberal education policy, *Journal of Educational Policy* 21(2), pp. 187–200.

Francis, B. & Skelton, C. (2001) Men teachers and the construction of heterosexual masculinity in the classroom, *Sex Education* 1(1), pp. 9–21.

——(2005) *Reassessing gender and achievement: Questioning contemporary key debates*, London: Routledge.

Fraser, N. (1997) *Justice interruptus: Critical reflections on the 'postsocialist' condition*, New York: Routledge.

Fynes-Clinton, M. (2006) A killer in the lunch box, *The Courier-Mail, QWeekend* 10–11 June, pp. 12–17.

Gilbert, R. & Gilbert, P. (1998) *Masculinity goes to school*, Sydney: Allen & Unwin.

Gill, Z. (2005) Boys—getting it right: The 'new' disadvantaged or 'disadvantage' redefined?, *Australian Educational Researcher* 32(2), pp. 105–24.

Giroux, H. (2003) Public pedagogy and the politics of resistance: Notes on a critical theory of educational struggle, *Educational Philosophy and Theory* 35(1), pp. 5–16.

——(2006) *Beyond the spectacle of terrorism: Global uncertainty and the challenge of the new media*, London: Paradigm Publishers.

Glasser, W. (1992) *The quality school: Managing students without coercion*, New York: Harper Perennial.

——(1998) *Choice theory: A new psychology of personal freedom*, New York: Harper Collins.

Gurian, M. (1999) *A fine young man: What parents, mentors, and educators can do to shape adolescent boys into exceptional men*, New York: Jeremy P. Tarcher/Putnam.

Gurian, M. & Ballew, A. (2003) *The boys and girls learn differently: Action guide for teachers*, San Francisco: Jossey Bass.

Hargreaves, A. (2003) *Teaching in the knowledge society: Education in the age of insecurity*, New York: Teachers College Press.

Hayes, D., Mills, M., Christie, P. & Lingard, B. (2006) *Teachers and schooling making a difference: Productive pedagogies, assessment and performance*, Sydney: Allen & Unwin.

Hickey, C. & Fitzclarence, L. (2004) Regimes of risk: The need for a pedagogy for peer groups, *Asia-Pacific Journal of Teacher Education* 32(1), pp. 49–63.

Hickey, C. & Keddie, A. (2004) Peer groups, power and pedagogy: The limits to an educational paradigm of separation, *Australian Educational Researcher* 31(1), pp. 57–79.

hooks, b. (2003) *Teaching Community: A pedagogy of hope*, New York: Routledge.

House of Representatives Standing Committee on Education and Training (2002) *Boys' education: Getting it right*, Canberra: Commonwealth Government.

Jackson, C. (2002) 'Laddishness' as a self-worth protection strategy, *Gender and Education* 14(1), pp. 37–51.

——(2006) *Lads and Ladettes: Gender and a fear of failure*, Maidenhead: Open University.

Jones, K. (1993) *Compassionate authority: Democracy and the representation of women*, New York: Routledge.

Kamler, B., Maclean, R., Reid, J. & Simpson, A. (1994) *Shaping up nicely: The Formation of Schoolgirls and schoolboys in the first month of school*, Canberra: Department of Employment, Education and Training.

Keddie, A. (2003) Little boys: tomorrow's macho lads, *Discourse: Studies in the Cultural Politics of Education* 24(3), pp. 289–306.

——(2005) A framework for gender justice: Evaluating the transformative capacities of three key Australian schooling initiatives, *Australian Educational Researcher* 32(3), pp. 83–102.

——(2006a) Fighting, frustration, anger and tears: Matthew's story of hegemonic masculinity, *Oxford Review of Education* 32(4), pp. 521–34.

——(2006b) Pedagogies and critical reflection: Key understandings for transformative gender justice, *Gender and Education* 18(1), pp. 99–114.

——(2007) Games of subversion and sabotage: issues of power, masculinity, class, rurality and schooling. *British Journal of Sociology of Education* 28(2), pp. 181–94.

Keddie, A. & Churchill, R. (2004) Power, control and authority: Issues at the centre of boys' relationships with their teachers, *Queensland Journal of Teacher Education* 19(1), pp. 13–27.

Kenway, J. (1996) Reasserting masculinity in Australian schools, *Women's Studies International Forum* 19(4), pp. 447–66.

Kenway, J. & Fitzclarence, L. (1997) Masculinity, violence and schooling: Challenging 'poisonous' pedagogies', *Gender and Education* 9(1), pp. 117–33.

Kenway, J., Willis, S., Blackmore, J. & Rennie, L. (1998) *Answering back: Girls, boys and feminism in schools*, London: Routledge.

Kindlon, D. & Thompson, M. (1999) *Raising Cain: Protecting the emotional life of boys*, London: Michael Joseph.

Lemon, P. (1995) New ways of reading, in H. Fraser (ed.), *Challenging the text*, Townsville: James Cook University, p. 41.

Lesko, N. (ed.) (2000) *Masculinities at school*, Thousand Oaks: Sage.

Levy, A. (2005) *Female chauvinist pigs: Women and the rise of raunch culture*, Melbourne: Schwartz Publishing.

Lingard, B. (2003) Where to in gender policy in education after recuperative masculinity politics? *International Journal of Inclusive Education* 7(1), pp. 33–56.

Lingard, B. & Douglas, P. (1999) *Men engaging feminisms: Profeminism, backlashes and schooling*, Buckingham: Open University Press.

Lingard, B., Hayes, D., Mills, M. & Christie, P. (2003) *Leading learning: Making hope practical in schools*, Maidenhead: Open University Press.

Lingard, B., Ladwig, J., Mills, M., Hayes, D., Bahr, M., Christie, P., Chant, D., Gore, J., Luke, A. & Warry, M. (2001) *Queensland school reform—longitudinal study*, Brisbane: Queensland Government.

Lingard, B., Martino, W., Mills, M. & Bahr, M. (2002) *Addressing the educational needs of boys*, Canberra: DEST.

Lingard, B., Mills, M. & Hayes, D. (2000) Teachers, school reform and social justice: challenging research and practice, *Australian Educational Researcher* 27(3), pp. 99–118.

Mac an Ghaill, M. (1994) *The making of men*, Buckingham: Open University Press.

McGregor, G. & Mills, M. (2006) RMXing the curriculum: Boys and music education, *Pedagogy, Culture and Society* 14(2), pp. 221–33.

McKay, J., Messner, M. & Sabo, D. (eds) (2000) *Masculinities, gender relations, and sport*, Thousand Oaks: Sage.

McLaren, P. & Farahmandpur, R. (2005) *Teaching against global capitalism and the new imperialism: a critical pedagogy*, Lanham, Md, Rowman & Littlefield.

McLean, C. (1997) Engaging with boys' experiences of masculinity: Implications for gender reform in schools, *Curriculum Perspectives* 17(1), pp. 61–64.

McLeod, J. (2004) Neo-liberal agendas and gender equity: From social justice to individual performance, *Redress: Journal of the Association of Women Educators* 13(3), pp. 10–15.

MacNaughton, G. (2000) *Rethinking gender in early childhood education*, Sydney: Allen & Unwin.

Mahony, P. (1985) *Schools for the boys?*, London: Hutchinson.

——(1998) Girls will be girls and boys will be first, in D. Epstein,

J. Elwood, V. Hey & J. Maw (eds), *Failing boys? Issues in gender and achievement*, Buckingham: Open University Press, pp. 37–55.

Mahony, P. and Hextall, I. (2000) *Reconstructing teaching: Standards, performance and accountability*, London: Routledge/Falmer.

Marsh, J. (2007) New literacies and old pedagogies: Recontextualising rules and practices, *International Journal of Inclusive Education*, 11(3), pp. 267–82.

Martino, W. (1999) 'Cool boys', 'party animals', 'squids' and 'poofters': Interrogating the dynamics and politics of adolescent boys at school, *British Journal of Sociology of Education* 20(2), pp. 239–63.

——(2000) The boys at the back, *English in Australia*, 127, pp. 35–50.

Martino, W. & Berrill, D. (2003) Boys, schooling and masculinities: Interrogating the 'right' way to educate boys, *Education Review* 55(2), pp. 99–117.

Martino, W. & Frank, B. (2006) The tyranny of surveillance: Male teachers and the policing of masculinities in a single sex school, *Gender and Education* 18(1), pp. 17–33.

Martino, W., Lingard, B. & Mills, M. (2004) Issues in boys' education: A question of teacher threshold knowledges, *Gender and Education* 16(4), pp. 435–54.

Martino, W. & Mellor, B. (1995) *Gendered fictions*, Cottesloe: Chalkface Press.

Martino, W. & Meyenn, B. (eds.) (2001) *What about the boys? Issues of masculinity and schooling*, Buckingham: Open University Press.

Martino, W., Mills, M. & Lingard, B. (2005) Interrogating single-sex classes for addressing boys' educational and social needs, *Oxford Review of Education* 31(2), pp. 237–54.

Martino, W. & Pallotta-Chiarolli, M. (2003) *So what's a boy? Addressing issues of masculinity and schooling*, Maidenhead: Open University Press.

——(2005) *Being normal is the only way to be: Adolescent perspectives on gender and school*, Sydney: University of NSW Press.

Mills, M. (1996) Homophobia kills: Disruptive moments in the educational politics of legitimation, *British Journal of Sociology of Education* 17(3), pp. 315–26.

——(1997) Towards a disruptive pedagogy: Creating spaces for student and teacher resistance to social injustice, *International Studies in Sociology of Education* 7(1), pp. 35–55.

——(1998) The human relationships education curriculum and gender and violence programs, *Change: Transformations in Education* 1(2), pp. 68–81.

——(2000) Issues in implementing boys' programmes in schools: Male teachers and empowerment, *Gender and Education* 12(2), pp. 221–38.

——(2001) *Challenging violence in schools: An issue of masculinities*, Buckingham: Open University Press.

——(2003) Shaping the boys' agenda: The backlash blockbusters, *International Journal of Inclusive Education* 7(1), pp. 57–73.

Mills, M. & Keddie, A. Teaching Boys and Gender Justice, *International Journal of Inclusive Education,* 11(3), pp. 335–54.

Mills, M., Martino, W. & Lingard, B. (2004) Issues in the male teacher debate: Masculinities, misogyny and homophobia, *British Journal of Sociology of Education* 25(3), pp. 354–69.

——(2007) Getting boys' education 'right': The Australian Government's Parliamentary Inquiry Report as an exemplary instance of recuperative masculinity politics, *British Journal of Sociology of Education* 28(1), pp. 5–21.

Munns, G. (2007) A sense of wonder: Pedagogies to engage students who live in poverty, *International Journal of Inclusive Education* 11(3), pp 301–16.

Newmann & Associates (1996) *Authentic achievement: Restructuring schools for intellectual quality*, San Francisco: Jossey-Bass.

NSW Department of Education and Training (2003) *Quality teaching in NSW public schools: Starting the discussion*, Sydney: State of NSW Department of Education and Training.

Ofsted (2003a) *Yes he can—schools where boys write well*, London: Ofsted.

——(2003b) *Boys' achievement in secondary schools*, London: Ofsted.

Pallotta-Chiarolli, M. (1995) Can I use the word 'gay'?, in R. Browne & R. Fletcher (eds), *Boys in schools: Addressing the real issues, behaviour, values and relationships*, Sydney: Finch, pp. 66–80.

Pollack, W. (1999) *Real boys: Rescuing our sons from the myths of boyhood*, New York: Henry Holt.

Reay, R. (2001) 'Spice girls', 'nice girls', 'girlies' and 'tomboys': Gender discourses, girls' cultures and femininities in the primary classroom, *Gender and Education* 13(2), pp. 153–66.

Reid, J. (1999) Little women/little men: Gender, violence, and embodiment in an early childhood classroom, in B. Kamler (ed.), *Constructing gender and difference*, New Jersey: Hampton Press, pp. 167–90.

Renold, E. (2001) Learning the 'hard' way: Boys, hegemonic masculinity and the negotiation of learner identities in the primary school, *British Journal of Sociology of Education* 22(3), pp. 369–85.

——(1997) 'All they've got on their brains is football', Sport, masculinity and the gendered practices of playground relations, *Sport, Education and Society* 2(1), pp. 5–23.

Rizvi, F. (2004) Debating globalisation and education after September 11, *Comparative Education* 40(2), pp. 157–71.

Robinson, K. (2000) 'Great tits, Miss!' The silencing of male students' sexual harassment of female teachers in secondary schools: A focus on gendered authority, *Discourse* 21(1), pp. 75–90.

Rosenstock, L. & Steinberg, A. (1999) Beyond the shop: Reinventing vocational education, in M. Apple & J. Beane (eds), *Democratic schools: Lessons from the chalkface*, Buckingham: Open University Press, pp. 48–67.

Roulston, K. & Mills, M. (2000) Male teachers in feminised teaching areas: Marching to the men's movement drums,

Oxford Review of Education 26, pp. 221–37.

Salisbury, J. & Jackson, D. (1996) *Challenging macho values*, London: Falmer.

Saltmarsh, S. (2005) Complicit institutions: representation, consumption and the production of school violence, unpublished PhD thesis, Macquarie University, Sydney.

Scutt, J. (1990) *Even in the best of homes: Violence in the family*, Melbourne: McCulloch.

Seidman, S. (1993) Identity and politics in a 'postmodern' gay culture: Some historical and conceptual notes, in M. Warner (ed.), *Fear of a queer planet: Queer politics and social theory*, Minneapolis: University of Minnesota Press, pp. 105–42.

Sewell, T. (1997) *Black masculinities and schooling: How black boys survive modern schooling*, Stoke-on-Trent: Trentham Books.

——(1998) Loose cannons: Exploding the myth of the 'black macho' lad, in D. Epstein, J. Elwood, V. Hey & J. Maw (eds), *Failing boys? Issues in gender and achievement*, Buckingham: Open University Press, pp. 111–27.

Simpson, L., McFadden, M. & Munns, G. (2001) 'Someone has to go through': Indigenous boys, staying on at school and negotiating masculinities, in W. Martino & B. Meyenn (eds), *What about the boys? Issues of masculinity and schooling*, Buckingham: Open University Press, pp. 154–68.

Skelton, C. (1997) Primary boys and hegemonic masculinities, *British Journal of Sociology of Education* 18(3), pp. 349–69.

——(2000) 'A passion for football': Dominant masculinities and primary schooling, *Sport, Education and Society* 5(1), pp. 5–18.

——(2001) *Schooling the boys: Masculinities and primary education*, Buckingham: Open University Press.

——(2002) The 'feminisation of schooling' or 'remasculinising' primary education? *International Studies in Sociology of Education* 12, pp. 77–96.

Summers, A. (1975) *Damned Whores and God's Police*, Ringwood: Penguin.

Swain, J. (2000) 'The money's good, the fame's good, the girls are good': The role of playground football in the construction of young boys' masculinity in a junior school, *British Journal of Sociology of Education* 21(1), pp. 95–109.

Taylor, S. & Henry, M. (2000) Challenges for equity policy in changing contexts, *The Australian Educational Researcher* 27(3), pp. 1–15.

Teese, R., Davies, M., Charlton, R. & Polesel, J. (1995) *Who wins at school?* Canberra: Australian Government Publishing Service.

Thorne, B. (1993) *Gender play*, New Jersey: Rutgers University Press.

Warrington, M. & Younger, M. (2002) Speech at the 'Raising Boys' Achievement conference', Homerton College, Cambridge, 11 July.

Weaver-Hightower, M. (2003) The 'boy turn' in research on gender and education, *Review of Educational Research* 73(4), pp. 471–98.

Weedon, C. (1999) *Feminism, theory and the politics of difference*, Oxford: Blackwell.

Wright, C., Weekes, D., McGlaughlin, A. & Webb, D. (1998) Masculinised discourses within education and the construction of black male identities amongst African Caribbean youth, *British Journal of Sociology of Education* 19(1), pp. 75–87.

Yates, L.M. & McLeod, J. (1994) Masculinity, femininity, class, rurality and schooling (first stages of a qualitative longitudinal research project), paper presented at the Australian Association for Research in Education conference, Newcastle, 28 November.

Yeatman, A. (1995) Interlocking oppressions, in B. Caine & R. Pringle (eds), *Transitions: New Australian feminisms*, Sydney: Allen & Unwin, pp. 42–56.

Young, I. (1990) *Justice and the politics of difference*, Princeton: Princeton University Press.

INDEX